EDUCATORS PRAISE THE CORE KNOWLEDGE SERIES

"Our school hired a curriculum specialist. He introduced me to **Core Knowledge**. With *What Your Kindergartner Needs to Know*, I have found hope and excitement for my Crow Indian students. I thank you for believing in the best for our children."

—*Jennifer Flatlip, teacher, St. Charles School, Pryor, Montana*

"For three years, we have been using elements of the **Core Knowledge** program, and I have watched as it invigorated our students. These books should be in every classroom in America."

—*Richard E. Smith, principal, Northside Elementary School, Palestine, Texas*

"Hirsch made it quite clear [in *Cultural Literacy*] that respect for cultural diversity is important but is best achieved when young people have adequate background knowledge of mainstream culture. In order for a truly democratic and economically sound society to be maintained, young people must have access to the best knowledge available so that they can understand the issues, express their viewpoints, and act accordingly."

—*James P. Comer, M.D., professor, Child Study Center, Yale University (in* Parents *magazine)*

The
CORE KNOWLEDGE
Series

Resource Books for
Kindergarten Through Grade Six

Bantam Books Trade Paperbacks

New York

Core Knowledge®

What Your Kindergartner Needs to Know

Preparing Your Child for a Lifetime of Learning

Edited by E. D. Hirsch, Jr., and John Holdren

Library of Congress Cataloging-in-Publication Data
What your kindergartner needs to know : preparing your child for a lifetime of learning /
edited by E. D. Hirsch, Jr., and John Holdren. — Bantam books trade paperback edition.
pages cm
Includes bibliographical references and index.
ISBN 978-0-345-54373-8 (alk. paper) — ISBN 978-0-345-54374-5 (ebook)
1. Kindergarten—Curricula—United States.   2. Curriculum planning—United States.
I. Hirsch, E. D. (Eric Donald).   II. Holdren, John.
LB1180.W53 2013
372.21'8—dc23
2013004494

Book design by Diane Hobbing

Editor-in-Chief of the Core Knowledge Series: E. D. Hirsch, Jr.

Editor: John Holdren

Project Manager and Art Editor: Alice Wiggins

Writers: Curriculum Concepts, Inc. (Mathematics, Music); Diane Darst (Visual Arts); Susan Hitchcock (History and Geography, Science, Music, Visual Arts); John Holdren (Literature and Language, History and Geography, Music, Mathematics, Science); Mary Beth Klee (History and Geography)

Artists: Gail McIntosh and Lina Chesak-Liberace, Jennifer Eichelberger, Leslie Evans, Barbara L. Gibson, Julie Grant, Shari Griffiths, Steve Henry, Jared Henry, Bob Kirchman, Kristin Kwan, Alvina Kwong, Amanda Larson, Michael McCurdy, Dustin McKay, Rebecca Miller, Steve Morrison, Julia Parker, Mary Parker, Michael Parker, Charles Peale, Giuseppe Trogu

Research Assistant: Deborah Hyland

Acknowledgments

This series has depended on the help, advice, and encouragement of 2,000 people. Some of those singled out here already know the depth of our gratitude; others may be surprised to find themselves thanked publicly for help they gave quietly and freely for the sake of the enterprise alone. To helpers named and unnamed we are deeply grateful.

2013 revision: Emma Earnst, Scott Ritchie, Liza Greene, Kim Berrall, Susan Hitchcock, Caroline HirstSion, Robert Pondiscio.

Advisers on multiculturalism: Minerva Allen, Barbara Carey, Frank de Varona, Mick Fedullo, Dorothy Fields, Elizabeth Fox-Genovese, Marcia Galli, Dan Garner, Henry Louis Gates, Cheryl Kulas, Joseph C. Miller, Gerry Raining Bird, Connie Rocha, Dorothy Small, Sharon Stewart-Peregoy, Sterling Stuckey, Marlene Walking Bear, Lucille Watahomigie, Ramona Wilson.

Advisers on elementary education: Joseph Adelson, Isobel Beck, Paul Bell, Carl Bereiter, David Bjorklund, Constance Jones, Elizabeth LaFuze, J. P. Lutz, Sandra Scarr, Nancy Stein, Phyllis Wilkin.

Advisers on technical subject matter: Marilyn Jager Adams, Diane Alavi, Richard Anderson, Judith Birsh, Cheryl Cannard, Paul Gagnon, David Geary, Andrew Gleason, Blair Jones, Connie Juel, Eric Karell, Joseph Kett, Mary Beth Klee, Michael Lynch, Joseph C. Miller, Jean Osborne, Margaret Redd, Nancy Royal, Mark Rush, Janet Smith, Ralph Smith, Nancy Strother, Nancy Summers, James Trefil, Nancy Wayne, Linda Williams, Lois Williams.

Conferees, March 1990: Nola Bacci, Joan Baratz-Snowden, Thomasyne

Beverley, Thomas Blackton, Angela Burkhalter, Monty Caldwell, Thomas M. Carroll, Laura Chapman, Carol Anne Collins, Lou Corsaro, Henry Cotton, Anne Coughlin, Arletta Dimberg, Debra P. Douglas, Patricia Edwards, Janet Elenbogen, Mick Fedullo, Michele Fomalont, Mamon Gibson, Jean Haines, Barbara Hayes, Stephen Herzog, Helen Kelley, Brenda King, John King, Elizabeth LaFuze, Diana Lam, Nancy Lambert, Doris Langaster, Richard LaPointe, Lloyd Leverton, Madeline Long, Allen Luster, Marcia Mallard, William J. Maloney, Judith Matz, Joseph McGeehan, Janet McLin, Gloria McPhee, John Morabito, Robert Morrill, Roberta Morse, Karen Nathan, Dawn Nichols, Valeta Paige, Mary Perrin, Joseph Piazza, Jeanne Price, Marilyn Rauth, Judith Raybern, Mary Reese, Richard Rice, Wallace Saval, John Saxon, Jan Schwab, Ted Sharp, Diana Smith, Richard Smith, Trevanian Smith, Carol Stevens, Nancy Summers, Michael Terry, Robert Todd, Elois Veltman, Sharon Walker, Mary Ann Ward, Penny Williams, Charles Whiten, Clark Worthington, Jane York.

Schools: Special thanks to Three Oaks Elementary for piloting the *original Core Knowledge Sequence* in 1990. Thanks also to the schools that have offered their advice and suggestions for improving the *Core Knowledge Sequence*, including (in alphabetical order) Academy Charter School (CO), Coleman Elementary (TX), Coral Reef Elementary (FL), Coronado Village Elementary (TX), Crooksville Elementary (OH), Crossroads Academy (NH), Gesher Jewish Day School (VA), Hawthorne Elementary (TX), Highland Heights Elementary (IN), Joella Good Elementary (FL), Mohegan School–CS 67 (NY), The Morse School (MA), Nichols Hills Elementary (OK), Ridge View Elementary (WA), R. N. Harris Elementary (NC), Southside Elementary (FL), Three Oaks Elementary (FL), Washington Core Knowledge School (CO). To the many other schools teaching Core Knowledge—too many to name here, and some of which we have yet to discover—our heartfelt thanks for "sharing the knowledge"!

Benefactors: The Brown Foundation, The Challenge Foundation, Mrs. E. D. Hirsch Sr., The Walton Family Foundation.

Our grateful acknowledgment to these individuals does not imply that we have taken their (sometimes conflicting) advice in every case, or that each of them endorses all aspects of this project. Responsibility for final decisions must rest with the editors alone. Suggestions for improvements are very welcome, and we wish to thank in advance those who send advice for revising and improving this series.

With much gratitude to Linda Berilacqua, who directs the
good work of the Core Knowledge Foundation
EDH

To my mother and father
JH

A Note to Teachers

We hope you will find this book useful, especially those of you who are teaching in the growing national network of Core Knowledge schools. Throughout the book, we have addressed the suggested activities and explanations to parents, since you as teachers know your students and will have ideas about how to use the content of this book in relation to the lessons and activities you plan. If you are interested in the ideas of the Core Knowledge Foundation, please write or call the Core Knowledge Foundation (801 East High Street, Charlottesville, VA 22902; (434) 977-7550) for information on accessing collections of lessons created and shared by teachers in Core Knowledge schools. Also, you can get access to more lessons and ideas shared by teachers through the Core Knowledge home page on the Internet at www.coreknowledge.org.

Contents

I. Language and Literature

II. History and Geography

III. Visual Arts

IV. Music

V. Mathematics

VI. Science

General Introduction to the Core Knowledge Series

Schools and Your Child

If Charles Dickens were alive today observing the state of American schools, he might be tempted to observe anew that it is the best of times and the worst of times. Seldom has there been more attention and energy aimed at our nation's education system. Unacceptable inequities in achievement between income and ethnic groups, long viewed with alarm, are being addressed with unprecedented urgency and resources. Years of dismay over lackluster performance have created a sense of crisis, even fear, that if we do not set our educational house in order, American competitiveness, our economy, and even our way of life are at risk. The response has been an unprecedented era of educational dynamism and innovation. Seen through this lens, it might seem to be the best of times for American education.

Yet for all our admirable focus, urgency, and investment, we have surprisingly little to show for it. Reading test scores for American 17-year-olds, the ultimate report card for our schools, have hardly budged in 40 years. That's two generations with no discernible progress. How can this be? We have tried testing every child and holding teachers accountable. We have built charter schools and filled classrooms with computers. We have even made it the law of the land that every child read on grade level, but to no avail. Surely it is the worst of times.

Do not blame teachers. They are among our most committed and generous-spirited citizens. We have not lacked urgency, idealism, or even resources. What we have lacked is a coherent plan for educating all children to proficiency.

The book you hold in your hand exemplifies an essential building block of that coherent plan.

Why Knowledge Matters in the Era of Google

American public education sprang from the 19th-century idea of the common school. We sent our children to learn reading and writing, but also a common curriculum of history, geography, math, and other subjects. Such schools also strived to create virtuous, civic-minded citizens for the new nation. As America matured and became more diverse, the idea of a common curriculum gradually melted away. Today we have all but abandoned the idea that there is a body of knowledge that every child should learn in school, and the broad mission of education is to maximize each individual's potential. But there is good reason to believe that the idea of common schooling is even more relevant and effective today than ever before.

Ask yourself this question: Would I rather have my child go to school to gain knowledge of history, science, art, or music? Or should schools emphasize skills such as critical thinking and problem solving? The answer should ideally be both. Knowledge and skills are not two different things; they are two sides of the same coin. Thinking skills are what psychologists call "domain specific." In plain English, this means that you cannot think critically about a subject you know little about. If we want our children to be broadly competent readers, thinkers, and problem solvers, it is not possible unless they have a rich, broad store of background knowledge to call upon, enabling them to flex those mental muscles.

Unfortunately, too many of our schools have lost touch with this critical insight. It is commonly believed to be a fool's errand to think we can teach children all they need to know—far better simply to spark in children a lifelong love of learning. Indeed, many well-intentioned educators believe the in-depth study of a few topics, practice with a variety of "thinking skills," and access to the Internet are all anyone needs today. Why clutter our minds with facts and trivia when you can just Google it? Today's classroom and curriculum, it is commonly argued, should be built around "21st-century skills" such as media literacy and working cooperatively to solve "authentic" problems. These are the skills that will ensure them a lifetime of learning, productivity, and engaged citizenship. The rest is mere trivia. Right?

On its surface, the idea that skills are more important than knowledge has a basic, commonsense appeal. Why should your child learn about the American Revolution, the parts of an atom, or who painted the *Mona Lisa*? What child hasn't asked, "Why do we need to know this?" Unfortunately this benign, even obvious-sounding idea contains a great paradox: it takes knowledge to gain knowledge. Those who repudiate a coherent, knowledge-rich curriculum on the grounds that you can always look things up have failed to learn an important lesson from cognitive science: deemphasizing factual knowledge actually prevents children from looking things up effectively. When you have just a little bit of information about a subject, you cannot readily evaluate the importance of new knowledge. When you know nothing, you're flying blind, like reading a book whose words you don't know. Thus emphasizing procedural skill at the expense of factual knowledge actually hinders children from learning to learn. Yes, the Internet has placed a wealth of information at our fingertips. But to be able to use that information—to absorb it, to add to our knowledge—we must already possess a storehouse of knowledge. That is the paradox disclosed by cognitive research.

Common Knowledge, Not "One Size Fits All"

All children are different. Like the idea that skills are more important than knowledge, there is a warm, intuitive appeal to the idea that we should tailor schooling to allow every child to find what most excites and engages him, and let those interests drive his "child-centered" education. But again, this ignores some fundamental facts about how we learn.

Language and vocabulary—like critical thinking and problem solving—also depend a great deal on a broad base of shared knowledge. When a sportscaster describes a surprising performance by an underdog basketball team as "a Cinderella story," or when a writer compares an ill-fated couple to Romeo and Juliet, they are making an assumption that their audience will know and understand the reference. So much of our language is dependent on a shared body of knowledge. Yes, you must know the words. But you must also understand the context in order to understand and be understood. The word "shot," for example, means something different in a doctor's office, on a basketball court, or when a repairman says your dishwasher is shot. Fluency depends on context, and context is largely a function of shared background knowledge.

Yet it remains all too easy to deride a knowledge-rich curriculum as "mere facts" and "rote learning." The idea that there is a common body of knowledge that all children should know to enable them to read, communicate, and work cooperatively with others does sound old-fashioned. But the overwhelming evidence argues that this is precisely the case. Learning builds on learning: children (and adults) gain new knowledge only by building on what they already know. It is essential to begin building solid foundations of knowledge in the early grades, when children are most receptive, because for the vast majority of children, academic deficiencies from the first six grades can permanently impair the success of later learning. Poor performance of American students in middle and high school can be traced to shortcomings inherited from elementary schools that have not imparted to children the knowledge and skills they need for further learning.

All of the highest-achieving and most egalitarian elementary school systems in the world (such as those in Sweden, France, and Japan) teach their children a specific core of knowledge in each of the first six grades, thus enabling all children to enter each new grade with a secure foundation for further learning. U.S. schools, with their high student mobility rates, would especially benefit from a carefully sequenced core curriculum in the elementary and middle school years.

Commonly Shared Knowledge Makes Schooling More Effective

We know that the one-on-one tutorial is the most effective form of schooling, in part because a parent or teacher can provide tailor-made instruction for the individual child. But in a non-tutorial situation—in, for example, a typical classroom with 25 or more students—the instructor cannot effectively impart new knowledge to all the students unless each one shares the background knowledge that the lesson is being built upon.

Consider this scenario. In third grade, Ms. Franklin is about to begin a unit on early explorers—Columbus, Magellan, and others. In her class she has some students who were in Mr. Washington's second-grade class last year and some students who were in Ms. Johnson's second-grade class. She also has a few students who have moved in from other towns. As Ms. Franklin begins the unit on explorers, she asks the children to look at a globe and use their fingers to trace a route across the Atlantic Ocean from Europe to North America. The students who had Mr. Washington look blankly at her: they didn't learn that last year. The students who had Ms. Johnson, however, eagerly point to the proper places on the globe, while two of the students who came from other towns pipe up and say, "Columbus and Magellan again? We did that last year."

When all the students in a class do share the relevant background knowledge, a classroom can begin to approach the effectiveness of a tutorial. Even when some children in a class do not have elements of the knowledge they were supposed to acquire in previous grades, the existence of a specifically defined core makes it possible for the teacher or parent to identify and fill the gaps, thus giving all students a chance to fulfill their potentials in later grades.

Commonly Shared Knowledge Makes Schooling Fairer and More Democratic

When all the children who enter a grade can be assumed to share some of the same building blocks of knowledge, and when the teacher knows exactly what those building blocks are, then all the students are empowered to learn. In our current system, children from disadvantaged backgrounds too often suffer from unmerited low expectations that translate into watered-down curricula. But if we specify the core of knowledge that all children should share, then we can guarantee equal access to that knowledge and compensate for the academic advantages some students are offered at home. In a Core Knowledge school, all children enjoy the benefits of important, challenging knowledge that will provide the foundation for successful later learning.

Commonly Shared Knowledge Helps Create Cooperation and Solidarity in Our Schools and Nation

Diversity is a hallmark and strength of our nation. American classrooms are usually made up of students from a variety of cultural backgrounds, and those different cultures should be honored by all students. At the same time, education should create a school-based culture that is common and welcoming to all because it includes knowledge of many cultures and gives all students, no matter what their background, a common foundation for understanding our cultural diversity.

Commonly Shared Knowledge Creates the Conditions That Make Higher-Order Thinking Possible

"We don't just read about science. We do science," a teacher in New York City recently wrote. One of the greatest misconceptions in contemporary education is the idea that in order to best prepare students for college and careers, we should train them to "think like an expert." In other words, we should help them understand and practice what scientists, historians, and other highly skilled professionals do. But it is clear from cognitive science that in order to think like an expert, you must know what the expert knows. Unfortunately, there are no shortcuts to expertise. Deep knowledge and practice are essential. Yet our schools, under the mistaken idea that knowledge is less important than skills, try to teach children to engage learning by doing, under the assumption that skills trump knowledge. They do not. You cannot have one without the other.

All of our most cherished goals for education—reading with understanding, critical thinking, and problem solving—are what psychologists call "domain-specific" skills. Simply put, there is no such thing as an all-purpose critical thinker or problem solver. Such skills are a function of your background knowledge.

What Knowledge Needs to Be Taught?

One of the primary objections to a content-rich vision of education is that it offends our democratic sensibilities. The title of this book—*What Your Kindergartner Needs to Know*—can easily be viewed as presumptuous: "Who are you to say what knowledge matters? Why do you get to decide what goes in my child's curriculum and what gets left out?" Deciding what we want our children to know can be a politically and emotionally charged minefield. No grade-by-grade sequence of knowledge or course of study will satisfy everyone. But it is educationally reckless to ignore what we know about the importance of a broad knowledge base. The effort may be difficult, but we are duty-bound to try.

The content in this and other volumes in the Core Knowledge Series is based on a document called the *Core Knowledge Sequence*, a grade-by-grade sequence of specific content guidelines in history, geography, mathematics, science, language arts, and fine arts. As the core of a school's curriculum, it offers a solid, coherent foundation of learning while allowing flexibility to meet local needs. The entire sequence, from preschool to eighth grade, can be downloaded for free at the Core Knowledge Foundation's website (www.coreknowledge.org/download-the -sequence).

The Core Knowledge Foundation invested a considerable amount of time, energy, and resources in an attempt to find a consensus on the most enabling knowledge—the content that would most enable all children to read, write, listen, and speak with understanding.

Shortly after the establishment of the Core Knowledge Foundation in 1987, we analyzed the many reports issued by state departments of education and by professional organizations—such as the National Council of Teachers of Mathematics and the American Association for the Advancement of Science—that recommend general outcomes for elementary and secondary education. We also tabulated the knowledge and skills, through grade six, specified in the successful educational systems of several other countries, including France, Japan, Sweden, and Germany.

In addition, we formed an advisory board on multiculturalism that proposed a specific knowledge of diverse cultural traditions that American children should all share as part of their school-based common culture. We sent the resulting materials to three independent groups of teachers, scholars, and scientists around the country, asking them to create a master list of the knowledge children should have by the end of grade six. About 150 education professionals (including college professors, scientists, and administrators) were involved in this initial step.

These items were amalgamated into a master plan, and further groups of teachers and specialists were asked to agree on a grade-by-grade sequence of the items. That sequence was then sent to some 100 educators and specialists who participated in a national conference that was called to hammer out a working agreement on an appropriate core of knowledge for the first six grades; kindergarten, grades 7 and 8, and preschool were subsequently added to the sequence.

This important meeting took place in March 1990. The conferees were elementary school teachers, curriculum specialists, scientists, science writers, officers of national organizations, representatives of ethnic groups, district superintendents, and school principals from across the country. A total of 24 working groups decided on revisions in the *Core Knowledge Sequence*. The resulting provisional sequence was further fine-tuned during a year of implementation at a pioneering school, Three Oaks Elementary, in Lee County, Florida.

In only a few years many more schools—urban and rural, rich and poor, public and private—joined in the effort to teach Core Knowledge. Based largely on suggestions from these schools, the *Core Knowledge Sequence* was revised in 1995; separate guidelines were added for kindergarten, and a few topics in other grades were added, omitted, or moved from one grade to another, in order to create an even more coherent sequence for learning. Because the sequence is intended to be a living document that provides a foundation of knowledge that speakers and writers assume their audiences know, it has been—and will continue to be—periodically updated and revised. In general, however, there is more stability than change in the sequence.

The purpose of the *Core Knowledge Sequence* is not to impose a canon. It is an attempt to *report* on a canon—to identify the most valuable, empowering knowledge across subject areas, and to create a plan for imparting it from the first days of school.

Knowledge Still Matters

This book, as well as the work of the Core Knowledge Foundation and the efforts of Core Knowledge teachers in hundreds of schools nationwide, swims strongly against the anti-knowledge tide of mediocrity that threatens to drag down our schools, our children, and ultimately our nation.

A broad, rich store of background knowledge is not merely nice to have. Knowledge is the essential raw material of thinking. Cognitive scientist Daniel Willingham observes, "Knowledge is not only cumulative, it grows exponentially. Those with a rich base of factual knowledge find it easier to learn more—the rich get richer. In addition, factual knowledge enhances cognitive processes such as problem solving and reasoning. The richer the knowledge base, the more smoothly and effectively these cognitive processes—the very ones that teachers target—operate. So, the more knowledge students accumulate, the smarter they become."

If all of our children are to be fully educated and participate equally in civic life, then we must provide each of them with the shared body of knowledge that makes literacy and communication possible. This concept, so central to the new Common Core State Standards adopted by more than 40 states, and to the Core Knowledge Foundation's goal of equity and excellence in education, manifests itself in the *Core Knowledge Sequence*—and in these popular grade-by-grade books. It is a pleasure to introduce this latest refinement of them to a new generation of readers.

E. D. Hirsch, Jr.
Charlottesville, Virginia

I
Language
and Literature

Reading, Writing, and Your Kindergartner

Acquiring the Skill of Reading

Literate adults are constantly interacting with text in one form or another. Think about the reading and writing you do on any given day. Perhaps you start the morning with a glance at a newspaper or headlines on your iPad. You might hastily scribble a note for your daughter's lunch bag. Billboards and road signs compete for your attention as you drive around town. At work there are memos, reports, and emails to read and write. Your child's knapsack carries home forms to fill out and announcements from his school or teacher. There are recipes to be read, bills to be paid, and account statements to be examined. When time allows, perhaps you end the day with a novel, a magazine, or Facebook posts from friends and family.

Each of these activities, and countless others, involves reading and writing. But we rarely think about our ability to make or make sense of printed words. It feels like something we do without thinking about it at all. In reality, our ability to make sense of the printed word is one of our greatest intellectual achievements. Most of us learn to speak and listen naturally, without formal instruction. But reading and writing are different. There's nothing at all natural about acquiring these abilities.

Reading Is Not a Skill

Most of us think learning to read is like learning to ride a bike. It's a skill we acquire as children and never lose. Moreover, riding a bike is also a transferable skill. Once you learn how, you can safely ride almost any bike. Surely it's the same with reading: some of us may read faster or slower than others, but reading is reading is reading. Once you learn how to read, you can read anything, right?

Unfortunately, it's not that simple. Your ability to translate written symbols into sounds—what reading experts call "decoding"—is a transferable skill. This explains why you can "read" nonsense words, even if you've never seen them before, such as those found in the famous Lewis Carroll poem "Jabberwocky."

> 'Twas brillig, and the slithy toves
> Did gyre and gimble in the wabe:
> All mimsy were the borogoves,
> And the mome raths outgrabe.

Few of us would disagree on how to pronounce words such as "brillig" and "mimsy," even though they don't exist. But there's more to reading than simply decoding the words on a page. Reading is about comprehension—your ability to make meaning from written words. If we can't make sense of the words on the page, we really cannot be said to be "reading." Unlike decoding, reading comprehension is not a transferable skill at all. It's the result of years and years of vocabulary growth, and of building up a store of knowledge about the world that helps you make sense of what you read. Reading about a subject that you know little about can be awkward and disorienting. For example, in his book *The Making of Americans*, Core Knowledge founder E. D. Hirsch describes reading this account of a cricket match in a British newspaper:

> *Thus, as the final day dawned and a near capacity crowd lustily cheered every run Australia mustered, much depended on Ponting and the new wizard of Oz, Mike Hussey, the two*

overnight batsmen. But this duo perished either side of lunch—the latter a little unfortunate to be adjudged leg-before—and with Andrew Symonds, too, being shown the dreaded finger off an inside edge, the inevitable beckoned, bar the pyrotechnics of Michael Clarke and the ninth wicket.

You probably know nearly all the words in this passage, but it's nearly impossible to understand what the writer is trying to say. Even common words such as "lunch" and "overnight" suddenly seem awkward and strange. Knowing that this is an account of a cricket match played by a team from Australia doesn't help. Your lack of knowledge about how the game is played keeps you from understanding what the words mean. This might strike you as an extreme example, but think of how it feels when you try to make sense of directions for installing an operating system on your computer, or struggle to understand a product warranty. Your rate of reading slows. You read and reread, struggling to understand.

Why is this so hard? Isn't reading like riding a bike?

Your ability to make sense of what you read depends heavily on your prior knowledge—the stuff you already know. "Prior knowledge is vital to comprehension because writers omit information," notes University of Virginia cognitive scientist Daniel Willingham. Suppose you read, "He just got a new puppy. His landlord is angry." According to Willingham, you easily understand the logical connection between those sentences because you have prior knowledge of puppies (they aren't housebroken), carpets (urine stains them), and landlords (they are protective of their property). But what if you didn't know those things? You would be confused, and comprehension breaks down.

In short, it's deeply misleading to think of reading as a "skill" at all. Reading is really a two-part process. The first part is decoding, which is a skill. The second part is comprehension, which depends almost entirely on vocabulary and background knowledge—you need to know all the words. But critically, you also need to know the things to which those words refer. And comprehension is most certainly not a skill. It's the product of years and years of language growth and knowledge acquisition. The work of acquiring that knowledge begins in earnest the day your child sets foot in kindergarten.

The Knowledge Connection

When we use this lens, it becomes clear that "knowing stuff" is critical to reading comprehension. Broad general knowledge is not merely nice to have; it's essential if we want our children to be able to read widely with understanding. When children struggle with comprehension, it is usually not because they cannot "read." More often it's because they lack the vocabulary and background knowledge to understand what the writer is trying to say.

The Core Knowledge approach to reading is built on this essential understanding: broad general reading ability correlates with broad general knowledge. If we want our children to become literate adults, they first must be explicitly taught to decode writing at a very early age. But their education must also furnish the broad, rich knowledge that educated Americans take for granted and assume that others have as well. Without that background knowledge, children will struggle to be fully literate and read fluently and with comprehension.

Kindergarten and Your Child

Most of us do not take on the task of teaching our children how to read and write. We send our children off to school and encourage them to work hard and pay attention, and we assume their teachers are caring and competent. But you would not be holding this book in your hand if you were not deeply concerned about your child's education. Thus, it's useful to know what a good kindergarten language arts program should look like. It's worth paying careful attention, since the first days of a child's formal education are critical to the goal of helping your child become a proficient reader.

Listening and Learning

We tend to think of the three R's—reading, writing, and arithmetic—as the foundations of a good, skills-based early childhood education. But to build this foundation, a good kindergarten classroom should probably be equally focused on the two L's—listening and learning.

Think of the way language develops. Oral language development (speaking and listening) precedes written language development (reading and writing). Nearly all children learn to listen and speak long before they can read and write. Science confirms what we know from common sense: children must be able to understand words before they can produce and use them independently—

attention paid to listening and speaking will provide a solid foundation for later reading and writing.

Listening comprehension also develops faster than reading comprehension and remains more advanced for far longer than you might expect: your child's ability to independently comprehend material on the printed page probably won't catch up to his or her ability to listen and understand the same material read out loud until the end of middle school. Our brains can only do so much at one time. When a child is learning to read, a significant amount of mental energy is devoted to decoding and reading with fluency. When she listens to text read out loud, attention is freed up to focus on the material itself. Thus, a good kindergarten classroom is one in which children are given lots of opportunities to be exposed to rich language by being read aloud to often.

Most kindergarten teachers read to their students. They know that small children love a good story. But the wisest teachers understand the importance of building vocabulary and background knowledge. They read nonfiction picture books and take advantage of a child's curiosity to begin building background knowledge of the world around us—knowledge that is critical to mature reading comprehension.

Read-alouds—both fiction and nonfiction—yield another important benefit: the language of books is richer and more formal than spoken English. By listening to stories or nonfiction selections read aloud, children can experience the complexities of written language without expending cognitive energy on decoding.

Helping young children develop the ability to listen to and understand written texts read aloud must be an integral part of any initiative designed to build literacy. A good kindergarten takes advantage not just of the natural benefits of listening and learning but also of the nuanced benefits provided when read-alouds are done in a coherent, systematic fashion. To achieve this, careful consideration should first be given to the selection of text read aloud, to ensure that the vocabulary and syntax presented are rich and complex. Furthermore, to make efficient use of instructional time, read-alouds must build a broad knowledge base while simultaneously building listening comprehension and language skills. To do this, the selection of read-alouds within a given grade level and across grade levels should not be random but rather should be guided by a coherent, sequenced approach to building knowledge.

Common Core State Standards and Your Child

One of the most important changes in U.S. schools in the last few decades is the creation of Common Core State Standards in English Language Arts and Math. By 2013, the standards describing what every child should know and be able to do were adopted by 45 states. State tests to determine if children were meeting those standards became a dominant feature of schooling in the era of the No Child Left Behind Act, which was passed in 2001. But 50 different states meant 50 different sets of standards and assessments, making it difficult to know whether children were truly proficient at reading and math or whether states were just lowering the bar to create the illusion of student achievement.

By establishing a single set of standards and common assessments, Common Core State Standards were designed to ensure clarity and consistency across the country. In many kindergarten and early elementary school classrooms, the new standards may mean dramatic changes in teaching and learning. Here are a few of the changes you should expect to see in your child's classroom—and how you can support high-level learning at home.

A Balance of Fiction and Nonfiction

For more than 25 years, the Core Knowledge movement has been built on the understanding that a rich, knowledge-based curriculum isn't merely "nice to have" but essential. A well-rounded curriculum is fundamental to reading comprehension, vocabulary development, and language proficiency. Common Core State Standards (CCSS) reflect this understanding. Indeed, some have described CCSS as "adding nonfiction to the curriculum," but what it really does is to *restore* art, music, history, and literature to the curriculum.

The same idea of domain-specific reading—that knowing a little bit (or, sometimes, a lot) about the subject you are studying is important in order to understand what you read about it—is also true about creativity, critical thinking, and problem solving. Indeed, nearly all of our most cherished goals for schooling are knowledge dependent. The more general knowledge you possess, the more fluid your thinking skills are. Yet how many times have we heard it said that schools are going to get away from teaching "mere facts" and focus on skills such as critical thinking, creativity, and problem solving? Unfortunately, it doesn't work that way. Common Core State Standards rescue knowledge from those who would trivialize it or who simply don't understand its fundamental role in human cognition.

Common Core State Standards call for an even balance between fiction and nonfiction in the early grades. Elementary classrooms will always rely heavily on stories, poems, and imagination. But a child's sense of wonder and awe is just as easily captured by animals, castles, and flying machines. To your child, those are fun things to learn about, play with, and talk about. To a teacher, it's building background knowledge. Both engagement and knowledge are essential ingredients, encouraging children to learn, explore, and grow. As a parent, you should be seeing your child exposed to a wide range of subjects in school. And you can support that at home by reading with your child on a wide variety of subjects—not just stories and fables—and encouraging his or her interest in real-world topics.

Explore the World Through Reading and Listening

Many teachers try to encourage young children to be independent readers by helping them to find books that are the right level for them to read on their own.

There's nothing wrong with that; however, that shouldn't be the only opportunity that your child has to interact with printed text in school, or even the most important one. Research tells us that children are able to understand text at a much higher level of sophistication when it's read out loud. Indeed, a child's ability to comprehend text read independently generally doesn't catch up to their ability to understand text read out loud until about the eighth grade.

In the early grades, read-alouds are a valuable way to help children interact with written text well above their ability to read independently. Most teachers understand this, but Common Core encourages teachers to use read-alouds not just for fictional stories and poems, but to build background knowledge and language skills across subject areas. If schools wait for a child to develop mature reading comprehension and read independently about nonfiction topics of interest, they're wasting valuable time that could be spent building background knowledge and exposing children to rich language and content that will pay dividends for the rest of their reading lives. Under Common Core State Standards, early childhood teachers are expected to devote significant time during language arts to reading aloud on a wide range of nonfiction topics, not just stories and poems.

One of the primary architects of the new standards put it eloquently: Common Core "restores elementary school teachers to their rightful place as guides to the world." As parents, you can support this in the same way—open your child's eyes to the world around them. And through books, videos, visits to museums and travel where possible, expose them to the wonders of the world around them.

A Focus on Evidence

Common Core Standards require students to pay greater attention to evidence in reading, writing, speaking, and listening. To meet standards, children are more likely to be asked not just to offer an opinion about a book or story but to back up their opinions with facts and details from the story. This may sound like a heavy lift for very young children, but it needn't be. When discussing stories with your children, ask probing questions. When discussing the Three Little Pigs, ask your child how she knows the third little pig was the smartest. What makes Anansi such a clever trickster? Questions that require your child to give examples from a story or text will prepare her for more complex reading and writing tasks later on.

Similarly, Common Core State Standards require that children spend less time writing "responses" to what they read and more time making coherent arguments in writing backed by evidence. It is far more common for children and parents to read together at home than to write. But to the degree that you do encourage your child to write at home—or that she enjoys writing independently—encourage your child not just to write stories but to create her own "books" that use real-life details and afford the opportunity for her to show what she knows about a topic.

Academic Vocabulary

The Common Core State Standards call on schools and teachers to help develop "academic vocabulary" in children. This merely means that certain words in our language tend to be subject-specific. You are unlikely to encounter the words "invertebrate" or "exoskeleton" unless you're reading about animals and insects, for example. Children love learning and saying "big words" and you should encourage them to do so. But academic vocabulary is more than just technical jargon. Learning about a subject encourages general vocabulary growth. We learn new words not by memorizing lists of words but by encountering them in everyday speech and reading. Academic vocabulary supports this general language and vocabulary growth. When a child is learning about ancient Egypt, for example, he may learn that "annual flooding in the Nile Delta was predictable enough for the Egyptians to plan agriculture around it." Your child's teacher may want him to know the academic vocabulary terms "agriculture" and "delta." But knowing those terms also allows children to make sense of the unfamiliar words such as "annual" and "predictable," which they will encounter again and again.

In this way academic vocabulary and general word growth support each other seamlessly.

Vocabulary is a slow-growing plant. We learn new words in context. Thus, the surest way to grow your child's vocabulary is to expose her to the richness of language in reading and speech. Do not be shy about speaking and reading to your child using as much sophisticated vocabulary as possible.

Coherence

Common Core asks not just for more nonfiction but for a knowledge-rich curriculum in English Language Arts. Yes, there's a difference. Perhaps the gravest disservice done to children in recent memory is the misguided attempt to teach and test reading comprehension not just as a skill but as a transferable skill—a set of tips and "reading strategies" that can be applied to virtually any text, regardless of subject matter. "The mistaken idea that reading is a skill," Daniel Willingham has said, "may be the single biggest factor holding back reading achievement in the country. Students will not meet standards that way. The knowledge base problem must be solved." CCSS aims to solve it with a curriculum "intentionally and coherently structured to develop rich content knowledge within and across grades." You can support this at home by identifying your child's interests and encouraging her to learn more and more about those things. Again, the benefit is not just learning about an interesting subject; knowing a lot about a subject is a sure way to grow language proficiency. By some estimates vocabulary growth occurs four times faster when students are familiar with the knowledge domain in which they encounter a new word. Thus the knowledge-rich classroom or home is also a *language-rich* classroom or home.

Perhaps the most important thing to understand is that standards are not curriculum. Common Core State Standards note that "by reading texts in history/social studies, science, and other disciplines, students build a foundation of knowledge in these fields that will also give them the background to be better readers in all content areas. Students can only gain this foundation when the curriculum is intentionally and coherently structured to develop rich content knowledge within and across grades." This is the fundamental insight upon which the Core Knowledge movement was built decades ago. Note that Common Core is silent on *which* texts and *what* knowledge is important. Decisions on the content of your child's education will largely be made at the state and local levels. But understanding that broad, rich, coherent knowledge is the key to vocabulary growth and language ability will allow you to be a watchful, effective advocate for your child and work with her school and teachers to ensure the knowledge- and language-rich education she deserves.

Building Literacy at Home

You don't need to be an early childhood literacy expert to help your son or daughter become a strong reader and writer. A few basic ideas and activities pursued diligently will pay big dividends and set your child on the road to full literacy.

Read to Your Kindergartner

Read to your child daily.

Without question, the single most important and helpful thing you can do is to set aside 20 minutes or more regularly, daily if possible, to read aloud to your child.

Remember that your child's ability to follow and enjoy a story when read aloud far surpasses her ability to read independently. Plus, studies confirm that the language of children's books is richer and more complex than the spoken language of even college graduates. Thus, reading aloud to your child is an unparalleled opportunity to expose your child to sophisticated language, vocabulary, and background knowledge. As you read, stop and talk about the story with your child to engage her in the story and check for understanding. Make inferences, predictions, and connections ("What do you think is going to happen next?" "This reminds me of the time when we . . ."), and encourage your child to do the same. And while small children love hearing familiar stories over and over, use your reading time to expand your child's horizons and knowledge, through nonfiction picture books as well as fictional stories.

Talk to Your Child

Engage your child in conversation and ask lots of questions.

A home that's rich in spoken words confers a tremendous boost to a child's language development. In a landmark study, published in 1995, researchers Betty Hart and Todd R. Risley found that the number of words children heard in their homes from birth to age four accurately predicted how many words they understood and how fast they could learn new words in kindergarten. In some cases the differences amounted to tens of millions of words heard before a child even set foot in a classroom for the first time.

"With few exceptions, the more parents talked to their children, the faster the children's vocabularies were growing and the higher the children's IQ test scores at age three and later," the researchers observed. Indeed, five years later, in third grade, early language competence still predicted language and reading comprehension. The preschoolers who had heard more words at home between birth and age four, and subsequently learned more words orally, became better readers.

The richest, most productive use of parent talk is back-and-forth conversation with your child. Don't just talk at your child; engage her in conversation and ask questions. Provide as many opportunities as possible for children to listen to and speak adult language. And don't feel compelled to simplify your vocabulary. Longer and more complex conversations with sophisticated words are a good way to expose your child to rich language.

Limit TV Time

Comparison studies of language complexity show that the language used on television is far less rich and complex than the language used in children's books and the typical conversation of college-educated parents. In addition, television distracts children from play and interaction with others. Most parents understand that television, like candy, is something that children may love but should have limited access to. The American Academy of Pediatrics has warned that screen time has no educational value at all for children under age two. Very young children learn more efficiently through interactions with people and things, not screens. For older children, TV can afford opportunities for learning and building knowledge. But it's no substitute for more enriching activities, and contributes less to language growth than reading and speaking.

Choose Activities That Build Background Knowledge

Every activity you do with your child, in the home or outside, is an opportunity to build background knowledge, vocabulary, and language skill. Trips to the park, the zoo, and a children's museum are an opportunity to expose your child to new things and ideas. Even a trip to the grocery store can be a way to engage your child, teaching the names of fruits and vegetables and where they come from. ("What do milk, cheese, and yogurt have in common?" "How come bananas don't grow where we live?" "How do you think those peaches got inside this can?")

Watching educational TV shows about animals or faraway places is a way to expand your child's awareness of other cultures and lands. Talking about what you see and do together builds language skill and vocabulary. If your child shows an interest in a particular topic, visit your local library. It will encourage your child's curiosity and teach her that books are a great way to learn more about interesting things.

Be a Reader, Raise a Reader

A large and comprehensive study across 27 different countries found that growing up in a home where there are lots of books, compared with a "bookless home," has as great an effect on the level of education a child will attain as having parents who are barely literate, compared with college-educated parents—about 3.2 years of advantage, on average. It may seem strange to suggest that merely having books in the home is enough to give kids an advantage, but the presence of books sends an unmistakable signal to children about what their parents value. When a child sees a parent reading on his or her own, it reinforces the idea that reading is an important and valuable use of time. Take every opportunity not just to read with your child but to demonstrate by example the importance of literacy in your own life.

Want to Learn More?

The Core Knowledge Foundation website (www.coreknowledge.org) offers a wide variety of information and resources for parents and professional educators. The *Core Knowledge Sequence* is designed to provide schools with a coherent, cumulative, and content-specific curriculum. In Core Knowledge schools, teaching and learning are more effective as teachers help students build upon prior knowledge and make more efficient progress from one year to the next. All students enjoy more equal educational opportunities as they are motivated by consistently challenging content. And all children are prepared to become members of the wider national community, respectful of diversity while strengthened by the shared knowledge that helps unite us on common ground.

To learn more, visit the Core Knowledge Reading Room on our website (www.coreknowledge.org/reading-room).

You can also find the following articles and video online:

"Building Knowledge: The Case for Bringing Content into the Language Arts Block and for a Knowledge-Rich Curriculum Core for All Children"
By E. D. Hirsch, Jr.
American Educator, Spring 2006
http://archive.aft.org/pubs-reports/american_educator/issues/spring06/hirsch.htm

"How Knowledge Helps: It Speeds and Strengthens Reading Comprehension, Learning—and Thinking"
By Daniel T. Willingham
American Educator, Spring 2006
http://archive.aft.org/pubs-reports/american_educator/issues/spring06/willingham.htm

Teaching Content Is Teaching Reading
www.youtube.com/watch?v=RiP-ijdxqEc

"The Early Catastrophe: The 30 Million Word Gap by Age 3"
By Betty Hart and Todd Risley
American Educator, Spring 2003
http://archive.aft.org/pubs-reports/american_educator/spring2003/catastrophe.html

Literature

Introduction: Worlds of Meaning

There is one simple practice that can make a world of difference for your kindergartner: read aloud to your child often, daily if possible. Reading aloud opens the doors to a world of meaning that most children are curious to explore but cannot enter on their own.

In reading aloud, you can offer your child a rich and varied selection of literature, including poetry, fiction, and nonfiction. Good literature brings language to life and offers children new worlds of adventure, knowledge, and humor.

Kindergartners enjoy traditional rhymes and fairy tales, like those found in the following pages. Even as adults, we find bits and pieces of fairy-tale lore entering our language, as when a sportscaster refers to the triumph of an underdog team as "a Cinderella story," or when a successful businessman is described as having "a Midas touch."

For children, fairy tales can delight and instruct, and provide ways of dealing with the darker human emotions, such as jealousy, greed, and fear. As G. K. Chesterton observed, fairy tales "are not responsible for producing in children fear, or any of the shapes of fear . . . The baby has known the dragon intimately ever since he had an imagination. What the fairy tale provides for him is a St. George to kill the dragon." And as Wanda Gag, the celebrated writer of children's tales, wrote in 1937, "A fairy story is not just a fluffy puff of nothing . . . nor is it merely a tenuous bit of make believe. . . . Its roots are real and solid, reaching back into man's past . . . and into the lives and customs of many people and countries." Whatever the geographical origin of the traditional tales we tell here—Africa, Japan, Europe, America, and so on—the stories have universal messages and lasting appeal across cultures and generations.

There are also, of course, many good books for young children by modern writers, such as Dr. Seuss, Maurice Sendak, Bill Martin, Jr., Verna Aardema, Shirley Hughes, Richard Scarry, Jack Prelutsky, Rosemary Wells, and many others. Your local library has a treasury of good books, and you might want to consult the lists of recommended works in such guides as:

Books That Build Character, by William Kilpatrick et al. (Simon and Schuster/Touchstone, 1994)
Books to Build On: A Grade-by-Grade Resource Guide for Parents and Teachers, edited by John Holdren and E. D. Hirsch, Jr. (Dell, 1996)
The Read-Aloud Handbook, 6th ed., by Jim Trelease (Penguin Books, 2006)
The New York Times Parent's Guide to the Best Books for Children, rev. ed., by Eden Ross Lipson (Times Books, 2000)

Beyond stories and poems, you can share appropriate works of nonfiction with your child. Kindergartners are fascinated by illustrated books that explain what things are and how they work, by biographies of famous people when they were children, and by books about animals and how they live.

Reading Aloud

As adults, we sometimes think that hearing the same story repeated is boring. Not so for young children! They love hearing the same stories over and over, and they discover something new and interesting every time. Here's a plan: just remember STORY!

[S]tart with Title and Pictures

First look at the book's cover or illustrated title page together. Read the title out loud, pointing to each word as you read it. Talk about what the title might mean, using pictures nearby for clues. Name the author and illustrator, if they are identified, so your child learns that real people make books.

Focus next on the pictures. Help your child name and describe what she sees. Then, before starting to read, ask her what she thinks the story will be about. The point is not to tell the story accurately but rather to find picture clues about character, theme, location, or plot. Hers may differ from the actual story, but that's okay!

[T]ell the Story

Read aloud, one or two pages at a time. Read the words clearly and expressively. At first, point to each word as you read. Granted, it would be tedious to do this throughout the entire story, but start by doing it on the first page or so.

Read with animation. Use different voices for different characters. For example, when you read "Goldilocks and the Three Bears," use a loud, assertive voice for Papa Bear, a quieter voice for Mama Bear, and a teeny-tiny squeak for Baby Bear.

[O]ffer Information

At the end of every page or two, pause and look at the illustrations together. Talk about them with your child. Ask what he sees. Use this conversation to confirm and clarify the words you have just read.

Look out for words or phrases that your child might not understand. Feel free to pause as you read in order to explain, rephrase, or give examples. We have identified in bold font a few words in these anthology readings that might be new to a kindergartner, but you know your child best and may notice other words that need some explaining. An ever-growing vocabulary is a rich reward for a child whose parent reads aloud.

When you are offering information, you are doing the essential task of building your child's vocabulary. The importance of helping develop a rich oral vocabulary during the preschool years cannot be overstated. Reading stories and nonfiction books aloud is one of the surest ways. Every time your child listens to a book or story, he will be exposed to words that often are not part of everyday spoken language.

Unlike many contemporary children's books, the selections in this anthology have been expressly written to include words that are challenging and evocative, designed to paint vivid pictures in the reader's and listener's minds. The parent notes in this anthology highlight a few such words, giving suggestions as to how to explain them to your child. Once you have talked about these words in the context of the story, make an effort to incorporate them into everyday conversations with your child, as the occasion arises.

For example, the "New Word" for the poem "Little Boy Blue" suggest that you explain the word "meadow" as meaning a large piece of land covered with grass. After reading this story, you might make a conscious effort to use the word "meadow" soon with your child: "We can fly a kite in the meadow behind your school. There's lots of room to run in the grass." It is only in hearing you use these new words in repeated, familiar contexts that your child will really begin to make sense of them. And as he hears them often, he will begin to use them comfortably and appropriately himself, in his own growing vocabulary.

A word of caution, though. While each anthology selection has a lot of colorful and interesting language likely to be unfamiliar to your kindergartner at the start, it is important not to bombard her with explanations for lots of new words in a single sitting. Don't try to discuss more than three or four new words per read-aloud session. Remember that young children like to hear the same story read over and over, and so each reading of a story with rich vocabulary represents another opportunity to talk about the new and interesting words it contains.

There are many ways to explain new words to your kindergartner as you come upon them during read-aloud time. Do all you can to keep your explanation at a level that your child can understand. Wordy, dictionary-like definitions—definitions that use more difficult words to explain the one in question—will not work. Instead, try simple, careful paraphrasing. Read the sentence from the story that contains a new word, and then repeat the very same sentence, this time substituting a synonymous word or phrase that your child already knows.

For example, in the story of the "Three Little Pigs," one sentence says, "The first little pig met a man with a bundle of straw . . ." Perhaps you have a hunch that your child is not familiar with this use of the word "straw." Read this sentence one more time slowly, pausing on the word. After the second reading, you might say, "That means the man had a bundle of dried grass. He had long pieces of dried grass tied in a bundle."

To further illustrate the meaning of a word unfamiliar to your kindergartner, you can also point to the pictures alongside the story. In the case of "The Story of the Jumping Mouse," when the the word "plains" is encountered, show your child the picture of the plains on page 175.

Another way to help your child understand a new word is to relate it to something within your child's own experience. "The City Mouse's house was stylish," you can say. "These jeans that you are wearing, with the colorful embroidery on them, are really stylish, too. They are very fancy and just the latest thing. I think they are cool—don't you? They are such stylish jeans." By relating the word to your child's own experience, you help her see how to use it in her own world and in her own vocabulary.

Using any or every one of these tactics to introduce new words to your child, you will be taking advantage of each read-aloud to help your child discover the richness of our language. Introducing new vocabulary is one of the most important things you do as you read together with your child, whether you are reading the stories and nonfiction selections of this anthology or reading other books, stories, and magazines. Always keep your eyes and ears attuned for new words—words that deserve an extra few minutes to be introduced deliberately to your child, then used consciously during the course of your day today, so that those words come to form part of your child's working vocabulary. Remember, we have used a bold font for some examples of new words that might deserve a few extra minutes of explanation.

We strongly recommend that before you read any selection aloud with your child, you take the time to read it to yourself. Do all that you can to read the passage through the eyes of a kindergartner. Make a mental note of the words that may be unknown to your child, and pick out a few to explain when you sit down together to share the story.

In this way, these anthology selections will never get old. They will grow with your child as you share them again and again throughout her early school years.

[R]eview and Discuss

At the end of each page or two, pause to make sure your child understands not only the vocabulary that has been part of the story but also the plot itself. Ask a question about a character or about something that has just happened.

As you read together more, your child will become more skillful at listening and answering simple questions. Then you can ask questions that require him to go beyond recalling immediate details. Some of the parent notes alongside the stories in this anthology suggest such questions, but your own child's experience and interests will bring up other possibilities as well.

[Y]our Child's Turn

During or after a story, asking questions is a good way to help your child understand. Here are a few that work well:

"Have you ever [done what one of the characters in the story is doing]?"

"Have you ever felt [an emotion felt by a character in the story]? When?"

"What do you think might happen next?"

"Why [did something happen, does a character feel a certain way]?"

"How do you think the story will end?"

After you finish the story, ask your child to tell it to you. (If her attention is lagging, postpone this request to another read-aloud time.) At first, retelling the story might be hard. There are good ways to help her. Move through the book, looking at each illustration, and ask her to tell you what is happening as a way to retell the story. Her early attempts may be disjointed, but that's all right.

You can also ask key questions about each illustration, then restate in complete sentences what your child tells you. Use standard phrases and story connectors, such as "Once upon a time," "First," "Next," "Then," and "The end." Soon he will be using those, too.

Reading Nonfiction?

Nonfiction read-alouds are just as important as stories. From them, your child can learn about all sorts of fascinating subjects. In this anthology, we include selections in history, science, and art. The five-step STORY approach can be more difficult to use when reading nonfiction, which is dense in vocabulary and information. Read only a couple of nonfiction pages at a time, spend lots of time talking about the illustrations, and find ways to relate the contents to your child's own experience.

The Pleasures of Reading Aloud

The hours you spend reading aloud with your kindergartner are precious—not only for your child, as a learning experience and as a time to feel close and comfortable with a caring adult, but also for you, as the person who is helping to nurture this child in so many important and wonderful ways. You will look back with pride and satisfaction, remembering these times and knowing that your child's engagement in learning began during the time you spent reading aloud.

Familiar and Favorite Poems

PARENTS: Here you will find a selection of traditional Mother Goose rhymes and other favorite poems. Children delight in hearing them read aloud, and they will enjoy and take pride in learning a few of their favorite rhymes by heart.

We also suggest some activities to go along with the poems. By playing with rhyming words, your child can sharpen her awareness of the sounds of spoken words. The activities are for speaking aloud; your child is not expected to read any words.

Activities for Poetry

- Read a rhyming poem aloud to your child. Then reread it and emphasize the rhyming words. Read the poem again and ask your child to "fill in the blank" with the rhyming word. For example:

"Jack be nimble, Jack be quick.

Jack jump over the candle _____." ("stick")

- Read a rhyming poem to your child several times. As you talk about the poem, give your child one member of a pair of rhyming words from the poem, then ask what rhymes with it. For example, after many readings of "Twinkle, Twinkle, Little Star," you might ask, "What rhymes with 'star'?" ("are"). And "What rhymes with 'high'?" ("sky"). Later you can extend this activity by asking, for example, "Can you think of any other words that rhyme with 'star'?" ("far," "bar," "car," etc.).
- Ask your child to be the "mistake finder." Say a poem that has grown familiar through repetition, but replace a rhyming word with a "wrong"

word that doesn't rhyme. Tell your child to clap when she hears a mistake. (Be sure to use a familiar poem so your child can do this activity successfully.) For example:

"One, two,
Buckle my shoe;
Three, four,
Shut the gate."

At times you can also ask her to correct your "mistake" by supplying the right rhyming word.

- Ask your child to repeat a word you say and then say a rhyming word. For example:

You say: "cat"
Child says: "cat, bat"
Here are some words to start with:

cat	*bed*	*map*	*pig*	*fan*
game	*toe*	*pin*	*fun*	*bug*
cake	*bump*	*boat*	*light*	*ball*

You can extend this activity by asking your child to say as many words as he can think of that rhyme with the word you say.

Some Poetry Collections for Children

Favorite Nursery Rhymes from Mother Goose, by Scott Gustafson (Greenwich Workshop Press, 2007)

The Random House Book of Poetry for Children, edited by Jack Prelutsky (Random House, 1983)

The Rooster Crows: A Book of American Rhymes and Jingles, edited by Maud and Miska Petersham (Macmillan/Aladdin, 1987)

Read-Aloud Rhymes for the Very Young, by Jack Prelutsky (Knopf Books for Young Readers, 1986)

Time to Rise

by Robert Louis Stevenson

A birdie with a yellow bill
Hopped upon the window-sill.
Cocked his shining eye and said:
"Ain't you 'shamed, you sleepy-head?"

Happy Thought

by Robert Louis Stevenson

The world is so full
of a number of things,
I'm sure we should all
be as happy as kings.

Hickory, Dickory, Dock

Hickory, dickory, dock,
The mouse ran up the clock.
The clock struck one,
The mouse ran down,
Hickory, dickory, dock.

Early to Bed

by Benjamin Franklin, from *Poor Richard's Almanac*

Early to bed and early to rise,
Makes a man healthy, wealthy,
and wise.

Diddle, Diddle, Dumpling

Diddle, diddle, dumpling, my son John,
Went to bed with his stockings on;
One shoe off, and one shoe on,
Diddle, diddle, dumpling, my son John.

A Diller, a Dollar

A diller, a dollar,
A ten o'clock scholar
What makes you come so soon?
You used to come at ten o'clock
But now you come at noon!

Hey, Diddle, Diddle

Hey, diddle, diddle,
The cat and the fiddle,
The cow jumped over the moon;
The little dog laughed
To see such sport,
And the dish ran away with the spoon.

Little Bo Peep

Little Bo Peep has lost her sheep,
And can't tell where to find them;
Leave them alone, and they'll come home,
Wagging their tails behind them.

Little Boy Blue

Little Boy Blue,
Come blow your horn,
The sheep's in the **meadow**,
The cow's in the corn;
But where is the boy
Who looks after the sheep?
He's under a haystack,
Fast asleep.

Baa, Baa, Black Sheep

Baa, baa, black sheep
Have you any wool?
Yes, sir, yes, sir,
Three bags full.
One for the master,
And one for the dame,
And one for the little boy
Who lives down the lane.

> **New Word**
> Does your child
> know what a
> **meadow** is? A
> meadow is a piece
> of land covered in
> grass.

One, Two, Buckle My Shoe

One, two,
Buckle my shoe;
Three, four,
Shut the door;
Five, six,
Pick up sticks;
Seven, eight,
Lay them straight;
Nine, ten,
A big fat hen;
Eleven, twelve,
Dig and delve;
Thirteen, fourteen,
Maids a-courting;
Fifteen, sixteen,
Maids in the kitchen;
Seventeen, eighteen,
Maids in waiting;
Nineteen, twenty,
My plate's empty.

Make a Connection

After sharing this rhyme with your child, try one of the Numbers and Number Sense activities from the math chapter.

Rain, Rain, Go Away

Rain, rain, go away,
Come again another day.

It's Raining, It's Pouring

It's raining, it's pouring,
The old man is snoring.
He bumped his head
And went to bed,
And he couldn't get up in the morning.

April Rain Song
by Langston Hughes

Let the rain kiss you.
Let the rain beat upon your head with silver liquid drops.
Let the rain sing you a lullaby.

The rain makes still pools on the sidewalk.
The rain makes running pools in the gutter.
The rain plays a little sleep-song on our roof at night—

And I love the rain.

The More It Snows
by A. A. Milne

The more it
SNOWS-tiddely-pom,
The more it
GOES-tiddely-pom
The more it
GOES-tiddely-pom
On
Snowing.

And nobody
KNOWS-tiddely-pom,
How cold my
TOES-tiddely-pom
How cold my
TOES-tiddely-pom
Are
Growing.

Make a Connection

After sharing these weather-related rhymes with your child, read about seasons and weather in the science chapter.

My Nose

by Dorothy Aldis

It doesn't breathe;
It doesn't smell;
It doesn't feel
So very well.

I am discouraged
With my nose:
The only thing it
Does is blows.

Roses Are Red

Roses are red,
Violets are blue,
Sugar is sweet,
And so are you.

Mary, Mary, Quite Contrary

Mary, Mary, quite contrary
How does your garden grow?
With silver bells, and cockle shells,
And pretty maids all in a row.

Make a Connection

Have you read about the five senses in the science chapter? Use these rhymes to talk about sight, smell, and taste.

Tommy

by Gwendolyn Brooks

I put a seed into the ground
And said, "I'll watch it grow."
I watered it and cared for it
As well as I could know.

One day I walked in my back yard,
And oh, what did I see!
My seed had popped itself right out,
Without consulting me.

Make a Connection
Reread this poem after you have read about plants in the science chapter.

Jack and Jill

Jack and Jill went up the hill
To fetch a pail of water;
Jack fell down and broke his crown,
And Jill came tumbling after.

Jack Be Nimble

Jack be nimble,
Jack be quick,
Jack jump over
The candlestick.

There Was a Little Girl

There was a little girl
Who had a little curl
Right in the middle of her forehead;
When she was good, she was very, very good,
And when she was bad, she was horrid.

Little Miss Muffet

Little Miss Muffet
Sat on a tuffet,
Eating her curds and whey;
Along came a spider,
Who sat down beside her
And frightened Miss Muffet away.

Georgie Porgie

Georgie Porgie, pudding and pie,
Kissed the girls and made them cry;
When the boys came out to play,
Georgie Porgie ran away.

Humpty Dumpty

Humpty Dumpty sat on a wall,
Humpty Dumpty had a great fall.
All the king's horses,
And all the king's men,
Couldn't put Humpty together again.

Little Jack Horner

Little Jack Horner
Sat in a corner,
Eating his Christmas pie;
He put in his thumb,
And pulled out a plum,
And said, "What a good boy am I!"

Mary Had a Little Lamb

from the poem by Sarah Josepha Hale

Mary had a little lamb,
Its fleece was white as snow;
And everywhere that Mary went,
The lamb was sure to go.

It followed her to school one day,
That was against the rule;
It made the children laugh and play
To see a lamb at school.

And so the teacher turned it out,
But still it lingered near,
And waited patiently about
Till Mary did appear.

"Why does the lamb love Mary so?"
The eager children cry.
"Why, Mary loves the lamb, you know,"
The teacher did reply.

Hot Cross Buns!

Hot cross buns!
Hot cross buns!
One a penny, two a penny,
Hot cross buns!

If you have no daughters,
Give them to your sons;
One a penny, two a penny,
Hot cross buns!

Simple Simon

Simple Simon met a pieman
Going to the fair;
Says Simple Simon to the pieman,
"Let me taste your ware."

Says the pieman to Simple Simon,
"Show me first your penny";
Says Simple Simon to the pieman,
"Indeed, I have not any."

Old Mother Hubbard

Old Mother Hubbard
Went to the cupboard
To get her poor dog a bone,
But when she got there,
The cupboard was bare,
And so her poor dog had none.

Old King Cole

Old King Cole
Was a merry old soul,
And a merry old soul was he;
He called for his pipe,
And he called for his bowl,
And he called for his fiddlers three.

Sing a Song of Sixpence

Sing a song of sixpence,
A pocket full of rye;
Four and twenty blackbirds
Baked in a pie.

When the pie was opened,
The birds began to sing;
Wasn't that a dainty dish
To set before the king?

The king was in his counting-house
Counting out his money;
The queen was in the parlor
Eating bread and honey.

The maid was in the garden
Hanging out the clothes,
Along came a blackbird
And pecked off her nose.

Ladybug, Ladybug

Ladybug, ladybug,
Fly away home,
Your house is on fire,
And your children are gone.

Three Blind Mice

Three blind mice,
Three blind mice,
See how they run!
See how they run!
They all ran after the farmer's wife,
Who cut off their tails with a carving knife,
Did you ever see such a sight in your life,
As three blind mice?

Jack Sprat

Jack Sprat could eat no fat,
His wife could eat no lean,
And so between the two of them
They licked the platter clean.

See Saw, Margery Daw

See Saw, Margery Daw
Jenny shall have a new master;
She shall have but a penny a day,
Because she can't work any faster.

A. RACKHAM

Three Little Kittens

by Eliza Lee Follen

Three little kittens lost their mittens
And they began to cry,
"Oh, mother dear,
We very much fear
That we have lost our mittens."
"Lost your mittens!
You naughty kittens!
Then you shall have no pie!"
"Mee-ow, mee-ow, mee-ow."
"No, you shall have no pie."
"Mee-ow, mee-ow, mee-ow."

The three little kittens found their
mittens
And they began to cry,
"Oh, mother dear,
See here, see here!
See, we have found our mittens!"
"Put on your mittens,
You silly kittens,
And you may have some pie."
"Purr-r, purr-r, purr-r,
Oh, let us have the pie!
Purr-r, purr-r, purr-r."

The three little kittens put on their
mittens,
And soon ate up the pie;
"Oh, mother dear,
We greatly fear
That we have soiled our mittens!"
"Soiled your mittens!
You naughty kittens!"
Then they began to sigh,
"Mee-ow, mee-ow, mee-ow."
Then they began to sigh,
"Mee-ow, mee-ow, mee-ow."

The three little kittens washed their
mittens,
And hung them out to dry;
"Oh, mother dear,
Do not you hear
That we have washed our mittens?"
"Washed your mittens!
Oh, you're good kittens!
But I smell a rat close by,
Hush, hush! Mee-ow, mee-ow."
"We smell a rat close by,
Mee-ow, mee-ow, mee-ow."

There Was an Old Woman Who Lived in a Shoe

There was an old woman who lived in a shoe
She had so many children she didn't know what to do;
She gave them some broth without any bread;
And spanked them all soundly and put them to bed.

Star Light, Star Bright

Star light, star bright,
First star I see tonight,
I wish I may, I wish I might,
Have the wish I wish tonight.

Aesop's Fables

A fable is a special kind of story that teaches a lesson. People have been telling some fables over and over for hundreds of years. It is said that many of these fables were told by a man named Aesop (EE-sop), who lived in Greece a very, very long time ago.

Aesop knew bad behavior when he saw it, and he wanted people to be better. But he knew that we don't like to be told when we're bad. That is why many of his fables have animals in them. The animals sometimes talk and act like people. In fact, the animals behave just as well and just as badly as people do. That's because, even when a fable is about animals, it is really about people. Through these stories about animals, Aesop teaches us about how we should act.

At the end of the fable, Aesop often tells us a lesson we should learn. The lesson is called the moral of the story.

Here are four of Aesop's fables. The first three end by telling you the moral of the story. But the last one does not tell you the moral. When you read the last fable, "The Grasshopper and the Ants," talk about what you think the moral of that story is.

The Dog and His Shadow

One day a dog was carrying home a large bone, which he held in his mouth. On his way he had to cross a bridge over a stream. As he crossed, he happened to look down into the water. There he saw his shadow, like a reflection in a mirror. He thought his reflection was another dog with a bigger bone than his own. He decided he wanted the other dog's bone, so he opened his mouth and barked. But when he did, the bone in his mouth dropped into the water and was gone forever.

Moral: If you are greedy, you may lose everything.

The Lion and the Mouse

One day a little mouse was running along when he happened to run across the paws of a big sleeping lion. This woke the lion—and the lion did not like to be woken up before he was ready! The lion was very angry at being disturbed, and he grabbed the mouse in his big paw. He was just about to swallow him when the mouse cried out, "Please, kind sir, I didn't mean to disturb you. If you will let me go, I will be grateful to you forever. And if I can, I will help you someday."

The lion laughed a big laugh. How, he thought, could such a little creature as a mouse ever help so great a creature as a lion? All the same, the lion decided to let the mouse go.

Not long after, the mouse was running along when he heard a great roaring nearby. He went closer to see what the trouble was, and there he saw the lion, caught in a hunter's net. The mouse remembered his promise to the lion, and he began gnawing the ropes of the net, and kept gnawing until he had made a hole big enough so that the lion could get free.

Moral: Little friends may be great friends.

The Hare and the Tortoise

There once was a hare who was always boasting about how fast he could run. One day he said to the other animals, "I'm so fast that no one can beat me. I dare anyone here to a race."

The tortoise said quietly, "I will race you."

"You!" laughed the hare. "That's a joke! Why, I could run circles around you all the way."

"Save your boasting until you've won," said the tortoise. "Shall we race?"

So the race began. The hare darted almost out of sight at once, and very soon he was far ahead of the tortoise, who moved along at a steady, even pace.

The hare knew he was far ahead, so he stopped and said, "I think I'll take a little nap. When I wake up, I can zip ahead of the tortoise without even trying."

So the hare settled into a nice sleep. And he was still asleep when the tortoise passed by. And when the hare finally woke up, he looked ahead, and what did he see? The tortoise was just then crossing the finish line to win the race!

Moral: Slow and steady wins the race. (Being the most talented doesn't always mean you'll come out on top. Hard, steady work is very important, too.)

The Grasshopper and the Ants

In a field on a fine summer's day, a grasshopper was hopping about, singing and dancing and enjoying himself.

Nearby, a group of ants was hard at work. They had built their house underground, and they were filling it with food to last them through the long cold winter ahead.

"Why not come and play with me?" asked the grasshopper. "Why bother about winter? We have plenty of food now. Come, leave your work. Now's the time to dance and sing."

But the ants paid no attention to the grasshopper. They kept working hard, all day and every day.

But not the grasshopper. All summer long, while the ants worked, he jumped about the field, and danced, and sang. Sometimes he'd sit for hours and listen to the humming of the bees, or watch the butterflies flitting about, or take long, lazy naps in the warm sun. And when he woke up he would sing this song:

"The summertime's the time for me,
For then I'm happy as can be.
I watch the butterflies and bees,
I do whatever I may please.
I do no work the livelong day,
I pass the time in fun and play.
Oh, summertime's the time for me,
For I'm as happy as can be!"

Yes, the grasshopper was a happy fellow—but he never thought about the future. One day the grasshopper woke up and felt a chill in the air. Then he saw the leaves turn red, gold, and brown and begin to fall from the trees. Then the days kept getting cooler, and soon the grasshopper saw no butterflies or bees, and the fields where he liked to sing and dance turned bare and hard.

Now the cold days of winter were upon him, and the grasshopper was freezing and hungry. He came to the ants' house and knocked on the door.

"What do you want?" asked the ants.

"May I come in and share your food?" asked the grasshopper.

"What did you do all summer?" asked the ants. "Didn't you put away some food to use now?"

"No," said the shivering grasshopper. "I was too busy singing and dancing."

"So," said the ants, "you sang and danced all summer while we worked. Well, now you can sing and dance while we eat!"

And as the hungry grasshopper walked away, he sadly sang this song:

"I did no work all summer long
And now I know that I was wrong.
It isn't fair for me to play
While others work the livelong day.
Next time I'll work as well as dance,
Then I'll be ready, like the ants!"

What do you think the moral of this story is?

> **Make a Connection**
> After reading this fable, read the story of the Little Red Hen on page 64. Help your child to compare the two tales. Do they have the same moral?

Stories

. . . .

The Three Little Pigs

Once upon a time there was an old mother pig with three little pigs. They lived happily together, but then hard times came and there was not enough to go around. So the three little pigs set out to make their own way in the world.

The first little pig met a man with a bundle of **straw,** and said to him, "Please, sir, give me that **straw** so that I may build a house."

The man gave him the **straw,** and the little pig built a house with it.

But soon, along came a big, bad wolf, and he knocked at the door and said, "Little pig, little pig, let me come in."

And the pig answered, "Not by the hair of my chinny chin chin."

So the wolf said, "Then I'll huff, and I'll puff, and I'll blow your house down!" And he huffed, and he puffed, and he blew the house down. The little pigs ran away.

The second little pig met a man with a bundle of sticks, and said to him, "Please, sir, give me those sticks so that I may build a house."

> **New Word**
> "Straw" is a multi-meaning word. Does your child know what this meaning of **straw** is? It can be explained as a long dry piece of grass. Help your child find straw in the illustration.

The man gave him the sticks, and the little pig built a house with them.

Then along came the wolf, and he said, "Little pig, little pig, let me come in."

"Not by the hair of my chinny chin chin."

"Then I'll huff, and I'll puff, and I'll blow your house down!" And he huffed, and he puffed, and he puffed and he huffed, and at last he blew the house down. The little pig ran to find his brothers.

The third little pig met a man with a load of bricks, and said to him, "Please, sir, give me those bricks so that I may build a house."

The man gave him the bricks, and the little pig built a house with them.

Then along came the wolf, and he said, "Little pig, little pig, let me come in."

"Not by the hair of my chinny chin chin."

"Then I'll huff, and I'll puff, and I'll blow your house down!" Well, he huffed, and he puffed, and he puffed and he huffed, and he huffed and he puffed, but he could not blow that house down. And when he found that all his huffing and puffing was for nothing, he said, "Little pig, I know where there is a nice apple tree."

"Where?" asked the pig.

"Down at Merry Garden," said the wolf. "If you will be ready tomorrow morning, I will come and get you, and we will go together and pick some apples."

"Very well," said the pig. "I will be ready. What time do you want to go?"

"Oh, at five o'clock," said the wolf.

Well, the next morning the little pig got up at four o'clock, an hour before the wolf said he would come. And the little pig picked the apples before the wolf arrived.

This made the wolf very angry indeed, and he declared that he would eat up the little pig, and that he would come down the chimney to get him. When the little pig saw what was happening, he and his brothers made a blazing fire, and put over it a big pot full of water. The wolf came down the chimney and—splash!—fell in the burning hot water, and that was the end of the wolf. And the little pigs lived happily ever after.

Goldilocks and the Three Bears

Once upon a time there were three bears who lived in a house in the woods.

Papa Bear was a great big bear. Mama Bear was a middle-sized bear. And Baby Bear was a wee little bear.

Each bear had a bowl for his **porridge**. Papa Bear had a great big bowl. Mama Bear had a middle-sized bowl. And Baby Bear had a wee little bowl.

One morning Mama Bear made some nice **porridge**. She put it into the bowls and set them on the table. But the **porridge** was too hot to eat. So, to give the **porridge** time to cool, the bears all went out for a walk.

While they were gone, a little girl named Goldilocks came to the house.

First she looked in at the window.

Then she peeped in at the door.

Then she knocked, but no one answered.

Now, you might think that she would turn right around and go home. But no—Goldilocks walked right into the house!

She was very glad when she saw the three bowls of **porridge**. First she tasted the porridge in the great big bowl, but it was too hot.

Then she tasted the **porridge** in the middle-sized bowl, but it was too cold.

Then she tasted the **porridge** in the wee little bowl, and it was just right. She liked it so much that she ate it all up!

Then Goldilocks saw three chairs and decided to sit down and rest. First she sat in Papa Bear's great big chair, but it was too hard.

> **New Word**
> Does your child know what **porridge** is? **Porridge** is like oatmeal.

Then she sat in Mama Bear's middle-sized chair, but it was too soft.

Then she sat in Baby Bear's wee little chair, and it was just right.

She sat and sat till suddenly—*plump!*—the bottom of the chair fell out.

Goldilocks picked herself up and looked for another place to rest. She went upstairs and found three beds.

First she lay down on Papa Bear's great big bed, but it was too high.

Then she lay down on Mama Bear's middle-sized bed, but it was too low.

So she lay down on Baby Bear's wee little bed, and it was just right.

She covered herself up, and then fell fast asleep.

About this time the three bears came back from their walk. They went straight to the table, and suddenly Papa Bear cried out in his great big voice, "Someone has been eating my **porridge**!"

Then Mama Bear looked at her dish, and she said in her middle-sized voice, "Someone has been eating my **porridge**!"

Then Baby Bear looked at his dish, and he said in his wee little voice, "Someone has been eating my **porridge**, and has eaten it all up!"

Then the three bears began to look all around them. Papa Bear said in his great big voice, "Someone has been sitting in my chair!"

Then Mama Bear said in her middle-sized voice, "Someone has been sitting in my chair!"

Then Baby Bear said in his wee little voice, "Someone has been sitting in my chair and has broken the bottom out of it!"

The three bears ran upstairs to their bedroom.

What About You?

Ask your child, "How do you think Goldilocks must have felt when the tiny chair broke into pieces and she fell onto the floor?"

Papa Bear said in his great big voice, "Someone has been lying in my bed!"

Then Mama Bear said in her middle-sized voice, "Someone has been lying in my bed!"

Then Baby Bear looked at his bed, and he cried out in his wee little voice, "Someone has been lying in my bed—and here she is!"

Baby Bear's squeaky little voice startled Goldilocks, and she sat up wide awake.

When she saw the three bears, she gave a cry, jumped up, and ran away as fast as she could. And to this day, the three bears have never seen her again.

Do It Yourself!
Encourage your child to repeat what the bears say, using a different voice for each bear. Repeat this participation throughout the story.

The Three Billy Goats Gruff

Once upon a time there were three billy goats who were all named Gruff.

The three Billy Goats Gruff longed to go up a hillside covered with thick green grass. They wanted to eat that grass, and so grow nice and fat.

To get to the hillside, they had to cross a brook. Over the brook was a bridge. And under the bridge lived a mean, ugly troll.

Now, the first to cross the bridge was the Little Billy Goat Gruff.

"Trip-trap, trip-trap!" went the bridge.

"Who's that trip-trapping over my bridge?" roared the troll.

And the tiny goat said in a wee small voice, "It is only I, Little Billy Goat Gruff. And I'm going to the hillside to make myself fat."

"Oh-ho!" said the troll. "I am coming to gobble you up."

"Oh, please don't eat me," said the Little Billy Goat Gruff. "I'm too little, yes I am. Wait a bit until my brother comes. He's much bigger."

"Well, be off with you!" said the troll.

Soon the Middle Billy Goat Gruff came to cross the bridge.

"Trip-trap! Trip-trap! Trip-trap!" went the bridge.

"Who's that trip-trapping over my bridge?" roared the troll.

And the goat said in a not-so-small voice, "It is only I, Middle Billy Goat Gruff, and I'm going to the hillside to make myself fat."

"Oh-ho!" said the troll. "I am coming to gobble you up."

"Oh no, don't eat me. Wait till my brother comes along. He's much bigger."

"Very well; be off with you!" said the troll.

And just then up came the great Big Billy Goat Gruff.

"*Trip-trap! Trip-trap! Trip-trap!*" went the bridge, for the Big Billy Goat Gruff was so heavy that the bridge creaked and groaned under him.

"Who's that trip-trapping over my bridge?" roared the troll.

And a deep, loud voice boomed, "It is I, Big Billy Goat Gruff."

"Oh-ho!" said the troll. "I am coming to gobble you up."

"Well, then, come and try it!" said the Big Billy Goat Gruff.

So the troll climbed up on the bridge.

And the Big Billy Goat Gruff rushed at that troll, and he bumped him and thumped him, and he danced and pranced all over him, till the troll rolled off the bridge into the water, never to be seen again.

After that, the Big Billy Goat Gruff went to the hillside, where he joined his brothers. And they all three got so fat they were scarcely able to walk home again.

Snip, snap, snout,

This tale's told out.

> **Do It Yourself!**
> This is a great story to act out. You don't need any props, and with only two children, or a child and an adult, you can do all the parts just by changing your voice a bit. Try it!

Momotaro: Peach Boy

(A Folktale from Japan)

Once upon a time, in a small village in the country of Japan, there lived a kind old man and his good, honest wife.

One fine morning the old man went to the hills to cut firewood, while his wife went down to the river to wash clothes. The old woman was scrub-scrub-scrubbing the clothes on a stone when something strange came floating down the river. It was a peach—a very big, round peach! She picked it up—oof!—and carried it home with her, thinking to give it to her husband to eat when he returned.

The old man soon came down from the hills, and the good wife set the peach before him. She lifted a knife and brought it close to the big peach. Suddenly a little voice cried out, "Stop! Don't hurt me." And as the old man and woman looked on in amazement, the peach split apart and out came a baby boy.

The old man and woman took care of the baby. They were kind to him and raised him as their own son. They called him Momotaro, a fine name, as it means "Peach Boy."

Momotaro grew up to be strong and brave—which was a good thing for the people in the village, because for many years they had been attacked and robbed by the oni, who were mean and greedy monsters. Everyone in the village was afraid of the oni.

One day, when Momotaro had grown to be a young man, he said to his parents, "I am going to the island of the oni monsters who steal from our village. I will bring back what they have stolen, and stop them from harming us ever again. Please make some millet cakes for me to take along on my journey."

The old man and woman were worried, but they made the millet cakes for Momotaro. And so he started on his way.

He had not gone far when he met a dog. "Where are you going, Momotaro?" asked the dog.

"I am going to the island of the oni monsters to bring back what they have stolen from my village," said Momotaro.

"And what are you carrying in that sack?" asked the dog.

"I'm carrying the best millet cakes in all Japan," said Momotaro. "Would you like one?"

"Mmm, yes!" said the dog. "And I will come with you to the island of the oni monsters. I will help you."

The dog ate the millet cake, then he and Momotaro walked on. They soon met a monkey.

"Where are you going, Momotaro?" asked the monkey.

"I am going to the island of the oni monsters to bring back what they have stolen from my village," said Momotaro.

"I will come with you," said the monkey. And Momotaro thanked him and gave him a millet cake.

The three of them were walking along when they heard a call: "Momotaro, Momotaro! Where are you going?"

Momotaro looked around to see who was calling. A big pheasant flew out of a field and landed at his feet. Momotaro told him that he and his new friends were going to the island of the oni monsters. "Then I will come with you and help you," said the pheasant. Momotaro thanked him and gave him a millet cake.

So Momotaro went on his way, with the dog, the monkey, and the pheasant following close behind.

They soon came to the island of the oni monsters. The monsters lived in a big stone castle. The pheasant flew over the high castle walls. He swooped down and used his sharp beak to peck-peck-peck at the oni monsters. The monsters shouted and screamed and ran about in confusion.

Just then Momotaro, with the help of the dog and monkey, broke through the gate of the castle. Oh, what a battle! The dog and monkey scratched and bit the monsters' legs. Momotaro slashed left and right with his sharp sword. Many of the monsters ran away, and soon Momotaro captured their king. When they saw their king held prisoner, the other oni monsters bowed down before Momotaro.

Momotaro ordered the monsters to collect all the treasure they had stolen. They brought out beautiful gowns and jewels, and gold and silver, and much more besides.

And so Momotaro took all the riches back to the village. The village was never again bothered by the oni monsters. And Momotaro and the old man and the old woman lived in peace and plenty for the rest of their lives.

What Is an Illustrator?

Do you like to draw? Meet Gail McIntosh. She loves to draw. In fact, drawing is her job. She's an artist—a special kind of artist called an illustrator.

An illustrator makes the pictures—the illustrations—that go in a book. Illustrations can be drawings, paintings, even paper cutouts.

Gail drew the pictures for the story "The Three Little Pigs." She also drew and painted many other illustrations in this book (you can see some on these pages: 48, 56, and 125.)

Before she draws a picture, Gail begins by imagining, by making pictures in her mind. When someone reads you a story, do you sometimes see pictures in your mind of what's happening in the story? That's what Gail does: she sees pictures in her mind—and then she draws them!

"What I do," says Gail, "is draw, draw, and draw." And even when she's not drawing, she's thinking about drawing. If someone asks her to illustrate a story, she has to think about what she's going to draw. She has to make choices, such as, "How mean should the wolf in 'The Three Little Pigs' look?"

When you sit down with a book that has pictures, find out who the illustrator is. And the next time you draw or paint, think about those "pictures in your mind" from some of your favorite stories.

The Little Red Hen

Once a hardworking little red hen lived on a farm with a dog, a cat, and a pig. One day she decided to make bread.

"Who will help me cut the wheat to make my bread?" she asked.

"Not I," said the dog.

"Not I," yawned the cat.

"Not I," grunted the pig.

"Then I will do it myself," said the little red hen.

When she had cut the wheat, the little red hen asked, "Who will help me take the wheat to the miller for grinding?"

"Not I," growled the dog.

"Not I," hissed the cat.

"Not I," snorted the pig.

"Then I will do it myself," said the little red hen.

When the wheat had been **ground** into flour, the little red hen asked, "Who will help me make the flour into bread dough?"

"Not I," sighed the dog.

"Not I," whined the cat.

"Not I," sniffed the pig.

"Then I will do it myself," said the little red hen.

When she had mixed the dough, the little red hen asked, "Who will help me bake the bread?"

"Not I," muttered the dog.

"Not I," murmured the cat.

"Not I," grumbled the pig.

"Then I will do it myself," said the little red hen.

And so, all by herself, she baked a fine loaf of bread. "Now," said the little red hen, "who will help me eat the bread?"

"I will!" barked the dog.

"I will!" purred the cat.

"I will!" grunted the pig.

But the little red hen said, "No, you won't. I cut the wheat all by myself. I took it to the miller all by myself. I mixed the dough and baked it all by myself. And now I shall eat the bread—all by myself!"

Chicken Little

One fine morning Chicken Little went out to the woods. As she walked along, an acorn fell on her head.

"Oh, dear me!" she cried. "The sky is falling. I must go and tell the king!"

On the way she met Henny Penny. "Henny Penny, the sky is falling!" said Chicken Little.

"How do you know?" asked Henny Penny.

"A piece of it fell on my poor head," said Chicken Little.

"Then let us go and tell the king!" said Henny Penny.

So Henny Penny and Chicken Little went along until they met Goosey Loosey.

"Goosey Loosey, the sky is falling!" said Henny Penny.

"How do you know?" said Goosey Loosey.

"A piece of it fell on my poor head," said Chicken Little.

"Then let us go and tell the king!" said Goosey Loosey.

So Goosey Loosey, Henny Penny, and Chicken Little went along until they met Ducky Lucky.

"Ducky Lucky, the sky is falling!" said Goosey Loosey.

"How do you know?" said Ducky Lucky.

"A piece of it fell on my poor head," said Chicken Little.

"Then let us go and tell the king!" said Ducky Lucky.

So Ducky Lucky, Goosey Loosey, Henny Penny, and Chicken Little went along until they met Turkey Lurkey.

"Turkey Lurkey, the sky is falling!" said Ducky Lucky.

"How do you know?" said Turkey Lurkey.

"A piece of it fell on my poor head," said Chicken Little.

"Then let us go and tell the king!" said Turkey Lurkey.

So they went along until they met Foxy Loxy.

"Foxy Loxy, the sky is falling!" said Turkey Lurkey.

"Oh, is that so?" said sly Foxy Loxy. "If the sky is falling, you'd better keep safe in my den, and I will go and tell the king."

So Chicken Little, Henny Penny, Goosey Loosey, Ducky Lucky, and Turkey Lurkey followed Foxy Loxy into his den. And they never came back out again.

Make a Connection

Remind your child of the saying "Great oaks from little acorns grow" (see page 142). Ask your child what kind of trees must have been in the woods where Chicken Little was walking.

Little Red Riding Hood

(A Tale from the Brothers Grimm)

There was once a sweet little girl who was loved by all who knew her, but most of all by her grandmother, who could not do enough for her. Once she sent her a cloak with a red velvet hood, and the little girl was so pleased with it that she wanted to wear it always. And so she came to be called Little Red Riding Hood.

One day her mother said to her, "Little Red Riding Hood, I want you to go and see your grandmother, for she is feeling sick. Take her these cakes we baked yesterday; they will do her good. Go quickly, and mind that you stay on the path, and do not stop along the way. When you go into Grandmother's house, don't forget to say 'Good morning' instead of looking all around the house."

"I will do just as you say, Mother," promised Little Red Riding Hood, and she started on her way.

Her grandmother lived in a house in the wood, a half hour's walk from the village. Little Red Riding Hood had only just entered the wood when she came upon a wolf. But she did not know what a wicked animal he was, so she was not afraid of him.

"Good morning, Little Red Riding Hood," said the wolf.

"Good morning, Mr. Wolf," she answered kindly.

"And where are you going so early?" he asked.

"To my grandmother's house."

"And what's that you're carrying?"

"A little basket of cakes, for you see, Grandmother is sick and this will make her feel better."

"And where does your grandmother live?"

"In the wood, a little ways from here, in a **cottage** under three big oak trees," said Little Red Riding Hood.

"Mmm," said the wolf as he thought, "What a tender young morsel this little girl is. But she's not enough for a meal. I must manage somehow to eat both her and her grandmother."

He walked along beside Little Red Riding Hood for a while and then

> **New Word**
> Does your child know what a **cottage** is? Explain that a **cottage** is a small simple house.

said, "Why, look at all the pretty flowers. Why don't you stop to pick some of them? You're hurrying along as if you were late for school, yet the birds are singing and everything is so pleasant here in the wood."

Little Red Riding Hood looked up and saw the sunlight dancing in the leaves of the trees. She saw the lovely flowers around her, and she thought, "I am sure Grandmother would be pleased if I took her a bunch of fresh flowers." So she left the path and went out of her way into the wood to pick some flowers. Each time she picked one, she saw others even prettier farther on, and so she strayed deeper and deeper into the wood.

As for the wolf, he hurried straight to Grandmother's **cottage**. He knocked on the door.

"Who's there?" called Grandmother.

"It is I, Little Red Riding Hood," said the wolf in as gentle a voice as he could.

"Oh, lift the latch and come in, dear," said the old woman, "for I am too weak to get out of bed."

So the wolf lifted the latch, swung open the door, **pounced** upon Grandmother, and gobbled her up in one mouthful! Then he dressed himself in one of the old woman's nightgowns and nightcaps. With a wicked grin, he lay down on the bed and pulled up the covers.

Meanwhile, Little Red Riding Hood, having picked all the flowers she could carry, finally found her way back to the path. She walked on quickly until she came to Grandmother's house. She was surprised to find the door open, and as she stepped inside, she felt very strange. "Oh, dear," she said to herself, "this morning I was so glad to be going to see my grandmother. Why do I feel so frightened now?"

She took a deep breath and called out, "Good morning." But there was no answer. She went up to the bed. There she saw, as she thought, her grandmother, but she could see only her head, for the wolf had pulled the covers up under his chin and had pulled the nightcap down to his eyes. Little Red Riding Hood thought her grandmother looked strange indeed.

"Oh, Grandmother," she said, "what big ears you have!"

> **New Word**
> Does your child know what "pounced" means? "Pounced" means jumped quickly. The wolf jumped quickly on Grandmother and gobbled her up in one mouthful!

"The better to hear you with, my dear," said the wolf.

"And Grandmother, what big eyes you have!"

"The better to see you with, my dear."

"And Grandmother, what big teeth you have!"

"The better to eat you!" cried the wolf as he sprang out of bed and swallowed Little Red Riding Hood in one big gulp.

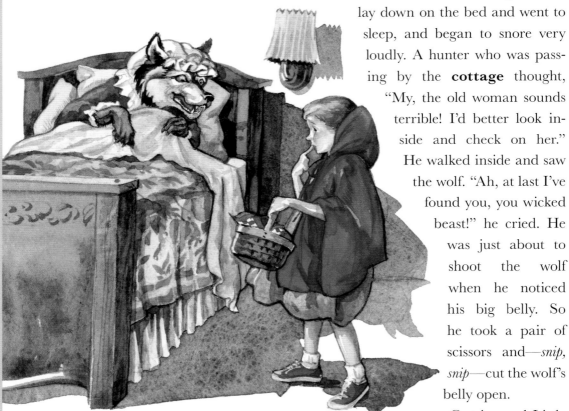

Now the wolf, feeling stuffed, lay down on the bed and went to sleep, and began to snore very loudly. A hunter who was passing by the **cottage** thought, "My, the old woman sounds terrible! I'd better look inside and check on her." He walked inside and saw the wolf. "Ah, at last I've found you, you wicked beast!" he cried. He was just about to shoot the wolf when he noticed his big belly. So he took a pair of scissors and—*snip, snip*—cut the wolf's belly open.

Out jumped Little Red Riding Hood! "Oh, I've been so afraid!" she said. "It's so dark inside the wolf!"

Then out came Grandmother, still alive.

Little Red Riding Hood fetched some large stones, and the hunter filled the wolf's belly with them. When the wolf woke up, he tried to run away, but the stones were so heavy that he sank down and fell dead.

Little Red Riding Hood sat down with her grandmother and the hunter, and together they ate the cakes Little Red Riding Hood had brought. And Little Red Riding Hood said to herself, "After this, I shall always do as my mother tells me, and I shall never leave the path again, not even to pick the pretty flowers."

PARENTS: The Brothers Grimm version of this tale ends with the moral of "Never leave the path." But you might come across other versions of this story (based on the re-telling by the seventeenth-century French tale-teller Charles Perrault), in which the story ends with the wolf gobbling up Little Red Riding Hood.

The Story of Jumping Mouse

(A Native American Legend of the Northern Plains People, Retold by Rosie McCormick)

Once there was a small mouse with a big dream. The small mouse had grown up listening to the elders tell wonderful stories about the far-off land. Now the small mouse lived in the brush near the sparkling river. On the other side of the sparkling river was the dry desert. The small mouse had been told that the far-off land was on the other side of the dry desert.

Although the mouse was small, he was brave. He intended to go to the far-off land. One day he said good-bye to his family and friends and set off. His first challenge was to find a way to cross the beautiful sparkling river. As he stared at the lapping water, a frog appeared beside him.

"You'll have to swim," said the frog.

"I don't know what you mean," replied the small mouse, for he had never swum before.

"Watch me," said the frog. And with that the frog jumped into the sparkling river and began to swim.

The small mouse watched the frog for several seconds before announcing, "I am afraid I cannot do that. I will have to find another way to cross the sparkling river."

The frog returned to the edge of the river.

"Why are you so determined to cross the sparkling river? Where are you going?" asked the frog.

"I am going to the far-off land," replied the small mouse.

"If you don't mind my saying, you are a very small mouse to cross such a big river and travel such a long distance to the far-off land." The frog stared at the small mouse for a short time, and seeing that he could not be swayed from following his plan, decided to help the small mouse.

"This is your lucky day," exclaimed the frog. "I am a magic frog and I will help you. I name you Jumping Mouse. You will soon discover that you can jump higher than you have ever jumped before. Follow me, Jumping Mouse, and I will take you across the sparkling river."

With that said, the frog and Jumping Mouse jumped very high and landed on a leaf in the middle of the sparkling river. They floated on the leaf to the other side of the sparkling river.

"Good-bye, my friend," said the frog. "Be brave and hopeful and you will surely reach the far-off land."

"Thank you," replied Jumping Mouse. "I will never forget your kindness."

Jumping Mouse set off across the dry desert. He jumped across stones and twigs on his strong legs. As the frog had promised, Jumping Mouse jumped higher than ever before. He traveled by day and by night, stopping only to eat berries wherever he found them.

Eventually Jumping Mouse came to a stream. The stream gave life to this part of the dry desert. Beside the stream grew many bushes. Underneath one of the bushes there lived a very fat mouse.

"Good day to you," the fat mouse said to Jumping Mouse.

"Good day," replied Jumping Mouse.

"Where are you going?" asked the fat mouse.

"To the far-off land," explained Jumping Mouse. "However, I would like to rest a while and eat some of the juicy berries that grow on the bushes beside the stream."

"Be my guest," said the fat mouse.

Jumping Mouse stayed with the fat mouse for several days. He ate berries and drank from the cool stream. Before long, he felt rested and ready to continue his journey.

"It is time for me to continue my journey," said Jumping Mouse one day.

"Why would you want to travel to a place you are not sure even exists? Stay here with me, where you can eat berries and drink from the stream to your heart's content! But, if you must go, be very careful for the journey will be perilous indeed for such a small mouse," warned the fat mouse.

"I will be careful. And I will find a way to pay forward the kindness you and the frog have shown me. Thank you for your generosity," replied Jumping Mouse, as his powerful legs carried him away. With hope in his heart, Jumping Mouse continued on his way.

Some time later, Jumping Mouse arrived at the great grassy **plain**. There he found a bison lying forlornly in the grass.

"Hello, bison," said Jumping Mouse. "I am Jumping Mouse."

"Hello, Jumping Mouse. Please tell me how beautiful the sky looks today," said the bison sadly.

"Have you lost your sight?" asked Jumping Mouse with compassion.

"Yes! I am blind now," replied the bison. "I do not know what I will do now that I cannot see."

Make a Connection
Show your child the picture of plains on page 175. Some Native Americans lived on the plains.

"I am just an ordinary mouse," replied Jumping Mouse, "but before I reached the great grassy **plain**, a magic frog gave me a new name. The frog named me Jumping Mouse. The name gave me extra strength in my legs. I will name you 'Eyes-of-a-Mouse' in the hope that your eyes will regain their strength."

No sooner had Jumping Mouse finished speaking, when the bison exclaimed, "I can see!"

At that very moment Jumping Mouse realized that he could no longer see.

"And I cannot see!" said Jumping Mouse.

"Dear Jumping Mouse," said the bison. "You have given me your eyes. I am so thankful! Let me do something for you."

"I am on my way to the far-off land," explained Jumping Mouse. "Though, how I will get there now, I do not know."

"Come, jump beneath my enormous hooves, and I will guide you across the grassy **plain** to the high mountain," said the bison gently. And with that they set off.

When they reached the high mountain, the bison bid farewell to Jumping Mouse. Jumping Mouse rested for a while and then began to climb the mountain. It was difficult, as Jumping Mouse could not easily tell which way to go. He sniffed the air and followed the scent of pine.

Jumping Mouse trod along on grass and rocks. But then he trod on something that felt alarmingly like fur. Jumping Mouse sniffed the air again.

"Wolf!" he said in a frightened voice.

"Do not fear me," replied the wolf, "for I am a very sad wolf. I have lost my sense of smell. I do not know how I will find food without it."

"My dear wolf," said Jumping Mouse, "it may seem strange, but I gave the bison my sight. I will call you 'Nose-of-a-Mouse' and we shall see what will happen."

No sooner had Jumping Mouse spoken these words than the wolf sniffed the air and cried, "I can smell you Jumping Mouse, and other wonderful fragrances as well. Thank you! I am so grateful. How can I repay you?"

"I am on my way to the far-off land. I am brave and I still have hope that I will get there even though I can no longer see or smell. Perhaps you can help me."

"I will help you, Jumping Mouse. Walk beneath my body and I will lead you onward," said the wolf.

Onward they went until at last the wolf exclaimed, "I can go no farther. We are on the top of the high mountain. I must bid you good-bye, my friend." And with that, the wolf retreated back down the mountainside. For the first time, Jumping Mouse felt fear. How would he ever get to the far-off land now that he could no longer see or smell?

A tiny tear drop fell to the ground. At that very moment, Jumping Mouse heard a familiar voice.

"Do not be fearful," said the magic frog, for it was he. "You could have misused my gift, but you did not. Instead, you showed kindness and helped others on your journey. Jump high into the sky, my friend."

Jumping Mouse hesitated for just a second, and then he jumped high into the sky. Immediately he felt the air lift him up into the clouds. He felt the warmth of the sun on his back. He looked down and saw the beauty of the land beneath him.

"Jumping Mouse," said the magic frog, "I am giving you a new name. It is Eagle. Fly away, my friend, and soar on to your new home in the far-off land." And that is exactly what Jumping Mouse did.

The Bremen Town Musicians

(A Tale from the Brothers Grimm)

Once upon a time there was a donkey who for many years had carried bags of **grain** on his back to and from the mill. But at last he grew so old that he could not carry the heavy bags. His master tried to think how he could get rid of his old servant so that he might not have to feed him. The donkey feared what was in his master's mind, so he ran away.

He took the road to Bremen, where he had heard a street band play sweet music, for he thought he could be a musician as well as they.

Soon he came upon an old dog panting for breath, as if he had been running a long way.

"What are you panting for, my friend?" asked the donkey.

"Ah," answered the dog, "now that I am old, and growing weaker every day, I can no longer go to the hunt. My master speaks of getting rid of me, so I have run away."

"Well," said the donkey, "come with me. I am going to be a street musician in Bremen. I can play the flute, and you can play the drum."

The dog was quite willing, and so they both walked on.

Soon they saw a cat sitting in the road with a face as long as three days of rainy weather.

"Now, what's the matter with you, old Tom?" asked the donkey.

"You would be sad," said the cat, "if you were in my place; for now that I am getting old and my teeth are gone, I cannot catch the mice, and I like to lie behind the stove and purr. They have thrown me out, and alas, what am I to do?"

"Come with us to Bremen," said the donkey. "I know that you sing well at night, so you can easily be a street musician in the town."

"That is just what I should like to do," said the cat; so he joined the donkey and the dog, and they all walked on together.

By and by, the three musicians came to a farmyard. On the gate stood a rooster, crying "Cock-a-doodle-doo!" with all his **might**.

New Word

"Grain" is a word used for some kinds of seeds. We make bread from flour, and flour is made from **grain**, or seeds of wheat.

New Word

"Might" is a multi-meaning word. Does your child know what "with all his **might**" means? Here "might" means strength.

"What are you making so much noise for?" asked the donkey.

"Ah," said the rooster, "I heard the cook say that I am to be baked for Sunday dinner. And so I am crowing as hard as I can while my head is still on!"

"Come with us, old Red Comb," said the donkey; "we are going to Bremen to be street musicians. You have a fine voice, and the rest of us are all musical, too."

"I will join you!" said the rooster. And all four went on together.

They could not reach the town in one day, and as evening came on, they began to look for a place to spend the night.

The donkey and the dog lay down under a large tree. The cat climbed up on one of the branches. The rooster flew to the top of the tree, where he could look all around.

"I see a light from a window," the rooster called to his friends.

"That means there is a house nearby," said the donkey. "Let us ask the people for supper."

"How good a bone would taste!" said the dog.

"Or a nice piece of fish!" said the cat.

"Or some corn!" said the rooster.

So they set out at once and soon reached the house.

The donkey, who was tallest, looked in the window.

"What do you see, old Long Ears?" asked the rooster.

The donkey answered, "I see a table spread with plenty to eat and drink. And robbers are sitting before it having their supper."

"Come down," said the dog, "and we shall think of a way to make the robbers' supper our own."

The four friends talked over what they could do to drive the robbers away. At last they hit upon a plan. This is what they did.

The donkey stood on his hind legs and placed his front feet on the windowsill. The dog stood on the donkey's back. The cat climbed up and stood on the dog's back. And the rooster perched on the cat's head.

Then the donkey gave the signal, and they all began to make their loudest music. The donkey brayed, the dog barked, the cat mewed, and the rooster crowed.

The robbers had never before heard such a noise, and they thought it must come from witches, or giants, or monsters.

They ran as fast as they could to the wood behind the house. Then our four friends rushed in and ate what the robbers had left on the table.

When the four friends had eaten as much as they could, they were full and ready to sleep. The donkey lay down in the yard, the dog lay behind the door, and the cat curled up in front of the fireplace, while the cock flew up to a high shelf. They were all so tired that they soon fell fast asleep.

When all was still and dark, the robber chief sent one of his bravest men back to the house. The man found everything quiet and still, so he went inside. He did not see the cat, and he stepped on his tail. The angry puss flew up, spit at the man, and scratched his face with his sharp claws. It gave the robber so great a fright that he ran for the door, but the dog sprang up and bit him in the leg as he went by.

In the yard the robber ran into the donkey, who gave him a great kick with his hind foot. All this woke the rooster, who cried with all his might, "Cock-a-doodle-doo! Cock-a-doodle-doo!"

The robber ran as fast as his legs could carry him back to his friends.

Gasping for breath, he said, "In that house is a wicked witch, who scratched my face with her long nails. Then by the door stood a man with a knife, who cut me in the leg. Out in the yard was a great giant, who struck me with a huge club. And all the while someone cried out, 'Kill the robber, do! Kill the robber, do!'"

The robbers were filled with fear and ran away as fast as they could. But our four friends liked the little house so well that they stayed there, and as far as I know, they are there to this day.

The Ugly Duckling

(Adapted from the Original by Hans Christian Andersen)

It was a lovely summer day in the country. The wheat was yellow, the oats were green, and the hay was stacked in the meadows.

All round the meadows were great forests, and in the middle of the forests lay deep lakes. By the water's edge grew plants with very large leaves, so large that a child could stand under them. Here, a mother duck had chosen to make her nest.

She sat on her eggs, waiting for them to hatch. She was growing tired of waiting. She had been sitting for so long and had so few visitors, because the other ducks preferred to swim around rather than sit among the leaves and quack with her.

At long last the eggs began to crack, one after another. "Cheep! Cheep!" One little head peeped forth, and then another. "Quack! Quack!" said the mother duck, and all the little ones stood up as well as they could and peeped about from under the green leaves.

"How big the world is!" cried the little ones—and of course it was big compared to being in an eggshell!

"Do you think this is the whole world?" said their mother. "It reaches far beyond the other side of the garden, to the edge of the wood, where I have never been. Well now, are you all here?" And she looked around and said, "Why, the biggest egg is still in the nest! Oh me, I've been sitting such a long time, and I'm so tired." But, tired as she was, she sat down on the egg.

Just then an old duck swam up and asked, "Well, how are you getting along?"

"This one egg is taking forever!" said the mother duck. "It just won't break. But look at the others! Aren't they the prettiest little ducklings you've ever seen?"

"Let me see the egg that won't break,"

said the old duck. "Ah yes, believe me, that's a turkey's egg. I was tricked by such an egg once myself, and I had such trouble with the little one. I quacked and I scolded, but I just couldn't get him into the water. Yes, that must be a turkey's egg. Just leave it behind and go teach your little ones to swim."

But the mother duck sighed and said, "I've been sitting so long that I may as well stay until the last egg is hatched."

"Do as you please," said the old duck, and away she waddled.

At long last the great egg cracked. "Cheep! Cheep!" said the little one, and out he tumbled—but oh, how big and ugly he was!

"Why, he's not at all like the others," said the mother. "Can it be a young turkey? We shall soon find out. He must go in the water, even if I have to push him in!"

And so the next day—and a beautiful day it was, with the sun shining on the big green leaves—the mother duck took her family down to the water. Splash! She went into the water and called to her ducklings, "Quack, quack!" One after another, the little ones jumped right in. The water closed over their heads, but they popped right back up and began swimming. Every one of them floated along pleasantly—even the ugly gray one.

"Why, he's no turkey!" said the mother duck. "See how well he uses his legs, and holds himself so straight. He's my very own duckling, he is. And really, if you look close, he's not so bad-looking after all. Quack, quack! Come, children, I will take you to the farmyard. Stay close to me or someone may step on you. And always look out for the cat!"

As they came to the farmyard, they could hear a horrid noise, a commotion of quacks, honks, hisses, clucks, and gobbles. "Keep together," said the mother duck, "and bow to the old duck yonder. She is a great lady. Now, bow your necks, children, and say 'Quack.'"

The ducklings did as they were told. But the other ducks looked at them and said, "Just look at that big gray one. How ugly he is! Let's drive him away." And one duck flew at him and bit him on the neck.

"Leave him alone!" cried the mother. "He is doing no harm."

"But he's so big and ugly!" said the other ducks. "We don't like him."

Then the great lady duck spoke up and said, "All of your children are pretty except the one. He has not turned out well. It's a pity you can't hatch him over again."

"Oh," said the mother, "that cannot be, Your Highness. And though he is not handsome, he is a good child, and a fine swimmer, and I think that, in time, he will grow to look more like the others."

"Well, make yourself at home, dears," said the old duck.

But the poor ugly duckling, who had come last out of his shell, was bitten, pecked, and teased by the ducks and the hens. Even the turkey puffed himself out **like a ship in full sail** and gobble-gobble-gobbled till he was red in the face, then charged at the duckling. The poor little thing scarcely knew what to do. He felt so sad, because he looked so ugly, and everyone was laughing at him. Even his brothers and sisters were mean to him, and said unkind things, such as "We hope the cat gets you, you ugly thing!"

> **Make a Connection**
> Show your child the ship on page 182. Help your child make a connection between a ship in full sail and how the turkey might look all puffed up.

At last the duckling ran away. He fluttered over the hedges, then on and on he ran, until he came to the marshes where the wild ducks lived. Here he lay the whole night, tired and lonely.

In the morning the wild ducks came to look at the newcomer. "Who are you?" they asked. The duckling bowed politely to them, but they rudely responded, "You are really ugly!" The poor duckling—all he wanted was to be left alone to drink a little marsh water.

He lay by the marsh for three days. Then he was visited by two wild geese. They were rude as well, and said, "Why, you're so ugly that we like you! Why don't you join us? Not far from here there are some sweet, adorable geese, really lovely maidens. You're so ugly, you'd be a big hit with them!"

Then suddenly—*bang! bang!*—shots rang out. The two wild geese lay dead, and the water became red with their blood. *Bang!*—another gun fired, and a whole flock of geese flew up, followed by more and more gunshots from hunters all around the marsh.

Smoke from the guns rose through the trees while the hunters' dogs splashed about in the mud. The little duckling was terrified. He turned his head to hide it under his wing, but then he saw, standing right next to him, a huge dog, with its tongue hanging out of its mouth and its eyes glowing like fire. The dog opened his jaws wide, showing his sharp white teeth, but then—*splash!*—he was gone, without touching the duckling at all.

"Well," sighed the duckling, "I should be thankful, I suppose, that I'm so ugly that even the dog won't eat me."

Hours later, when the shooting was over at last, the duckling hurried away from the marsh. He ran over fields and **meadows,** though the wind was so strong that he had to fight just to move ahead.

In the evening he came to a poor little cottage. The door was crooked, so he could creep inside through an opening. Inside this cottage lived an old woman with her cat and her hen. The cat could arch its back and purr. The hen laid very good eggs. When they noticed the duckling, the cat began to purr and the hen cackled and clucked.

Now, the cat and the hen thought they were the most handsome and clever creatures in the world. The duckling did not quite agree, but the hen would not allow him to say so.

"Can you lay eggs? Can you?" the hen asked.

"No," said the duckling.

And the cat spoke up: "Can you arch your back, like this? And can you purr?"

"No."

"Well then, you should just keep quiet when sensible persons are speaking!"

So the duckling sat alone in a corner and felt very sad. But then a thought came to him, a thought of fresh air and sunshine. And he felt such a strong wish to be floating on the water that he couldn't help telling the hen about it.

"What's gotten into you?" clucked the hen. "Where do you get such silly ideas? If you would either lay eggs or purr, you wouldn't have such strange thoughts."

"But it's so glorious to float on the water!" said the duckling. "It's so wonderful to duck your head under, then dive to the bottom."

> **New Word**
> Did you teach the word "**meadow**" on page 33? Can your child tell you what a **meadow** is?

"You must be crazy!" said the hen. "Do you think I would like to swim? Or ask the cat—he's the most sensible person I know. Do you think he would like to dive down to the bottom of the water? Humph!"

"But you don't understand me," said the duckling.

"Oh, and if we don't understand you, then I would like to know who does," said the hen. "Surely you don't think that you are wiser than we are. If you paid attention, you could learn from us. Now, get busy and lay some eggs or learn to purr!"

"I think," sighed the duckling, "that I shall go back out into the wide world."

"Well then, go!" snapped the hen.

So the duckling went. And he floated on the water, and he **plunged** under it. But he was lonely, for all the animals would have nothing to do with him because he was so ugly.

Month after month the ugly duckling swam upon the clear water of the great lake. By and by, autumn came. The leaves turned yellow and brown, and the wind caught them and made them dance about. The air was cold, and the clouds were heavy with snow. The poor duckling was cold, lonely, and unhappy.

One evening, just as the sun was setting, a flock of birds rose out of the bushes. Never before had the duckling seen anything so beautiful. Their feathers were white as snow, and they had long, graceful necks. With a strange, wild cry, they spread their splendid wings and soared high, so very high, on their journey away from the cold lake to far-off warmer lands.

The duckling turned round in the water, and stretched his neck to look after them, and let out a cry so loud and strange that he scared himself. He could not stop thinking of those noble, happy birds. They were swans, though the duckling did not know what they were called or where they were going. Still, he loved them as he had never before loved anything. He was not jealous of them, for how could he even wish for such beauty for himself? He would have been happy if the ducks in the farmyard would just put up with him—the poor, ugly duckling.

Winter came on, and it was terribly cold. The duckling had to keep swim-

> **New Word**
> Ask your child, "What do you think 'plunged' means?" "Plunged" means to go quickly. The duckling went under the water quickly.

ming round and round in the water to keep it from freezing. But every night the water froze more and more, till at last the duckling grew so tired that he could only lie still with water freezing around him.

The next morning a farmer passed by and saw the duckling frozen in the lake. He used his wooden shoe to break the ice, then took the duckling home to his wife and children.

The children wanted to play with the duckling, but he feared that they might hurt him, so he flew around and knocked over the milk pail, spilling milk all over the room. The woman screamed and waved her arms, which scared the duckling even more, and he jumped about and flew into a flour tin and a butter tub. The children shrieked and laughed and tumbled over each other trying to catch him. It was lucky for the duckling that the door stood a little open. He jumped out among the bushes into the snow, and there he lay in a daze.

It would be too sad to tell you about all the hard times the duckling had through the winter.

One day, as he was lying on the marsh, the sun began to shine warm again and the larks began to sing—spring, beautiful spring, had returned!

He stood up and shook his wings. They were stronger than they had ever been, and they lifted him easily. To his great surprise, he found that they carried him quickly to a large garden where the apple trees were in bloom. Then, on a nearby stream, he saw three beautiful swans floating gently on the water. When the duckling saw the lovely birds, he felt a strange sadness.

"I will fly right over to those noble birds," he said. "They may peck me to death because I'm so ugly, but I don't care. It's better to be killed by them than to be bitten by the ducks, pecked by the hens, and have to live through another painful winter."

He flew into the water and swam toward the beautiful creatures. They saw him and swam toward him. He bowed his head low, expecting to be bitten or even killed. But as he looked down, what did he see in the clear water? He saw his own reflection, as though he were looking in a mirror. And he no longer saw an ugly gray bird—for he himself was a swan!

So you see, being born in a duck yard doesn't matter when you've been hatched out of a swan's egg!

Some children came into the garden and threw bread into the water. The smallest child cried out, "Look, there's a new one. He's the nicest of all. He's so young and handsome!" And the old swans bowed their heads before him, which really quite embarrassed the young swan, so he tucked his head under his wing.

He felt so happy! He remembered how he had been hated and teased, and yet now he heard everyone say that he was the most beautiful of all the beautiful birds. As the sun shone warm and bright, he shook his feathers and stretched his slender neck, and said with all his heart, "Never, ever did I dare even to dream of such happiness, not when I was the ugly duckling!"

Tug-of-War

PARENTS: This is a folktale from Africa. People in different parts of Africa tell it with different small animals—a turtle, a porcupine, a rabbit—as the central character. All versions share a theme (found also in the American Brer Rabbit tales, which have their roots in Africa) of the large, strong characters outwitted by the small, clever ones.

If your child is not familiar with the game of tug-of-war, you may want to describe it before you read this story aloud.

Make a Connection
Use the map on page 150 to show your child where Africa is located.

Turtle was small, but he talked big. He loved to boast and brag and say things such as, "I'm as powerful as the biggest animals around here, indeed I am. And that includes Elephant and Hippopotamus. That's right: Elephant and Hippopotamus call me friend because I'm as powerful as they are."

One day Elephant and Hippopotamus happened to hear from some of the other animals what Turtle was going around saying. Elephant and Hippopotamus laughed. "So," they said, "Turtle says we call him friend? That's the silliest thing we've ever heard. We don't call him friend. He's so little we don't think of him at all."

And when the animals told Turtle what Elephant and Hippopotamus said, Turtle got mad, very mad. "So, they do not think of me because I'm so small? They do not call me friend? Well, I'll show them who is really powerful. And they will call me friend, just you wait and see!" Then Turtle set off to find Elephant and Hippopotamus.

He found Elephant lying down in the forest. Elephant was big as a mountain; his trunk was long as a river. But Turtle was bold. He walked right up and shouted, "Hey, friend, get up and say hello to your friend."

Elephant looked all around to see where the voice could be coming from. Finally he looked down—way down—and spotted Turtle. "Oh, it's you, is it?" said Elephant. "Go away, you small animal of no importance. And watch out whom you call friend."

"I call you friend because that's what you are—right, Elephant?"

"Wrong!" rumbled Elephant. "And what is this foolishness I hear, that you claim to be as powerful as I am? Do you dare to think of yourself as equal to me? Don't be stupid, little creature."

"Now, Elephant," said Turtle, "just listen. Yes, I call you friend, and yes, I say we are equal. You think that because you're so much bigger than me, that makes you better. Well, let's have a tug-of-war to find out."

"A tug-of-war?" said Elephant. He laughed so hard the earth shook for miles around. "Why," he said to Turtle, "you haven't got a chance."

"Maybe not, maybe so," said Turtle. "But if you're so sure, what have you got to lose?" Then Turtle cut a very long vine and gave one end to Elephant. "Here," said Turtle. "Now, if I pull you down, I am greater. If you pull me down, you are greater. We won't stop tugging until one of us pulls the other over or the vine breaks. And if the vine breaks, we are equal and will call each other friend."

And Turtle walked off with the other end of the long, long vine until, some time later, he found Hippopotamus bathing in the river.

"Oh, friend, I'm here!" shouted Turtle. "Come out of the water and give your friend a proper greeting, why don't you?"

Hippopotamus could hardly believe his ears. "Don't call me friend, you little good-for-nothing!" he bellowed.

"Now hold on, friend Hippo," said Turtle. "You think that because you're so much bigger than me, that makes you better. Well, let's have a tug-of-war to find out. Whoever pulls the other down is greater. We will keep pulling until one of us wins or the vine breaks. And if the vine breaks, we are equal and will call each other friend."

"You silly turtle, you must have no brain in that little head," said Hippopotamus. "I'll pull you down before you can blink."

"Well, let us see," said Turtle, and he gave Hippopotamus the other end of the long, long vine. "Now I'll go pick up my end," said Turtle, "and when you feel me start tugging, you tug back."

Turtle walked into the forest and picked up the middle of the vine. He gave it a good hard shake. When Hippopotamus felt this, he started to tug. When Elephant felt the tug, he tugged back.

Elephant and Hippopotamus both tugged so mightily that the vine stretched tight. Turtle settled into a comfortable spot and watched for a while as the vine moved just a little bit one way, then just a little the other way. He took out his lunch and munched on his food very slowly, enjoying every bite. Then he yawned and fell asleep.

He woke a couple of hours later, feeling very refreshed from his nap. He looked up to see the vine still stretched tight, and he smiled. Yes, Elephant and Hippopotamus were still pulling with all their might. Neither one could pull the other over.

"I suppose it's about time," said Turtle, and he cut the vine.

When the vine broke, both Elephant and Hippopotamus tumbled down, *whump bumpity-bump bam boom!*

Turtle went to see Elephant and found him sprawled on the ground, rubbing his head.

"Turtle," said Elephant, "you are powerful. You were right, we are equal. I guess that bigger doesn't mean better after all, my, uh, my—friend."

Then Turtle went to see Hippopotamus, who was also sprawled on the ground, rubbing his head.

"So, Turtle," said Hippopotamus, "we are equal after all. You were right, my friend."

From then on, whenever the animals held a meeting, there at the front sat Elephant, Hippopotamus, and Turtle. And they always called each other friend.

They are friends, yes—but tell me, do you think they are equal?

Cinderella

Once upon a time there was a rich man whose wife lay in bed, very sick. She felt the end of her life drawing near, and she called her only daughter to her bedside. "Dear child," she said, "always be good, and I will look down on you from heaven." Then she closed her eyes and died.

Every day the little girl went to her mother's grave and wept, and she tried always to be good. When the winter came, the snow covered the ground like a white blanket; and when the sun came in the spring and melted it away, the little girl's father married a new wife. And so the little girl had a stepmother—and this was the beginning of a bad time for the little girl.

For you see, the stepmother was the proudest, most disagreeable woman in the land. She had two daughters, who were as proud and hateful as herself. The stepmother could not bear the kind, sweet little girl, who was so unlike her own daughters. She forced her to do the hardest and dirtiest work in the house. The

poor girl scoured the dishes, scrubbed the floors, and washed the clothes. When her work was finally done, she would sit, tired and alone, on the hearth by the fireplace, among the ashes and **cinders**. And so she came to be called Cinderella.

Cinderella's stepsisters had fine rooms with soft beds and thick carpets and mirrors so large that they might see themselves at full length from head to foot. But poor Cinderella had only a small room in the attic with a wretched straw bed. Yet she bore it all patiently and did not complain to her father, for his new wife ruled him entirely.

> **New Word**
>
> Does your child know what **cinders** are? **Cinders** are burned pieces of the fire logs.

Now, it happened one day that the king's son, the prince, announced that he was going to hold a ball. When they heard the announcement, the stepsisters shrieked with excitement. All the young ladies in the kingdom were invited to the palace for a grand evening of dancing and merriment. For days the stepsisters primped in front of their mirrors and talked of nothing but what they would wear.

"For my part," said the older sister, "I shall wear my red velvet dress with lace trimming."

"And I," said the younger sister, "shall have a gold-flowered gown with a diamond belt, quite out of the ordinary!"

And the stepsisters snapped at Cinderella, "You must help us get ready for the ball. Clean our shoes! Comb our hair! Hurry!"

Anyone but Cinderella would have tied their hair in knots, but she helped her stepsisters without complaining. Silently, however, she longed to go to the ball and imagined herself dancing in the arms of the prince.

At last the day came. The stepsisters and their mother left for the palace. Cinderella watched them as long as she could. When she had lost sight of them, she began to cry, so miserable and alone did she feel.

But Cinderella was not alone after all. For she heard a gentle voice ask, "What's the matter, dear?"

She looked up and saw an old woman with a kind face. "I wish—I wish I could—" began Cinderella, but she could not finish for all her tears and sobbing.

"You wish to go to the ball—is that it?" said the kind old woman.

"Why, yes!" said Cinderella with surprise.

"Then it shall be so!" said the woman, for she was, you see, Cinderella's fairy godmother. "Now run into the garden," she said to Cinderella, "and bring me a pumpkin."

Cinderella went immediately to the garden, though she could not imagine what a pumpkin had to do with going to the ball. She watched her fairy godmother scoop out the inside of the pumpkin, leaving only the rind, which she then touched with her wand. Instantly the pumpkin turned into a dazzling coach lined with satin!

"Now, dear," said the fairy godmother, "bring me the mousetrap from the house." Cinderella brought the trap, which had six live mice in it. "Open the door of the trap, dear," said the fairy godmother. Then, as each mouse scurried out, she gave it a tap with her wand, turning them into a fine set of six horses, all a beautiful mouse-colored gray. Next, with a touch of her wand, she turned a big rat into a fat, jolly coachman with long fancy whiskers.

"Well," said the fairy godmother with a smile, "are you pleased? Are you ready to go to the ball?"

"Oh, yes!" cried Cinderella. "But . . . must I go in these dirty rags?"

Her godmother laughed and, with a touch of her wand, changed Cinderella's tattered clothes into a glittering gown of gold and silver. And on her feet appeared a pair of glass slippers, the prettiest in the world. Cinderella stepped into the coach. But before she left, her fairy godmother gave her this warning: "Do not stay at the ball after midnight, not even for a moment! When the clock strikes twelve, the coach will once again be a pumpkin; the horses, mice; the coachman, a rat; and your gown, the same old clothes you had on."

Cinderella promised she would leave before midnight. Then, calling out her thanks, away she rode in the coach, feeling happier than she had ever felt before.

At the palace the prince heard that a great princess had arrived, but that nobody knew who she was. So he went to meet her, and gave her his hand, and led her into the great ballroom filled with people. As they entered, a hush fell upon the room. The dancers stopped dancing, the musicians stopped playing: everyone stood still just to look upon the beauty of the unknown newcomer.

The prince asked Cinderella to dance with him. They danced together once,

then twice, then again and again. Cinderella's face shone with happiness. Everyone at the ball looked on in admiration—everyone, that is, but the two jealous stepsisters, who glared at the lovely lady, though they had no idea that they were glaring at Cinderella!

Soon a fancy dinner was served, but the prince didn't eat a bit, for he was too busy gazing into Cinderella's eyes. For Cinderella, the music, the dancing, the warm gaze of the prince—all seemed a wonderful dream.

How quickly time slips away when the heart is happy! As Cinderella began to dance again with the prince, she heard the great bell of the palace clock begin to toll: one . . . two . . . three . . .

"Oh!" she gasped. "The clock! What time is it?"

The prince answered, "Midnight."

Midnight! Cinderella's cheeks grew pale. She turned and, fast as a deer, ran out of the ballroom, down a long hallway, then down a long staircase. At the foot of the staircase she stumbled, and one of her glass slippers fell off! But Cinderella could not stop. Already the clock had sounded its eleventh stroke. As she leapt breathlessly out of the castle into the darkness, she heard the clock sound the last stroke of midnight—and felt her smooth gown turn into the rough cloth of her real clothes.

Talk and Think
Ask your child to explain why Cinderella has to be home by midnight.

Her dazzling coach had turned back into a pumpkin, so she ran home alone. When she got there, she was out of breath, but climbed the stairs to her cold attic room. Then she noticed: she was still wearing one glass slipper!

Now, when Cinderella had run from the palace, the prince had raced after her. And though he had not been able to catch her, he did find, at the bottom of the staircase, the glass slipper that had fallen off her foot.

And that is why, the very next morning, the sound of trumpets woke the kingdom, and the prince announced that he would marry the woman whose foot fit the glass slipper. The prince sent men to try the slipper on the foot of every lady in the land.

From house to house they went, trying the slipper on foot after foot. But on one foot the slipper was too long; on another, too short; on another, too wide; on another, too narrow.

And so it went until at last they came to the house of Cinderella and her stepsisters. One by one, the stepsisters squeezed, pinched, and pushed, but the slipper would not fit.

Then, from the shadows, Cinderella stepped forth and said, "Let me see if it will fit me."

"You!" the stepsisters cried. "Go back to the cinders where you belong!"

But one of the prince's men said that he had orders to try the slipper on every maiden in the kingdom. He placed the slipper on Cinderella's foot—and it fit

perfectly! The stepsisters' mouths dropped open in astonishment. And they were even more shocked when, from her pocket, Cinderella drew forth the other glass slipper.

And now the stepsisters recognized Cinderella as the beautiful lady they had seen at the ball. They threw themselves at her feet and begged her pardon for all of the ways they had treated her so badly. Cinderella was so kindhearted that she forgave them and embraced them.

Later, after Cinderella married the prince, she even invited her stepmother and stepsisters to live at the palace. And there Cinderella and the prince lived happily ever after.

The Wolf and the Seven Little Kids

(A Tale from the Brothers Grimm)

There was once a mother goat who had seven little **kids,** and she loved them as well as any mother has ever loved her children.

One day she gathered her seven kids around her and said, "Dear children, I must go into the forest to get food for us to eat. While I am away, be on your guard against the wolf. For if he gets inside, he will eat you up, bones and all! The wicked creature often disguises himself. But you can always know him by his rough voice and by the black fur on his paws."

"Don't worry, Mother," said the kids, "we will take good care of ourselves." So the mother goat bleated good-bye and went on her way with a calm mind.

> **New Word**
> Ask your child, "Did you know that young goats are called '**kids**' just like young humans?"

Soon there came a knock at the door, and a voice called out, "Open the door, my dear children. Your mother is back and has brought you each something." But oh, what a rough voice!

"No, we won't open the door!" cried the kids. "Our mother has a sweet, gentle voice, and your voice is rough. You must be the wolf!"

The wolf ran off to a store, where he bought a big lump of a special kind of chalk, which he ate to make his voice soft. Then he came back, knocked at the door again, and called out in a gentle voice, "Open the door, my dear children. Your mother is back and has brought you each something."

But the wolf had put his paws against the window, and the kids could see the black fur.

"No, we won't open the door!" cried the kids. "Our mother's feet do not have black fur. You must be the wolf!"

So the wolf ran to a baker. "Baker," he said, "I have hurt my foot. Spread some dough over it."

And when the baker had coated his paw with dough, the wolf went to the miller. "Miller," he said, "sprinkle some white flour over my paws." The miller said no, for he thought that the wolf must be planning to trick someone. But then the wolf cried, "If you won't do it, I'll eat you up!"

The miller was scared and did as the wolf demanded—which just goes to show how people can be.

For a third time the wolf went to the door, knocked, and said in a gentle voice, "Open the door, my dear children. Your mother is back and has brought you each something."

"First show us your paws," said the kids. And the wolf put his white, flour-covered paws against the window. "Yes, this must be our dear mother," said the kids, and they opened the door.

In pounced the wolf! The terrified kids tried to hide. The first ran under the table. The second crawled under the bed. The third got into the oven. The fourth ran into the kitchen. The fifth jumped into the cupboard. The sixth ran under a tub. And the seventh climbed inside a big grandfather clock.

But the wolf found them all and gobbled them up—all except the youngest, who was hiding in the grandfather clock.

The wolf, feeling fat and happy, strolled into the forest, lay down under a tree, and fell into a deep sleep.

A short while later the mother goat came home from the woods, and oh! what a sad sight met her eyes. The door stood wide open. Tables and chairs were thrown all about, dishes were broken, quilts and pillows were torn off the beds. She called out for her children, but they were nowhere to be found. She called each one again by name, but no one answered until she called the name of the youngest kid.

"Here I am, Mother," a frightened little voice cried, "here inside the big clock."

And so she helped him out, and heard how the wolf had come and eaten all the other kids. How she cried and cried for her poor children.

Still crying, she wandered outside with her youngest kid, and soon they came to the forest. There they saw the wolf, fast asleep under a tree, snoring so hard that he shook the branches. Then the mother goat saw something move inside the wolf's body!

"Dear me!" she thought. "Could my poor kids still be alive?" And she sent her youngest kid home to get scissors, needle, and thread. He hurried back, and then the mother goat cut open the wolf. No sooner had she made one snip than out came the head of one of the kids. She made another snip, and another, and one after the other all six of the kids jumped out alive and well—for in his greediness, the wolf had swallowed them whole.

"Now," said the mother to her kids, "fetch some good hard stones, and we will fill his body with them while he's still asleep."

The kids quickly picked up some stones, and they packed them inside the wolf. Then the mother used her needle and thread to sew him up, while he slept and snored all the while.

When the wolf at last awoke, he felt very thirsty. As he walked to the brook, the stones rattled inside him, and he said: "What is this knocking against my bones? I thought it was kids, but it feels like stones!"

He came to the brook, and he bent over to take a drink. The weight of the stones made him fall—*splash!*—into the water. He sank to the bottom and was never seen again.

"Hooray, hooray, the wolf is dead!" cried the kids, and they danced around their mother with joy.

King Midas and the Golden Touch

(A Myth from Ancient Greece, adapted from Nathaniel Hawthorne's Wonder Book*)*

Once upon a time there lived a very rich king whose name was Midas.

Although King Midas lived long ago, he was very like some people today: he was fond of gold. He loved gold more than anything in the world. If he happened to gaze for an instant at the gold-colored clouds of a beautiful sunset, he would wish that the clouds were real gold.

If King Midas loved anything as much or more than he loved gold, it was his little daughter, who was named Marygold. When Marygold would run to meet him with a bunch of buttercups and dandelions, King Midas would say, "Dear child, if these flowers were as golden as they look, then they would be worth picking."

King Midas had once loved flowers. Years before, he had planted a garden full of beautiful, sweet-smelling roses. But now, if he looked at the roses at all, it was only to wonder what they would be worth if each of the rose petals were a thin plate of gold.

Every day King Midas spent many hours locked away in a dark room in the basement of the palace. In this room he stored his treasures. He would go there and carefully lock the door behind him. Then he would take out bags of gold coins, pour the coins in piles, and run his hands through them. As he did this, he would whisper to himself, "Oh, rich King Midas, what a happy man you are!" But even as he said this, he felt that he was not quite as happy as he might be. For no matter how much he had, he always wanted more.

One day, as Midas was enjoying himself in his treasure room, he looked up and saw a strange young man, who seemed to shine with a golden glow. King Midas knew that he had carefully locked the door so that no one could get into the room, yet here stood this strange young man. And so, King Midas thought, the stranger must have some magic power. But the stranger had a kind smile, so King Midas felt no fear.

Then the stranger spoke to King Midas: "You are a rich man, friend Midas," he said.

"Yes, I have some gold," answered Midas, "but it is not enough."

"What!" cried the stranger. "Then you are not satisfied?"

Midas shook his head.

"What would satisfy you?" asked the stranger.

King Midas imagined one gold mountain heaped on top of another, and another, and another, yet still it seemed not enough. But then a bright idea occurred to him, and he said to the shining stranger, "I wish that everything I touch may turn to gold."

The stranger smiled and said, "A golden touch! Are you quite sure you would be satisfied then?"

"Yes, I would be perfectly happy, and ask for nothing more," answered Midas.

"Then it shall be as you wish," said the stranger. "Tomorrow, at sunrise, you shall find yourself gifted with the golden touch." Then suddenly a great brightness filled the room, causing Midas to squeeze his eyes shut. And when he opened them, the stranger was gone!

The next morning, when the sun had hardly peeped into his room, King Midas jumped out of bed.

He touched a chair. It turned to gold.

He touched the bed and a table, and they were changed to solid, shining gold.

He rushed to put on his shoes, and was amazed to see them turn to gold in his hands.

From his pocket he **drew** forth a handkerchief, on which his daughter, Marygold, had stitched a design. The cloth had turned to gold, as had his daughter's neat and pretty stitches. And somehow, this change did not quite please King Midas.

But he did not let it trouble him. In great excitement, he opened the door—and was pleased to see the doorknob turn into shining gold. He ran outside to the garden. He saw many roses in full bloom. He went from bush to bush and touched each one, until every flower, every leaf, and every bud was changed to gold.

Now King Midas was hungry, so he returned to the palace for his breakfast. He lifted his cup of coffee and sipped it, but the instant the liquid touched his lips it turned to gold. He tried to take a bite of a boiled egg, but it, too, turned to gold.

"I don't quite see how I am to get any breakfast!" said King Midas. Then he grabbed a hot potato from his plate and tried to cram it into his mouth and swallow it in a hurry. But the golden touch was too quick for him. He found his mouth full, not of soft potato, but of hot metal, which so burned his tongue that he began to dance and stamp around the room.

Just then Midas heard someone crying. He turned to see Marygold enter the room, sobbing as if her heart would break. In her hand she held one of the roses that her father had changed to gold.

"Why, my little lady!" said King Midas. "What is there in this beautiful golden rose to make you cry?"

> **New Word**
> "Drew" is a multi-meaning word. Does your child know what **"drew"** means here? It means "pulled."

"Dear Father," Marygold answered, "it is not beautiful! It is the ugliest flower that ever grew. As soon as I was dressed this morning, I ran to the garden to gather roses for you. But what do you think happened? All the beautiful, sweet-smelling roses have been spoiled!"

"My dear little girl," said Midas, who hated to see his daughter sad, "please don't cry." Then he bent down and kissed his child, who he felt was worth a thousand times more than anything he had gained by the golden touch.

"My precious Marygold!" he said. But Marygold did not answer.

Alas, what had he done? The moment King Midas's lips touched Marygold's head, her sweet rosy face turned a glittering yellow color. Little Marygold was a human child no longer, but a golden statue. Yet on her face there remained a questioning look of love and sadness.

King Midas cried out, and wrung his hands, and wished that he were the poorest man in the world if only he could have his daughter back again.

Then he noticed someone standing in the doorway. It was the young stranger, who had appeared the day before in Midas's treasure room. The stranger still shone with a soft glow, and he smiled as he asked the king, "Well, friend Midas, how do you like your golden touch?"

"I am very unhappy," said Midas.

"Unhappy?" asked the stranger. "But don't you have everything your heart desired?"

"No," said King Midas. "Gold is not everything. And I have lost all that my heart really cared for."

Then the stranger asked Midas, "Which of these two things do you think is worth the most: the golden touch or one cup of clear, cold water?"

"A cup of water!" cried the king.

"Which is worth more?" the stranger asked again. "The golden touch or a crust of bread?"

"A crust of bread," said Midas quietly.

"And," the stranger asked again, "the golden touch or your own little Marygold?"

"Oh, my child, my dear child!" cried poor Midas. "I would not give one hair of her head even for the power to change this whole big earth into a solid lump of gold!"

"You are wiser than you were, King Midas," said the stranger. "Go, and plunge into the river that runs by your garden. The water will take away the golden touch. And fill this pitcher with water, then sprinkle everything you have touched."

King Midas bowed low, and when he lifted his head, the shining stranger was gone. Then the king ran as fast as he could and jumped into the river. He filled the pitcher and ran back to the palace. The first thing he did, as you hardly need to be told, was to sprinkle handfuls of water over the golden figure of little Marygold.

The rosy color came back into her cheeks. She looked in surprise at her father, who was still throwing water on her!

"Father, please stop!" she cried. "See how you have soaked my dress!"

King Midas took Marygold in his arms and kissed her. "Now I am truly happy," he said. "My dear child, you mean more to me than all the gold in the world!"

Snow White

(Adapted from the Brothers Grimm)

It was the middle of winter, and the snowflakes were falling like feathers from the sky. A queen sat sewing near a window. The window was framed with a fine black wood called ebony. As the queen sewed, she gazed out the window at the snow. She pricked her finger with the needle, and three drops of blood fell on the snow. And when she saw how bright and red it looked, she said, "Oh, I wish I had a child as white as snow, as red as blood, and as black as the ebony round my window."

It was not long before she had a daughter with skin as white as snow, lips as red as blood, and hair as black as ebony. She was named Snow White, and when she was born, the queen died.

After a year had gone by, the king married again. The new queen was very beautiful, but she was terribly proud. She could not bear to think that anyone might be more beautiful than she. She had a magic mirror, and she would look into it and say:

"Mirror, mirror on the wall,
*Who is **fairest** of us all?"*

New Word

"Fairest" is a multi-meaning word. Does your child know what it means for the queen to be the **fairest**? "Fairest" means "most pretty" or "prettiest."

And the mirror would answer:

*"You, queen, are the **fairest** of all."*

And she was satisfied, for she knew the mirror spoke the truth.

Now, as Snow White grew up, she grew prettier and prettier, and when she was seven years old, she was as beautiful as the day and more beautiful than the queen herself. One day the queen went to her mirror and said:

"Mirror, mirror on the wall,
*Who is **fairest** of us all?"*

And the mirror answered:

"Though you are fair, O queen, 'tis true,
Snow White is fairer still than you."

When the queen heard this, she
turned green with jealousy, and from
that moment her heart turned against
Snow White. Envy and pride grew in
her like weeds, until one day she called
for a huntsman and said, "Take the
child into the woods so that I may set
eyes on her no more. Put her to death,
and bring me her heart to prove that
you have done it."

The huntsman took the child into
the forest. But when he drew his sword,
Snow White cried out, "Oh, dear
huntsman, let me live. I will go away,
far into the woods, and never come back again."

The huntsman took pity on her and said, "Go ahead then, poor child, run
away." But he thought that the wild animals of the forest would eat her anyway.
A wild boar came running by at just that moment, and the huntsman killed it and
took out its heart, which he gave to the queen.

When poor Snow White found herself alone in the woods, she felt afraid and
did not know what to do. Even the leaves on the trees seemed to threaten her. She
began to run over the sharp stones and through the thorn bushes, and the wild
beasts saw her but did not hurt her. She ran as long as her feet would carry her,
until at last, as evening fell, she came upon a little house deep in the woods.

She went inside to rest. Inside the house everything was very small, but as neat
and clean as possible. By the wall stood seven little beds, side by side, covered with
clean white quilts. Nearby there stood a little table, covered with a white cloth and

set with seven little plates, seven knives and forks, and seven little drinking cups. Snow White was very hungry, but she didn't want to eat anyone's whole meal, so she took a little porridge and bread from each plate, and a little sip from each cup. After that, she felt so tired that she lay down on one of the beds and fell asleep.

When it was quite dark, the owners of the little house came home. They were seven dwarfs, who worked every day in the mountains, digging with their picks and shovels for gold. When they had lighted their seven candles, they saw that everything in the house was not the same as they had left it.

The first dwarf said, "Who has been sitting in my chair?"

The second said, "Who has been eating from my plate?"

The third said, "Who has taken a bit of my bread?"

The fourth said, "Who has been tasting my porridge?"

The fifth said, "Who has been using my fork?"

The sixth said, "Who has been cutting with my knife?"

And the seventh said, "Who has been drinking from my cup?"

Then the seventh looked around and saw Snow White lying asleep in his bed. He cried out to the others, and they all came running up with their candles, and said, "Oh, goodness gracious! What a beautiful child!" They were so full of joy to see her that they did not wake her.

The next morning Snow White woke and saw the seven dwarfs, and at first she was frightened. But they seemed quite friendly, and asked her what her name was, and she told them. And she told them how her stepmother had wished her to be put to death, and how the huntsman had spared her life, and how she had run the whole day long, until at last she had found their little house.

Then the dwarfs said, "If you will keep house for us, and cook, and wash, and make the beds, and sew, and keep everything tidy, you may stay with us, and we will make sure you have everything you need."

"I'd be happy to," said Snow White. And so she stayed.

Every morning the dwarfs went to the mountain to dig for gold. When the dwarfs were away during the day, Snow White was alone in the house. The dwarfs warned her, saying, "Don't let anyone in the house! Beware of your stepmother, for she may find out you are here."

And indeed, one day the queen went to her mirror and said:

"Mirror, mirror on the wall,
*Who is **fairest** of us all?"*

And the mirror answered:

"O queen, you are of beauty rare,
But Snow White living in the glen
With the seven little men
Is a thousand times more fair."

The queen gasped. She knew the mirror spoke the truth, and so she knew that the huntsman must have tricked her, and Snow White must still be living. It filled the queen with rage to think that she was not the fairest in the land, so she thought of a plan to get rid of Snow White. She made herself look like an old peddler woman so that no one could tell she was the queen. Then she went across the seven mountains, until she came to the house of the seven dwarfs. She knocked at the door and cried, "Pretty things for sale! Come see my fine silk laces!"

Snow White peeped out the window. "I don't need to be afraid of letting in this good old woman," she thought. So she opened the door and bought the pretty lace.

"Come, child," said the old woman, "and let me lace you up properly." Snow White saw no reason not to trust the woman, so she let her tie the lace around her. But the old woman pulled the lace so tight that it took away Snow White's breath, and she fell down as though she were dead.

"Now," said the queen, "you are no longer the fairest in the land." And she hurried off.

Soon the seven dwarfs came home. They were horrified to see Snow White on the ground, lying so still they thought she must be dead. Then they saw the tight lace around her, and they cut it. She began to breathe again, and little by little she came to life. When she told the dwarfs what had happened, they said,

"That peddler woman was the wicked queen! Don't let anyone in when we are away!"

By this time the queen had returned home. She went straight to her mirror and said:

"Mirror, mirror on the wall,
*Who is **fairest** of us all?"*

And the mirror answered:

"O queen, you are of beauty rare,
But Snow White living in the glen
With the seven little men
Is a thousand times more fair."

"Still alive!" cried the queen. "Then I will think of something else to destroy her for sure!" And she used a magic spell to make a poisoned comb. Then she made herself look like a different old woman, and away she went, across the seven mountains, to the home of the seven dwarfs. She knocked at the door and cried, "Pretty things for sale!"

But Snow White said, "Go away. I must not let anybody in."

"Oh," said the old woman, "but surely it's all right for you just to take a look?" And she held up the pretty poisoned comb. And the child liked it so well that without thinking she opened the door.

"Now I shall comb your hair as it should be done," said the old woman. As soon as she ran the comb through Snow White's hair, the poison began to work, and the child fell down as though she were dead.

"So, my little beauty, that's the end of you," said the wicked queen as she hurried away.

It was good luck that the seven dwarfs came home soon. They saw the poisoned comb still in her hair, and as soon as they pulled it out, Snow White woke up and told them what had happened. Then they warned her once again never to let anyone in the door.

When the queen got home, she went straight to her mirror and said:

"Mirror, mirror on the wall,
*Who is **fairest** of us all?"*

And the mirror answered:

"O queen, you are of beauty rare,
But Snow White living in the glen
With the seven little men
Is a thousand times more fair."

The queen shook with anger. "Snow White shall die," she cried, "even if it costs me my own life!" Then she went to a dark and secret room, and there she made a poisonous apple. It was so big, beautiful, and red that any-one who saw it would long for it, but whoever ate even a piece of it would die. Then the queen made herself look like a poor old woman, and went across the seven mountains to the home of the seven dwarfs. When she knocked at the door, Snow White put her head out the window and said, "I dare not let anybody in. The seven dwarfs told me not to."

"All right, I'll go," said the old woman. "But here, let me give you one of my apples."

"No," said Snow White, "I'm not supposed to take anything."

"Goodness, child, you act like the apples are poisoned!" said the old woman. "Look here, I'll take a bite of this apple myself, all right?"

But the apple had been made so that all the poison was only in one side—the side that the old woman held out toward Snow White. Snow White looked at the lovely apple, and she wanted it so much that when she saw the old woman take a bite of the other side, she could not resist. She stepped outside, took the apple, bit it, and fell down dead.

The queen laughed out loud and said, "White as snow, red as blood, black as ebony you may be, but the dwarfs will not be able to help you this time!"

When she got home, she rushed to her mirror and asked:

"Mirror, mirror on the wall,
*Who is **fairest** of us all?"*

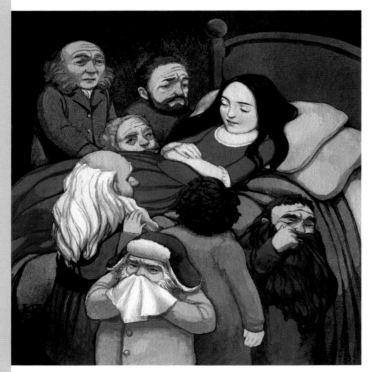

And the mirror answered:

*"You are now the **fairest** of all."*

The dwarfs came home and found Snow White dead. They lifted her up and looked for a lace to cut, or a comb to take out, but they found nothing, and nothing they did helped the child—she was dead. And they sat, all seven of them, around her and wept for three days. And they would have buried her, but still she looked so fresh and alive, with her beautiful red cheeks, that they said, "We cannot hide her away in the ground." So they made a coffin of clear glass, and laid her in it, and wrote her name on it in golden letters, and set it on the mountain, where one of them always kept watch over it. And the birds came and sang sad songs around the coffin of Snow White.

For many years Snow White lay in her coffin, and all the while she never changed, but looked as if she were asleep, with skin as white as snow, lips as red as blood, and hair as black as ebony. Then one day a prince was riding through the woods. He stopped at the dwarfs' cottage. From there he could see the coffin on the mountain, and beautiful Snow White in it. And he said to the dwarfs, "Let me have the coffin, and I will pay you whatever you ask."

But the dwarfs told him they could not part with it, not even for all the gold in the world. Then the prince said, "I beg you to give it to me, for I cannot live without looking upon Snow White." The good dwarfs felt sorry for him and gave him the coffin. The prince called his servants and told them to carry the coffin down from the mountain. As they were carrying it, they stumbled, which gave the coffin, and Snow White in it, a hard shake—and when this happened, the piece of poisoned apple came out of Snow White's throat!

Snow White sat up and cried, "Oh! Where am I?"

The prince, full of joy, said, "You are near me, and I love you more than anything in the world. Come with me to my father's castle and be my bride."

A splendid wedding was held for the prince and Snow White. Snow White's wicked stepmother, the queen, was invited to the wedding. When she had dressed herself in beautiful clothes, she went to her mirror and asked:

"Mirror, mirror on the wall,
*Who is **fairest** of us all?"*

And the mirror answered:

"Though you are fair, O queen, 'tis true,
The new bride is fairer still than you."

Do It Yourself!
Help your child count each dwarf in the illustration.

And the queen screamed with anger. First she thought she would not go to the wedding. Then she thought she had to go and see the new bride. And when she saw the new bride, she recognized her as Snow White, and she was filled with a terrible rage. In a wild fury, she screamed and stomped her feet and jumped up and down, as though she were wearing red-hot shoes, and then she fell down dead.

Snow White and the prince lived happily ever after.

How Many Spots Does a Leopard Have?

(An African Folktale Retold by Julius Lester)

One morning Leopard was doing what he enjoyed most. He was looking at his reflection in the lake. How handsome he was! How magnificent was his coat! And, ah! The spots on his coat! Was there anything in creation more superb?

Leopard's rapture was broken when the water in the lake began moving. Suddenly Crocodile's ugly head appeared above the surface.

Leopard jumped back. Not that he was afraid. Crocodile would not bother him. But then again, one could never be too sure about Crocodile.

"Good morning, Leopard," Crocodile said. "Looking at yourself again, I see. You are the vainest creature in all of creation."

Leopard was not embarrassed. "If you were as handsome as I am, if you had such beautiful spots, you, too, would be vain."

"Spots! Who needs spots? You're probably so in love with your spots that you spend all your time counting them."

Now there was an idea that had not occurred to Leopard. "What a wonderful idea!" he exclaimed. "I would very much like to know how many spots I have." He stopped. "But there are far too many for me to count myself."

The truth was that Leopard didn't know how to count. "Perhaps you will count them for me, Crocodile?"

"Not on your life!" answered Crocodile. "I have better things to do than count spots." He slapped his tail angrily and dove beneath the water.

Leopard chuckled. "Crocodile doesn't know how to count, either."

Leopard walked along the lakeshore until he met Weasel. "Good morning, Weasel. Would you count my spots for me?"

"Who? Me? Count? Sure. One-two-three-four."

"Great!" exclaimed Leopard. "You can count."

Weasel shook his head. "But I can't. What made you think that I could?"

"But you just did. You said, 'One-two-three-four.' That's counting."

Make a Connection
Turn to the map of the world and its continents on page 150 or, better yet, look together at a globe again. Help your child find Africa. Explain that this story was first told in Africa.

Weasel shook his head again. "Counting is much more difficult than that. There is something that comes after four, but I don't know what it is."

"Oh," said Leopard. "I wonder who knows what comes after four."

"Well, if you ask at the lake when all the animals come to drink, you will find someone who can count."

"You are right, Weasel! And I will give a grand prize to the one who tells me how many spots I have."

"What a great idea!" Weasel agreed.

That afternoon all the animals were gathered at the lake to drink. Leopard announced that he would give a magnificent prize to the one who could count his spots.

Elephant said he should be first since he was the biggest and the oldest.

"One-two-three-four-five-six-seven-eight-nine-ten," Elephant said very loudly and with great speed. He took a deep breath and began again. "One-two-three-four-five-si—"

"No! No! No!" the other animals interrupted. "You've already counted to ten once."

Elephant looked down his long trunk at the other animals. "I beg your pardon. I would appreciate it if you would not interrupt me when I am counting. You made me forget where I was. Now, where was I? I know I was somewhere in the second ten."

"The second ten?" asked Antelope. "What's that?"

"The numbers that come after the first ten, of course. I don't much care for those 'teen' things, thirteen, fourteen, and what have you. It is eminently more sensible to count ten twice and that makes twenty. That is multiplication."

None of the other animals knew what Elephant was talking about.

"Why don't you start over again?" suggested Cow.

Elephant began again and he counted ten twice and stopped. He frowned and looked very confused. Finally he said, "Leopard has more than twenty spots."

"How many more than twenty?" Leopard wanted to know.

Elephant frowned more. "A lot." Then he brightened. "In fact, you have so many more spots than twenty that I simply don't have time to count them now. I have an important engagement I mustn't be late for." Elephant started to walk away.

"Ha! Ha! Ha!" laughed Mule. "I bet Elephant doesn't know how to count higher than twenty."

Mule was right.

"Can you count above twenty?" Leopard asked Mule.

"Who? Me? I can only count to four because that's how many legs I have."

Leopard sighed. "Can anyone count above twenty?" he asked plaintively.

Bear said, "Well, once I counted up to fifty. Is that high enough?"

Leopard shrugged. "I don't know. It might be. Why don't you try and we will see."

Bear agreed. "I'll start at your tail. One-two-three-four-five-six . . . Hm. Is that one spot or two spots?"

All the animals crowded around to get a close look. They argued for some time and finally agreed that it should only count as one.

"So, where was I?" asked Bear.

"Five," answered Turkey.

"It was six, you turkey," said Chicken.

"Better start again," suggested Cow.

Bear started again and got as far as eleven. "Eleven. That's a beautiful spot right there, Leopard."

"Which one?" Leopard wanted to know.

"Right there. Oh, dear. Or was it that spot there? They're both exquisite. My, my. I don't know where I left off counting. I must start again."

Bear counted as far as twenty-nine this time and then stopped suddenly. "Now, what comes after twenty-nine?"

"I believe thirty does," offered Turtle.

"That's right!" exclaimed Bear. "Now, where did I leave off?"

"You were still on the tail," offered Lion.

"Yes, but was that the twenty-ninth spot, or was it this one here?"

The animals started arguing again.

"You'd better start again," suggested Cow.

"Start what again?" asked Rabbit, who had just arrived.

The animals explained to Rabbit about the difficulty they were having in counting Leopard's spots.

"Is that all?" Rabbit said. "I know the answer to that."

"You do?" all the animals, including Leopard, exclaimed at once.

"Certainly. It's really quite simple." Rabbit pointed to one of Leopard's spots. "This one is dark." He pointed to another. "This one is light. Dark, light, dark, light, dark, light." Rabbit continued in this way until he had touched all of Leopard's spots.

"It's simple," he concluded. "Leopard has only two spots: dark ones and light ones."

All the animals remarked on how smart Rabbit was—all of them, that is, except Leopard. He knew something was wrong with how Rabbit counted, but unless he learned to count for himself, he would never know what it was.

Leopard had no choice but to give Rabbit the magnificent prize.

What was it?

What else except a picture of Leopard himself!

What Is an Author?

Meet Julius Lester. He's a teacher and he's an author. An author is a writer. Authors write books. Many of these books tell stories.

Julius Lester loves to tell stories. He writes them down so that he can share them with you. Sometimes he makes up a story out of his own imagination, then writes it down. Sometimes he takes a story that people have been telling each other for many years—like the story called "How Many Spots Does a Leopard Have?"—and he writes it down in the way he likes to tell it.

Julius Lester is the author of many books. He has won awards for his writing. If you go to a library, you'll find lots of books that say, "By Julius Lester."

When you sit down with a book, find out who the author is. Do you have a favorite author? If you do, then the next time you're at the library, look for more books by that person.

Do you like to tell stories? Someday soon you'll learn to write them down. Then you can be an author, too!

Julius Lester, author

In Which Pooh Goes Visiting and Gets into a Tight Place

(A selection from Winnie-the-Pooh *by A. A. Milne)*

Edward Bear, known to his friends as Winnie-the-Pooh, or Pooh for short, was walking through the forest one day, humming proudly to himself. He had made up a little hum that very morning, as he was doing his Stoutness Exercises in front of the glass: *Tra-la-la, tra-la-la,* as he stretched up as high as he could go, and then *Tra-la—oh, help—la,* as he tried to reach his toes. After breakfast he had said it over and over to himself until he had learnt it off by heart, and now he was humming it right through, properly. It went like this:

Tra-la-la, tra-la-la,
Tra-la-la, tra-la-la,
Rum-tum-tiddle-um-tum.
Tiddle-iddle, tiddle-iddle,
Tiddle-iddle, tiddle-iddle,
Rum-tum-tum-tiddle-um.

New Word
"Bank" is a multi-meaning word. Does your child know what a "sandy **bank**" is? This kind of bank is a sloping piece of land—a little hill made of sand.

Well, he was humming this hum to himself, and walking along gaily, wondering what everybody else was doing, and what it felt like, being somebody else, when suddenly he came to a sandy **bank,** and in the bank was a large hole.

"Aha!" said Pooh. *(Rum-tum-tiddle-um-tum.)* "If I know anything about anything, that hole means Rabbit," he said, "and Rabbit means Company," he said, "and Company means Food and Listening-to-Me-Humming and such like. *Rum-tum-tum-tiddle-um.*"

So he bent down, put his head into the hole, and called out:

"Is anybody at home?"

There was a sudden scuffling noise from inside the hole, and then silence.

"What I said was, 'Is anybody at home?'" called Pooh very loudly.

"No!" said a voice; and then added, "You needn't shout so loud. I heard you quite well the first time."

"Bother!" said Pooh. "Isn't there anybody here at all?"

"Nobody."

Winnie-the-Pooh took his head out of the hole, and thought for a little, and he thought to himself, "There must be somebody there, because somebody must have *said* 'Nobody.'" So he put his head back in the hole, and said:

"Hallo, Rabbit, isn't that you?"

"No," said Rabbit, in a different sort of voice this time.

"But isn't that Rabbit's voice?"

"I don't *think* so," said Rabbit. "It isn't *meant* to be."

"Oh!" said Pooh.

He took his head out of the hole, and had another think, and then he put it back, and said:

"Well, could you very kindly tell me where Rabbit is?"

"He has gone to see his friend Pooh Bear, who is a great friend of his."

"But this *is* Me!" said Bear, very much surprised.

"What sort of Me?"

"Pooh Bear."

"Are you sure?" said Rabbit, still more surprised.

"Quite, quite sure," said Pooh.

"Oh, well, then, come in."

So Pooh pushed and pushed and pushed his way through the hole, and at last he got in.

"You were quite right," said Rabbit, looking at him all over. "It *is* you. Glad to see you."

"Who did you think it was?"

"Well, I wasn't sure. You know how it is in the Forest. One can't have *anybody* coming into one's house. One has to be *careful*. What about a mouthful of something?"

Pooh always liked a little something at eleven o'clock in the morning, and he was very glad to see Rabbit getting out the plates and mugs; and when Rabbit said, "Honey or condensed milk with your bread?" he was so excited that he said, "Both," and then, so as not to seem greedy, he added, "But don't bother about the bread, please." And for a long time after that he said nothing . . . until at last, humming to himself in a rather sticky voice, he got up, shook Rabbit lovingly by the paw, and said that he must be going on.

"Must you?" said Rabbit politely.

"Well," said Pooh, "I could stay a little longer if it—if you—" and he tried very hard to look in the direction of the larder.

"As a matter of fact," said Rabbit, "I was going out myself directly."

"Oh, well, then, I'll be going on. Good-bye."

"Well, good-bye, if you're sure you won't have any more."

"*Is* there any more?" asked Pooh quickly.

Rabbit took the covers off the dishes, and said no, there wasn't.

"I thought not," said Pooh, nodding to himself. "Well, good-bye. I must be going on."

So he started to climb out of the hole. He pulled with his front paws, and pushed with his back paws, and in a little while his nose was out in the open again . . . and then his ears . . . and then his front paws . . . and then his shoulders . . . and then—

"Oh, help!" said Pooh. "I'd better go back."

"Oh, bother!" said Pooh. "I shall have to go on."

"I can't do either!" said Pooh. "Oh, help *and* bother!"

Now by this time Rabbit wanted to go for a walk too, and finding the front door full, he went out by the back door, and came round to Pooh, and looked at him.

"Hallo, are you stuck?" he asked.

"N-no," said Pooh carelessly. "Just resting and thinking and humming to myself."

"Here, give us a paw."

Pooh Bear stretched out a paw, and Rabbit pulled and pulled and pulled. . . .

"*Ow!*" cried Pooh, "You're hurting!"

"The fact is," said Rabbit, "you're stuck."

"It all comes," said Pooh crossly, "of not having front doors big enough."

"It all comes," said Rabbit sternly, "of eating too much. I thought at the time," said Rabbit, "only I didn't like to say anything," said Rabbit, "that one of us was eating too much," said Rabbit, "and I knew it wasn't *me*," he said. "Well, well, I shall go and fetch Christopher Robin."

Christopher Robin lived at the other end of the Forest, and when he came back with Rabbit, and saw the front half of Pooh, he said, "Silly old Bear," in such a loving voice that everybody felt quite hopeful again.

"I was just beginning to think," said Bear, sniffing slightly, "that Rabbit might never be able to use his front door again. And I should *hate* that," he said.

"So should I," said Rabbit.

"Use his front door again?" said Christopher Robin. "Of course he'll use his front door again."

"Good," said Rabbit.

"If we can't pull you out, Pooh, we might push you back."

Rabbit scratched his whiskers thoughtfully, and pointed out that, when once Pooh was pushed back, he was back, and of course nobody was more glad to see Pooh than *he* was, still there it was, some lived in trees and some lived underground, and—

"You mean I'd *never* get out?" said Pooh.

"I mean," said Rabbit, "that having got *so* far, it seems a pity to waste it."

Christopher Robin nodded.

"Then there's only one thing to be done," he said. "We shall have to wait for you to get thin again."

"How long does getting thin take?" asked Pooh anxiously.

"About a week, I should think."

"But I can't stay here for a *week*!"

"You can *stay* here all right, silly old Bear. It's getting you out which is so difficult."

"We'll read to you," said Rabbit cheerfully. "And I hope it won't snow," he added. "And I say, old fellow, you're taking up a good deal of room in my house—*do* you mind if I use your back legs as a towel-horse? Because, I mean,

there they are—doing nothing—and it would be very convenient just to hang the towels on them."

"A week!" said Pooh gloomily. "*What about meals?*"

"I'm afraid no meals," said Christopher Robin, "because of getting thin quicker. But we *will* read to you."

Bear began to sigh, and then found he couldn't because he was so tightly stuck; and a tear rolled down his eye, as he said:

"Then would you read a Sustaining Book, such as would help and comfort a Wedged Bear in Great Tightness?"

So for a week Christopher Robin read that sort of book at the North end of Pooh, and Rabbit hung his washing on the South end . . . and in between Bear felt himself getting slenderer and slenderer. And at the end of the week Christopher Robin said, *"Now!"*

So he took hold of Pooh's front paws and Rabbit took hold of Christopher Robin, and all Rabbit's friends and relations took hold of Rabbit, and they pulled together. . . .

And for a long time Pooh only said *"Ow!"* . . .

And *"Oh!"* . . .

And then, all of a sudden, he said *"Pop!"* just as if a cork were coming out of a bottle.

And Christopher Robin and Rabbit and all Rabbit's friends and relations went head-over-heels backwards . . . and on the top of them came Winnie-the-Pooh—free!

So, with a nod of thanks to his friends, he went on with his walk through the forest, humming proudly to himself. But, Christopher Robin looked after him lovingly, and said to himself, "Silly old Bear!"

PARENTS: Check out A. A. Milne's *Winnie-the-Pooh* for more stories about Pooh and his friends: Rabbit, Piglet, Eeyore, Kanga and Roo, and Christopher Robin—but not Tigger: that bouncy fellow is introduced in another book, *The House at Pooh Corner,* a selection from which you'll find in *What Your First Grader Needs to Know* (revised edition).

The Velveteen Rabbit; or, How Toys Become Real

(Adapted from the Original by Margery Williams)

There was once a velveteen rabbit, and in the beginning he was really splendid. He was fat and bunchy, as a rabbit should be; his coat was spotted brown and white, he had real thread whiskers, and his ears were lined with pink satin. On Christmas morning, when he sat wedged in the top of the Boy's stocking, with a sprig of holly between his paws, the effect was charming.

There were other things in the stocking, nuts and oranges and a toy engine, and chocolate almonds and a clockwork mouse, but the Rabbit was quite the best of all. For at least two hours the Boy loved him, and then there was a great rustling of tissue paper and unwrapping of parcels, and in the excitement of looking at all the new presents, the Velveteen Rabbit was forgotten.

For a long time he lived in the toy cupboard or on the nursery floor, and no one thought very much about him. He was naturally shy, and being only made of velveteen, some of the more expensive toys quite snubbed him. The mechanical toys were very superior and looked down upon everyone else; they were full of modern ideas and pretended they were real. But the Rabbit didn't even know that real rabbits existed; he thought they were all stuffed with sawdust like himself. So the poor little Rabbit was made to feel very insignificant and commonplace, and the only person who was kind to him at all was the Skin Horse.

The Skin Horse had lived longer in the nursery than any of the others. He was so old that his brown coat was bald in patches, and most of the hairs in his tail had been pulled out. He was wise, for he had seen many mechanical toys arrive to boast and swagger, and by and by break their mainsprings and pass away, and he knew that they were only toys and would never turn into anything else. For nursery magic is very strange and wonderful, and only those play-things that are old and wise and experienced like the Skin Horse understand all about it.

"What is REAL?" asked the Rabbit one day. "Does it mean having things that buzz inside you and a stick-out handle?"

"Real isn't how you are made," said the Skin Horse. "It's a thing that happens to you. When a child loves you for a long, long time, not just to play with, but REALLY loves you, then you become Real."

"Does it hurt?" asked the Rabbit.

"Sometimes," said the Skin Horse, for he was always truthful. "When you are Real, you don't mind being hurt."

"Does it happen all at once, like being wound up," the Rabbit asked, "or bit by bit?"

"It doesn't happen all at once," said the Skin Horse. "It takes a long time. Generally, by the time you are Real, most of your hair has been loved off, and your eyes drop out, and you get very shabby. But these things don't matter at all, because once you are Real, you can't be ugly."

"I suppose you are Real?" said the Rabbit.

"The Boy's Uncle made me Real," the Skin Horse said. "That was a great many years ago; but once you are Real, you can't become unreal again. It lasts for always."

The Rabbit sighed. He longed to become Real, to know what it felt like; and yet the idea of growing shabby and losing his eyes and whiskers was rather sad. He wished that he could become real without these uncomfortable things happening to him.

There was a person called Nana who ruled the nursery. Sometimes she took no notice of the playthings lying about, and sometimes she went swooping about like a great wind and hustled them away in cupboards. She called this "tidying up," and the playthings all hated it. The Rabbit didn't mind it so much, for wherever he was thrown he came down soft.

One evening, when the Boy was going to bed, he couldn't find the china dog that always slept with him. Nana was in a hurry, so she simply looked about her, and seeing that the toy cupboard door stood open, she made a swoop.

"Here," she said, "take your old Bunny!" And she dragged the Rabbit out by one ear and put him into the Boy's arms.

That night, and for many nights after, the Velveteen Rabbit slept in the Boy's bed. At first he found it rather uncomfortable, for the Boy hugged him very tight, and sometimes he rolled over on him, and sometimes he pushed him so far under the pillow that the Rabbit could scarcely breathe. And he missed, too, those long moonlight hours in the nursery, when all the house was silent, and his talks with the Skin Horse. But very soon he grew to like it, for the Boy talked to him and made nice tunnels for him under the bedclothes that he said were like the burrows the real rabbits lived in. And when the Boy dropped off to sleep, the Rabbit would snuggle down close under his little warm chin and dream, with the Boy's hands clasped close round him all night long.

And so time went on, and the little Rabbit was very happy—so happy that he never noticed how his beautiful velveteen fur was getting shabbier and shabbier, and his tail coming unsewn, and all the pink rubbed off his nose where the Boy had kissed him.

Spring came, and they had long days in the garden, for wherever the Boy went the Rabbit went, too. He had rides in the wheelbarrow, and picnics on the grass, and lovely fairy huts built for him under the raspberry canes. And once, when the Boy was called away suddenly, the Rabbit was left out on the lawn until long after dusk, and Nana had to come and look for him with the candle because the Boy couldn't go to sleep unless he was there. He was wet through with the dew, and Nana grumbled as she rubbed him off with a corner of her apron.

"You must have your old Bunny!" she said. "Fancy all that fuss for a toy!"

The Boy sat up in bed and stretched out his hands.

"Give me my Bunny!" he said. "He isn't a toy. He's REAL!"

When the little Rabbit heard that, he was happy, for he knew that what the Skin Horse had said was true at last. The nursery magic had happened to him, and he was a toy no longer. He was Real. The Boy himself had said it.

That night he was almost too happy to sleep. And into his boot-button eyes, which had long ago lost their polish, there came a look of wisdom and beauty.

That was a wonderful summer!

Near the house where they lived there was a wood, and in the long June evenings the Boy liked to go there to play. He took the Velveteen Rabbit with him, and before he wandered off to play, he always made the Rabbit a little nest where he would be quite cozy. One evening, while the Rabbit was lying there alone, he saw two strange beings creep out of the tall grass near him.

They were rabbits like himself, but quite furry and brand-new. They must have been very well made, for their seams didn't show at all, and they changed shape in a queer way when they moved; one minute they were long and thin and the next minute fat and bunchy, instead of always staying the same as he did.

They stared at him, and the little Rabbit stared back. And all the time their noses twitched.

"Why don't you get up and play with us?" one of them asked.

"I don't feel like it," said the Rabbit, for he didn't want to explain that he couldn't get up.

"Can you hop on your hind legs?" asked the furry rabbit.

That was a dreadful question, for the Velveteen Rabbit had no hind legs at

Take a Look

Look at the picture of the Velveteen Rabbit. Now look at the rabbit on page 359. Ask your child what is the same about the two rabbits and what is different?

all! The back of him was made all in one piece, like a pincushion. He sat still and hoped that the other rabbits wouldn't notice. But wild rabbits have very sharp eyes. And this one stretched out his neck and looked.

"He hasn't got any hind legs!" he called out. And he began to laugh.

"I have!" cried the little Rabbit. "I have got hind legs! I am sitting on them!"

"Then stretch them out and show me, like this!" said the wild rabbit. And he began to whirl around and dance, till the little Rabbit got quite dizzy.

"I don't like dancing," he said. "I'd rather sit still!"

But all the while he was longing to dance, for a new tickly feeling ran through him, and he felt he would give anything to be able to jump about like these rabbits did.

The strange rabbit stopped dancing and came quite close.

"He doesn't smell right!" he exclaimed. "He isn't a rabbit at all! He isn't real!"

"I am Real!" said the little Rabbit. "I am Real! The Boy said so!" And he nearly began to cry.

Just then there was a sound of footsteps, and the Boy ran past near them, and with a flash of white tails the two strange rabbits disappeared.

"Come back and play with me!" called the little Rabbit. "Oh, do come back! I know I am Real!"

But there was no answer. The Velveteen Rabbit was all alone. For a long time he lay very still, hoping that they would come back. But they never returned, and presently the sun sank lower and the little white moths fluttered out, and the Boy came and carried him home.

Weeks passed, and the little Rabbit grew very old and shabby, but the Boy loved him just as much. He loved him so hard that he loved all his whiskers off, and the pink lining to his ears turned gray, and his brown spots faded. He even began to lose his shape, and he scarcely looked like a rabbit anymore, except to the Boy. To him, he was always beautiful, and that was all that the little Rabbit cared about.

And then, one day, the Boy was ill.

His little body was so hot that it burned the Rabbit when he held him close. Strange people came and went in the nursery, and a light burned all night, and

New Word

Beds don't have clothes! Ask your child what she thinks "bedclothes" might mean. Bedclothes are the sheets and blankets.

through it all the little Velveteen Rabbit lay there, hidden from sight under the **bedclothes,** and he never stirred, for he was afraid that if they found him, someone might take him away, and he knew that the Boy needed him.

It was a long, weary time, for the Boy was too ill to play. The little Rabbit snuggled down patiently, and looked forward to the time when the Boy would be well again and they would go out in the garden amongst the flowers and the butterflies and play splendid games in the raspberry thicket like they used to.

At last the Boy got better. He was able to sit up in bed and look at the picture books while the little Rabbit cuddled close at his side. And one day they let him get up and dress.

It was a bright, sunny morning. They had carried the Boy outside, wrapped in a shawl, and the little Rabbit lay tangled up among the bedclothes, thinking.

The Boy was going to the seaside tomorrow. Now it only remained to carry out the doctor's orders. They talked about it all the while the little Rabbit lay under the bedclothes and listened. The room was to be disinfected, and all the books and toys that the Boy had played with in bed must be burnt.

"Hurrah!" thought the little Rabbit. "Tomorrow we shall go to the seaside!" For the Boy had often talked of the seaside, and he wanted very much to see the big waves coming in, and the tiny crabs, and the sand castles.

Just then Nana caught sight of him.

"How about his old Bunny?" she asked.

"That?" said the doctor. "Why, it's a mass of scarlet fever germs! Burn it at once!"

And so the little Rabbit was put into a sack with the old picture books and a lot of rubbish, and carried out to the end of the garden. That was a fine place to make a bonfire, only the gardener was too busy just then to attend to it.

That night the Boy slept in a different bedroom, and he had a new bunny to sleep with him, but he was too excited to care very much about it. For tomorrow he was going to the seaside, and he could think of nothing else.

And while the Boy was asleep, dreaming of the seaside, the little Rabbit lay among the old picture books and rubbish, and he felt very lonely. The sack had been left untied, and so by wriggling a bit he was able to get his head through the opening and look out. Nearby he could see the thicket of raspberry canes in whose shadow he had played with the Boy on bygone mornings. He thought of those long sunlit hours in the garden—how happy they were—and a great sadness came over him. He thought of the Skin Horse, so wise and gentle, and all that he had told him. Of what use was it to be loved and lose one's beauty and become Real if it all ended like this? And a tear, a real tear, trickled down his shabby little velvet nose and fell to the ground.

And then a strange thing happened. For where the tear had fallen, a mysterious flower grew out of the ground. It had slender green leaves the color of emeralds; and in the center of the leaves, a blossom like a golden cup. It was so beautiful that the little Rabbit forgot to cry. And presently the blossom opened, and out of it there stepped the loveliest fairy in the whole world. Her dress was of pearl and dewdrops, and there were flowers round her neck and in her hair. And she came close to the little Rabbit and gathered him up in her arms and kissed him on his velveteen nose that was all damp from crying.

"Little Rabbit," she said, "I am the nursery magic Fairy. I take care of all the playthings that the children have loved. When they are old and worn out and the children don't need them anymore, then I come and take them away with me and turn them into Real."

"Wasn't I Real before?" asked the little Rabbit.

"You were Real to the Boy," the Fairy said, "because he loved you. Now you shall be Real to everyone."

And she held the little Rabbit close in her arms and flew with him into the wood. It was light now, for the moon had risen. All the forest was beautiful. In the open glade between the tree trunks, the wild rabbits danced with their shadows on the velvet grass, but when they saw the Fairy, they all stopped dancing and stood round in a ring to stare at her.

"I've brought you a new playfellow," the Fairy said. "You must be very kind to him and teach him all he needs to know, for he is going to live with you for ever and ever!"

And she kissed the little Rabbit again and put him down on the grass.

"Run and play, little Rabbit!" she said.

But the little Rabbit sat quite still for a moment and never moved. For when he saw all the wild rabbits dancing around him, he suddenly remembered about his hind legs, and he didn't want them to see that he was made all in one piece. He did not know that when the Fairy kissed him that last time, she had changed him altogether. And he might have sat there a long time, too shy to move, if just then something hadn't tickled his nose, and before he thought what he was doing, he lifted his hind toe to scratch it.

And he found that he actually had hind legs! Instead of dingy velveteen he had brown fur, soft and shiny, his ears twitched by themselves, and his whiskers were so long that they brushed the grass. He gave one leap, and the joy of using those hind legs was so great that he went springing about on them, jumping sideways and whirling round as the others did, and he grew so excited that when at last he did stop to look for the Fairy, she had gone.

He was a Real Rabbit at last, at home with the other rabbits.

Autumn passed and winter, and in the spring, when the days grew warm and sunny, the Boy went out to play in the wood behind the house. And while he was playing, two rabbits crept out and peeped at him. One of them was brown all over, but the other had strange markings under his fur, as though long ago he had been spotted, and the spots still showed through. And about his little soft nose and his round black eyes there was something familiar, so that the Boy thought to himself, "Why, he looks just like my old Bunny that was lost when I had scarlet fever!"

But he never knew that it really was his own Bunny, come back to look at the child who had first helped him to be Real.

Two Tall Tales

PARENTS: There's a bit of truth in the two tall tales we tell here: both Johnny Appleseed and Casey Jones were real people. But tall tales aren't known for being truthful, and like all tall tales, these two stories dish up a heaping portion of exaggeration. They present people and deeds bigger than life, but no bigger than the spirit of the people who love to tell tall tales.

Johnny Appleseed

This here is the story of John Chapman, better known as Johnny Appleseed. He lived in this country a long time ago, when America was still growing, and there weren't as many towns or cities, but there was a lot of wide-open land.

Now, Johnny was an unusual kind of hero. He didn't lead any soldiers in a war, and he didn't become the president, and he didn't sail ships across the oceans, and he didn't kill dragons or rescue princesses. But still, he was a real hero. And what he did best was—well, you'll see.

People say that when Johnny was a baby, he'd fuss and cry and keep the family awake until they put a twig with apple blossoms in his little hand. Then he wouldn't bang the petals off, or eat them, like other babies would. Instead, he'd just lie there in his crib, looking at those apple blossoms, sniffing at them now and then, as happy as an angel full of ice cream.

When Johnny was a little boy, his mother would wander with him in the woods and show him plants and squirrels and such. He loved the birds and animals almost as much as he loved apples and apple trees. He was never happier than when he was lugging around some little animal or other, even if it was a skunk. And whenever an animal in the neighborhood was sick or had a broken leg, people would say, "Just take it over to Johnny Chapman. He'll fix the little critter right up."

When Johnny grew up, he got an idea in his head, and he couldn't get it out. His idea was that there ought to be more apple trees, lots more, and that he was just the fellow to plant them. But he couldn't carry trees all over the country! What he needed was seeds, and plenty of 'em.

Near where Johnny lived there were mills where folks made apple cider. They pressed the juice out of the apples and had no use for the seeds. But Johnny could use them. He took the seeds, washed them off, and let them dry in the sun. When he finished, he had sacks and sacks full of seeds.

So Johnny set off westward, carrying his apple seeds. He carried so many seeds that he couldn't bring along much of anything else. He found a place for his two favorite books, the Bible and Aesop's Fables, and he needed a cooking pan, so he wore that on his head.

> **Make a Connection**
>
> Use the image on page 337 to show your child what Johnny's apple seeds looked like, and where they are found inside the apples.

Johnny walked all over the country, sleeping out in the open, eating whatever was handy, tramping through the mud and snow.

He walked and walked, stopping here and there to plant the seeds all along the rivers, in meadows, wherever people would let him. Whenever he met a family moving west (which a lot of families were doing in those days), he'd give them a little pouch of seeds so that they could grow their own apple trees. And that's how folks came to know him as "Johnny Appleseed."

Some people thought Johnny was foolish because he gave away his seeds for free—and these people thought that it only made sense to do something if you were going to make money doing it. But Johnny Appleseed would just say, "Money?" And he would snap his fingers. "What do you do with money? Just spend it for clothes or houses or food." Then, without taking a cent from anyone, he'd be on his way.

When anybody brought up the subject of animals, Johnny Appleseed was likely to go through that finger-snapping business again. "Leave animals alone," he'd say, "and they'll do the same by you. They're your brothers and sisters, sort of, only they don't borrow clothes, and they don't argue with you the way human brothers and sisters do."

Once, on a cold winter's day, Johnny was slushing through the snow, and night came. He looked around for some big hollow log to sleep in. He found a

dandy log, built a fire nearby, cooked his mush, ate it up, and started to crawl into the hollow log.

When he'd got in about to his hips, he heard a groaning grunt. Peeking in, he saw a big bear lying in there with his paws crossed on his chest, enjoying his winter snooze. Johnny backed out, inch by inch, slow as a snail, being quiet so as not to disturb the bear's sleep. "Beg your pardon, Brother Bear," he whispered. Then he yawned, stretched out, and curled up in the snow.

Johnny Appleseed had something he believed in, and he went to a lot of trouble to bring it about. He wanted to see a nation of apple orchards, with apple trees in bloom in the spring, and the men and women and children everywhere strong and good and healthy, like Johnny himself.

Johnny lived a long, long time ago, but people say that, even today, if you go to a certain part of Ohio in apple blossom time, and get up before sunrise, and go to a certain old apple tree, you'll see the smoke from Johnny's fire as it dies out. Maybe you'll even catch a glimpse of Johnny's spirit as it moves along westward with the spring, waking up the blossoms and tending the orchards.

> **Make a Connection**
> Read about the life cycle of a plant in the science chapter.

Casey Jones

PARENTS: Casey Jones was a real man, born John Luther Jones in 1864. When he began to work for the railroad at age fifteen, everybody called him "Casey" after his hometown, Cayce, Kentucky. His deeds as a railroad engineer have entered the realm of legend and tall tale. The story of the life and dramatic death (in 1900) of Casey Jones lives on mostly in a song, of which there are many different versions. This version of the story of Casey Jones weaves in some lines from the songs about him.

Now gather round, friends, for I want you to hear
The story of a brave engineer.

His name was Casey Jones, and let me tell you, there's never been a man who could drive a train as fast as Casey.

When Casey was a young man, the railroad was about the fastest way of getting round. This was back before the time of airplanes or rocket ships, even before fast cars or trucks.

Casey drove a train on the Illinois Central Line. He loved to sit way up in the cabin of the train with his hand on the throttle—that's the handle you use to make the train go slower or, in Casey's case, faster. He loved to see the trees and fields go whizzing by. He loved to make the whistle blow—and there was no other train with a whistle like Casey's: it started out soft, like a whippoorwill, then rose to a howl, like a coyote crying in the night, then faded away into a ghostly whisper.

People always knew when Casey was coming. Even before they could see the train, they could hear the powerful *chugga-chugga*, *chugga-chugga*, getting louder and louder. Then they'd hear that wild whistle howl. People used to say that when Casey blew his whistle, why, little babies would wake up from their naps, but they wouldn't cry. Instead, they'd make little *chugga-chugga*, *whoo-whoo* sounds, then fall right back asleep. And people said that when Casey blew his whistle, the cows would give an extra quart of milk, and the chickens lay at least a dozen eggs each.

And if you hurried, you could take one of those eggs and crack it into a cold frying pan and put out a piece of plain bread, and just as soon as Casey went blazing by, there in that pan would be a nicely fried egg, over easy, and on the side a plate of hot buttered toast.

Now the reason Casey drove so fast was, he took pride in always being on time. He wanted to get that train where it was going when it was supposed to be there, or even a little before. Whenever he started on a trip, the railroad men would wave and yell, "Bring her in on time, Casey!" And they knew he would.

But you can't make a train go fast all by yourself. Casey needed a good fireman to help him, and he had one of the best in Sim Webb. The fireman on a train doesn't put out fires—no, Sim Webb kept the fire going by shoveling coal into it, which got the flames a-roarin', which made a lot of steam, which made the train go fast—and got the train in on time.

Once, Casey and Sim almost didn't make it on time. They were carrying a load of mail to Memphis, Tennessee, and it was raining cats and dogs. Some people say

The rain had been falling for five or six weeks,
And the railroad track was like the bed of a creek.

At the station in Memphis, the railroad men waited for Casey to arrive. Some said, "There's no way he can make it on time in all this rain. He'll have to slow down." But others said, "Just you wait. Casey Jones always makes it on time. Running on time is his hobby." And sure enough, just then they saw a light on the tracks up ahead, and heard the lonesome whistle that could only be Casey's, and the train pulled into the station, dripping wet, puffing hard, but on time.

Casey and Sim were dog tired and looking forward to a good night's sleep. But they'd hardly settled into bed when a knock came at the door. It seems that the engineer who was supposed to drive the train on the southbound run was sick. Well, they didn't even have to ask Casey if he would take the man's place. Tired as he was, Casey got dressed and headed for the train. And when he got there, he found Sim Webb, already stoking the fire with coal, getting the train ready to carry mail, packages, and some passengers as well.

Now, friends, here's where I have to tell you the sad part of this story, about how Casey met his end.

As Casey mounted to the cabin and took the throttle in his hand, he heard someone shout, "Casey, you're already more than an hour and a half late." But Casey just smiled and said to himself, "Guess that means I'll have to go a little faster."

He opened up the throttle and the train plunged into the dark, wet night. Sim Webb shoveled the coal as fast as he could, and the train chugged on, faster and faster. "Casey!" Sim yelled. "You're running too fast."

And Casey said, "I believe we'll make it through,
For the engine is a-steamin' better than I ever knew."
And Casey said, "Fireman, don't you fret,
Keep knockin' at the fire door, and don't give up yet.
I'm going to run this train until she leaves the rail
Or we make it on time with the southbound mail."

Casey was "highballing" down the tracks—which means he was pushing the train just as fast as it would go. He was going so fast that it looked like they might even make it on time. But then, as they squealed around a curve, through the darkness Casey saw a light up ahead. But that light wasn't supposed to be there, not on this track. Then Casey knew: there was a train stuck on the track just ahead and he was speeding straight toward it!

Casey pulled the brake as hard as he could, and yelled, "Jump, Sim!"

"Casey, you come on!" said Sim.

"Jump!" Casey shouted, and Sim jumped. But Casey stayed on. He knew he couldn't stop the train in time, but he also knew he had to slow it down. He knew if he jumped and let go of the brake, it might mean death for the passengers on the train. So Casey pulled on the brake with all his might, and a terrible screeching, squealing sound ripped through the darkness.

The trains, they met in the middle of a hill
In a head-on tangle that was bound to kill.
He tried to do his duty, the men all said,
But Casey Jones, he ended up dead.

Casey Jones—mounted to the cabin.
Casey Jones—throttle in his hand.
Casey Jones mounted to the cabin
And took his farewell trip to the Promised Land.

Poor Casey. When they found him, he had one hand still tight on the throttle, and one hand tight on the brake. But Casey was the only person who died. The passengers lived because Casey stayed at his post and did his duty.

People say that if you look up in the sky at night and see a light flash across the sky—well, it might be a shooting star, but then again, it might be Casey Jones, highballing across the heavens, *chugga-chugga*, chugga-chuggin' now and forever, on time till the end of time.

Sayings

PARENTS: Every culture has phrases and proverbs that make no sense when carried over literally into another culture. To say, for example, that someone has "let the cat out of the bag" has nothing to do with setting free a trapped kitty. Nor—thank goodness— does it ever literally "rain cats and dogs"!

The sayings and phrases in this section may be familiar to many children, who hear them at home. But the inclusion of these sayings and phrases in the *Core Knowledge Sequence* has been singled out for gratitude by many parents and by teachers who work with children from home cultures that are different from the culture of literate American English.

For kindergartners, we have chosen to introduce a selection of very familiar sayings that are likely to have some connection to the child's world of experience. It will help your child to learn these sayings if you use them in meaningful situations. Look for some of them to appear in the "Make a Connection" text in the margins of this book.

April showers bring May flowers.

People use this saying to mean that something unpleasant can cause something pleasant to happen, just as spring rains cause flowers to bloom.

Bob had caught chicken pox and he couldn't go to the fair. "Cheer up, Bob," said his mother. "April showers bring May flowers: you have to stay home, but now we have time to work on that big new puzzle you've been wanting to put together."

Better safe than sorry.

People use this saying to mean it's better not to take a chance than to do something that might be very risky. They say this because you're less likely to be hurt or make a bad mistake when you're careful.

Make a Connection
Read about seasons and weather in the science chapter. Ask your child in which season April and May are found.

Alex dared Carlos to walk on the railing of the old bridge. "No way, Alex," said Carlos. "It's a long fall into the river. Better safe than sorry."

Do unto others as you would have them do unto you.

This saying is called the Golden Rule. When people use it, they mean you should treat other people as you would like to be treated yourself. It comes from the Bible.

"Molly, stop drawing on Becky's picture," said the babysitter. "Would you like Becky to mess up your picture? Remember, do unto others as you would have them do unto you."

A dog is man's best friend.

Some people think that a dog is more than a pet. They think a dog can also be a really good friend. That's because dogs, like good friends, can be loyal and loving.

Peter had lost his lunch money and torn his favorite shirt. As he walked home, he was feeling sad, but then he heard his dog, Prince, barking. Prince jumped up and licked Peter with his big wet tongue. "Prince," Peter laughed, "it's true: a dog is man's best friend."

The early bird gets the worm.

This saying means that you can usually get ahead of others if you get going before they do. Sometimes people say it to someone who needs a little extra push to do what he is supposed to do.

"Hey, Billy," said Juan, "did you hear? Cary's Card Shop is opening early on Saturday, and the first fifty people in the shop get free baseball cards!"

> **Make a Connection**
> Ask your child what kind of care "man's best friend" might need. Read about animals and their needs in the science chapter.

"That's great!" answered Billy. "Let's find out what time they open and be waiting at the door. The early bird gets the worm, you know."

Great oaks from little acorns grow.

This saying means that, just as a small acorn can grow into a towering oak tree, something that starts out small or not very important can turn out big or very important.

Abraham Lincoln was born in a log cabin and read books by firelight. Even though his family was poor, he became one of the greatest presidents of the United States. His life is true to the saying "Great oaks from little acorns grow."

> **Make a Connection**
> Read about the life cycle of a plant in the science chapter. Explain to your child that an acorn is a seed and will follow the same cycle to grow into a big tree.

Look before you leap.

This saying means you should be careful and think before you rush into doing something.

"Mom!" said Andrew with excitement. "Ben says he'll trade me all his toy cars for my bike. Isn't that great?"

"I don't know, Andrew. Is it?" asked his mother. "You ride your bike every day, and a bike costs a lot more than toy cars. Do you really want to trade? You'd better look before you leap."

A place for everything and everything in its place.

This saying means you should put things where they belong. We use this saying when we want people to be neat.

When Andrea came in from playing, she would always kick off her shoes in the hall. Her mother said, "Andrea, your shoes don't belong in the hall. Please put them in the closet. Remember: a place for everything and everything in its place!"

It's raining cats and dogs.

People use this saying to mean that it is raining very, very hard.

"We'd better ride the bus home today. If we walk, we'll get soaked. It's raining cats and dogs!"

Make a Connection

Read more about weather in the science chapter.

Practice makes perfect.

People use this saying to mean that doing something over and over makes you good at it.

Lucy liked taking piano lessons. She practiced every day. Sometimes it was hard, but she felt proud when she learned to play her first song without making any mistakes. She understood now why her teacher always said, "Practice makes perfect."

Where there's a will, there's a way.

This saying means if you want to do something badly enough, you'll find a way to do it.

Lillian had tried and tried to jump rope fifty times in a row, but she always messed up after forty jumps. "Aagh!" she said to her friend Betty. "I don't think I'll ever do fifty!"

"Oh, yes you will," said Betty. "Keep trying. Where there's a will, there's a way."

II
History and Geography

Introduction

In kindergarten, children often study aspects of their immediate world: the family, the school, the community, and so on. While such local studies should be encouraged, we should also take advantage of children's natural curiosity and begin to broaden their horizons. By introducing kindergartners to history and geography, we can foster their curiosity about the larger world and begin to develop their sense of the past and its significance. For young children, we need to emphasize the "story" in history. By appealing to children's naturally active imaginations, we can ask them to "visit" people and places in the past. We encourage you to go beyond these pages to help your child learn about history through art projects, drama, music, and discussions.

In the following pages, we introduce a variety of people and events. This is really just an introduction, though, and children will encounter most of these people and events more fully in their later schooling.

For example, we introduce July 4, 1776, as "the birthday of our nation," on the premise that kindergartners can understand the idea of a birthday. But we do not mention the American Revolution (which, by the way, we do introduce in the first-grade book of this series and explore in some detail in the fourth-grade book).

In beginning to tell children the story of the past, we have tried to be sensitive about the degree to which, and the manner in which, we expose children to the tragic aspects of history, such as the practice of slavery in the United States. In some cases, we have chosen to leave for later grades some of the darker aspects of history, although we have not painted a dishonestly pretty picture of the past. For example, here we tell the story of Columbus's first journey to the "New World," but we wait until later books in this series to tell about the devastation wrought on Native American peoples by the diseases that came with the European explorers. The goal in kindergarten, then, is less to explore historical events or ideas in depth than to orient the child to history and to a sense of the distant past—and to plant the seeds of knowledge that will grow in later years.

World History and Geography

Planet Earth

When you are standing outside and you look as far as you can, what do you see? Do you see streets and houses? Cars and big apartment buildings? Green fields and mountains? Maybe you see some water, such as a river, a lake, or an ocean.

Everything you see is a part of our world. The streets and houses, cars and buildings, fields and mountains, lakes and rivers all belong to planet Earth, which is another word for our world. The world stretches as far as you can see—in fact, the world stretches a whole lot farther than you can see!

What's the tallest thing you can think of in your neighborhood? Is it a building? Is it a tree? Imagine if you climbed up to the very top and looked around. What do you think you could see? You could see things you never saw from down here. You could see how this big world of ours goes on and on and on. Maybe you would see rows of houses, all lined up along streets that look like crisscrossed lines. Or maybe you would see the tops of trees and a big green field with a red barn that looks very tiny because it is so far away.

When people take trips in an airplane, they can look down in just this same way and see fields and houses, or lots of buildings in a city, or ocean water, stretching far into the distance.

And when astronauts go up in rockets, even higher than airplanes, they can see something amazing. When they look back at planet Earth, it looks like a big blue marble. Here is a picture of Earth that one astronaut took from way up in outer space.

Does it look like a big blue marble to you? What colors do you see? The blue is water. The green and brown parts are land. The white swirls are clouds. Somewhere on this picture of a blue marble, way too tiny to see, there are houses and barns and fields and trees and cars and people.

This is how our world, the planet Earth, looks from space.

Oceans and Continents, Maps and Globes

If you could take a deep breath and blow away all those clouds that are covering the planet Earth, you would see something like this.

Now you can see the blue and brown and green even better. The big patches of blue are all water. The brown and green patches are land.

What do you see more of, blue or green? Water or land? There's a lot more blue than green on this planet, isn't there? The biggest bodies of water are called oceans, and oceans cover a lot of the planet Earth.

If you could fly like an astronaut around the planet and count all the big pieces of land on Earth, like these, you would count up seven. These big pieces of land are called continents.

Sometimes it helps to draw a picture of all the continents of the planet Earth on a flat piece of paper. Imagine if we could carefully peel the skin off the Earth, as if it were an orange, and then lay that whole skin down flat. It would look something like this.

This kind of picture is called a map. Maps are special drawings of places. People use maps to show where they live or to see where they are going when they take trips. They might not draw people or cars or houses on a map, but they probably would include streets or important buildings. Maps show rivers and lakes. Some maps show where moun-

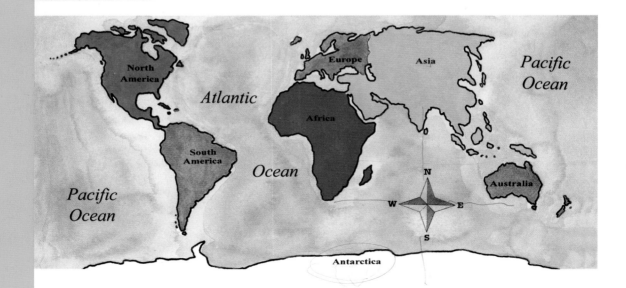

tains are and give their names. Some show highways and how they lead to towns and cities. All of these things—streets, buildings, rivers, lakes, mountains, highways, towns, and cities—are part of the geography of Earth, this big place where we live.

Do It Yourself!
Find a map that includes a key. Talk with your child about how the symbols on the map key represent different things. Are there symbols for mountains? Parks? Roads? Railroad tracks?

Earth's Seven Continents

Remember how we made the map by peeling the Earth and laying it down flat? Now what if we went the opposite way? What if we took a flat map and wrapped it tightly around a big ball so the two edges met on the other side? Then we would be making a special sort of map called a globe.

A globe is a model of the whole planet Earth, with all the oceans and continents. When you look at a globe, you can imagine that you are like an astronaut, flying far up in outer space and looking back at your home, Earth. But your globe is much, much, much tinier than the planet Earth.

Now let's look at a map or a globe and find the continents. How many are there? Let's count again.

Seven. Every continent has a name. They are called:

Asia
Europe
Africa
North America
South America
Australia
Antarctica

PARENTS: Feel free to point to each continent as you say its name, but don't focus your child on memorizing the names of continents unless he is eager to do so. More important is to convey the sense of large bodies of land that make up the planet.

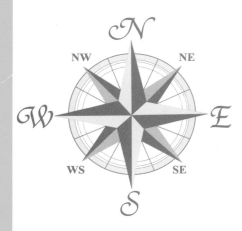

Which Way Are You Going?

Often people use maps to figure out where they are and where they are going. For instance, right now, if you wanted to show on this map where you and I are sitting, you would point to a place right about here. From here, we could travel in many directions, couldn't we? In order to talk about going in different directions, and in order to show those directions on a map, we use four important words: "north," "south," "east," and "west." Often on a map you will just see the first letters of each word: "N" stands for north, "S" for south, "E" for east, and "W" for west.

There are special ways you can know these four directions, no matter where you are. When you look at the sun coming up in the morning, you are always looking east, no matter where you are. When you look at a beautiful sunset, you are always looking west. By remembering where the sun rises and where the sun sets, you can find all four directions. Here's how.

Stick your arms straight out from your sides. Slowly turn until your right arm points to where the sun comes up. Your left arm is pointing to where the sun goes down, isn't it? Another way to say the same thing is that your right arm is pointing east and your left arm is pointing west. Now look straight ahead. Your nose is pointing north. And the back of your head is facing south. The four directions are just that simple.

Do It Yourself!

Take a break from reading now and then to connect these concepts to your kindergartner's own experience. When you talk about traveling in each direction, use a specific example, near or far, to symbolize that direction: "If we walk out the front door to the garage, we are walking west." "When we drive to Grandma's in Florida, we are driving south." Slowly help your child move from thinking about those specific places to the more abstract concept of direction.

North, South, East, West

Knowing the four directions is important when you are looking at maps.

Most of the time, the top of a map is north. When you put your finger on the map and move it up, your finger is moving north.

When north is at the top of a map, south is toward the bottom. So to make your finger trace a path going south, you move your finger down toward the bottom edge of the map.

If north is up and south is down on a map, then east is to the right. So start in the middle on this map and make your finger move east. That's right: your finger moves to the right.

The last direction is west. Which way do you think your finger moves to go west? When your finger moves to the left on this map, it is moving west.

Now let's look at the map again. The house is in the middle. There are four things on each side of the house. Can you tell me which direction each thing is from the house?

- The dog is _____ of the house.
- The tree is _____ of the house.
- The cat is _____ of the house.
- The car is _____ of the house.

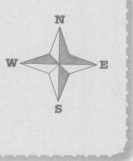

The North and South Poles

Polar bears live in the Arctic Region around the North Pole.

Let's take a look at the globe again. We are going to look for the North Pole and the South Pole.

If you start your finger in the middle, which direction do you move your finger to go north? You move it up—and up and up, and when you get to the top of the globe, you have reached the North Pole.

Now put your finger in the middle again and move your finger toward the south. You move it down, down, down— and when you get to the bottom of the globe, you have reached the South Pole!

The North Pole and the South Pole are special names for the very top and the very bottom of our world. You can tell by looking at the globe that they are far apart, but they do have something in common: it's icy cold at both the North and the South Pole!

The Seven Continents

PARENTS: It is not important that kindergartners be able to explain the difference between countries and continents. This level of abstract reasoning will develop in later years for most children. But because children will hear about both countries and continents at this age, we introduce both concepts, along with a working response to their likely question, "What's the difference?"

When we counted the continents on the globe, how many were there? There are seven continents, and they are named Asia, Europe, Africa, North America, South America, Australia, and Antarctica. And now you know another way to describe Antarctica—it is a continent at the South Pole!

When people ask you where you live, what do you say? There are many ways to talk about the place you live. You could talk about your house or say your family's address. You could name the town or community you live in. You could say the name of the country you live in: maybe that's the United States of America. Or you could say the name of the continent you live on. If you live in the United States, the continent you live on is North America. Let's find it on the globe.

The United States of America is a country on the continent of North America. There are other countries on the continent of North America. To the north of the United States is the country called Canada. To the south of the United States is the country called Mexico. Each one of these countries

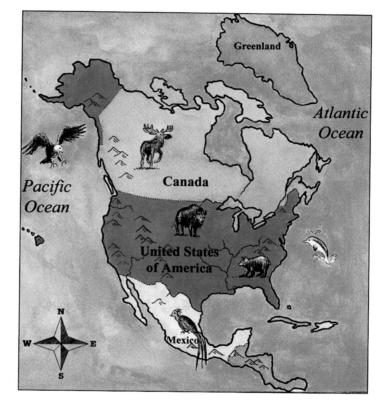

has a different leader and different laws. Each country uses a different kind of money. Each country has a different flag. But all three countries are on the same continent: North America.

Now let's take an imaginary trip around the world and visit all the continents.

Asia

The largest continent of all is Asia. Here is a map of Asia. What does this map tell us about Asia? Do you see mountains? Do you see water? Do you see pictures of animals? That means that these animals live on the continent of Asia.

Talk and Think

Pause on each continent map to talk over some of the things you see, using it to help your child become comfortable reading maps. For example, ask him to trace the shape of the continent. Ask him to show you where the land meets the water. If the map shows a river, ask him to trace that line starting in the continent's interior and ending in the ocean. Talk about each animal shown on the map, and once he can identify the animal, repeat the name of the animal and the continent where it lives. For example, "Camels live in Asia."

In the country called China, which is on the continent of Asia, there is a wall that is thousands of miles long, built a long time ago. It took many people many, many years to build this wall. Powerful kings wanted a wall to keep enemies out of their country. There are watchtowers and walkways built into this wall. Not only is it very long, but it is also so wide that six horses can run side by side along its top. The wall is called the Great Wall of China, and it plays an important part in the history of the continent of Asia.

Asia is such a big continent, it contains many different kinds of places: deserts, beaches, flat steppes with short grass, rivers that wind through jungles full of leaves and vines, mountains that stay cold all the time, and islands that stay hot all the time.

The Great Wall of China

Europe

Now let's visit Asia's neighbor, the continent called Europe. We can look at the world map to see how these two continents, Asia and Europe, touch each other. Compared with Asia, Europe is a small continent. But there are many interesting countries in Europe, as well as beautiful buildings—palaces, cathedrals, museums, and more!

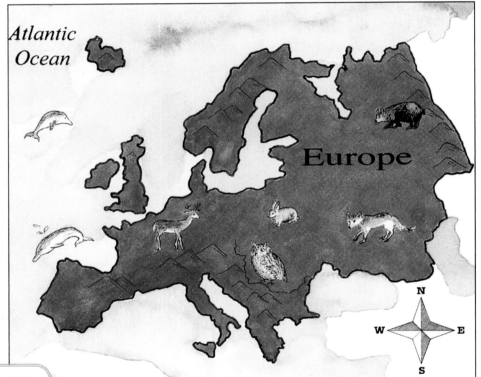

Do It Yourself!
As you introduce each new continent, turn back to the world map on page 150 and look together at the continent maps on these pages.

Here is a very famous building that we could visit in Europe. It is a complicated structure called the Eiffel Tower, and it was built more than one hundred years ago in the country called France. The Eiffel Tower is very tall, taller than most buildings. It is built out of metal. You can ride to the top of the Eiffel Tower in an elevator. When you get to the top, you can look out over the great city of Paris, France.

The Eiffel Tower is in Paris, France.

Here is another very famous building that we could visit in Europe, but it is in the city called London, England. This building is called Buckingham Palace, and it is the home of the king or queen of England. For many, many years through the history of England, kings and queens have lived here in Buckingham Palace. Long ago, the king or queen made all the decisions and rules in England. Nowadays, many other people help make the laws and decisions, but the king or the queen is still an important person to everyone who lives in England.

See those fellows with red coats and big, tall, fuzzy black hats standing outside the palace? They are the palace guards. Look for the guards in the bottom left and right corners of the picture (below).

Buckingham Palace

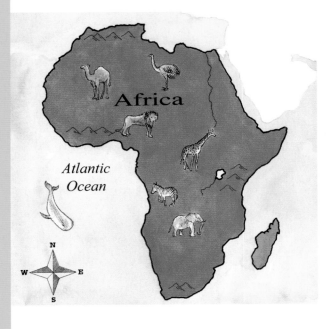

Atlantic
Ocean

Africa

Let's head south from Europe and go to another big continent called Africa. Africa is the second-largest continent in the world. We already visited the first largest continent—do you remember which one? (It's Asia.)

Because Africa is such a big continent, stretching far from north to south and east to west, it is a continent of amazing variety, which means many different kinds of places, weather, land, and animals.

In one part of Africa, we could travel through a hot, dry desert. In another part of Africa, we could go for miles and miles through land that grows tall grass and only a few trees. And in yet another part of Africa, we could visit a steamy jungle, where the trees and vines grow thick all around and there is always a little rain in the air. That's why it is called a rain forest.

Zebras live in Africa.

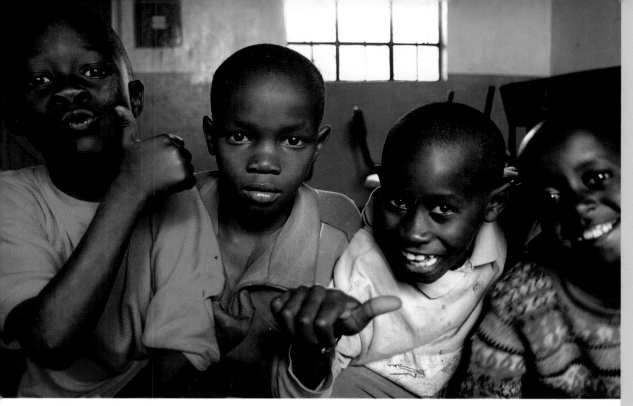

These boys are in their classroom in Nairobi, a city in the African country Kenya.

With so many different kinds of places in Africa, there are many different kinds of animals as well. There are hippos and hyenas, leopards and lions, elephants and rhinos, crocodiles and ostriches—and that's just the beginning.

In the east of Africa, there is a huge region called the Serengeti (sair-en-GET-ee) Plain. This is one of the parts of Africa where you see miles and miles of grassland and not very many trees. It is called a savanna. Many different wild animals make their homes in the Serengeti. Giraffes munch leaves from high up in the treetops. Lions lounge on rocks. Zebras, antelopes, and cheetahs roam across the grassland.

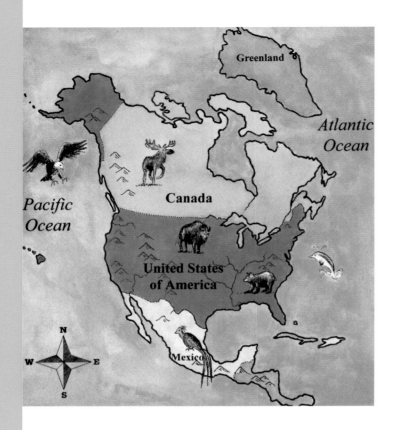

North America

Let's look at a map of the world again and find the continents we have read about so far: Asia, Europe, and Africa. Put your finger on the map and pretend you are in Europe. Now you want to go west to find more continents. To do that, you have to cross an ocean first. The name of this big ocean is the Atlantic Ocean.

So let's pretend your finger is a ship, sailing through the big waves of the Atlantic Ocean to another continent: North America. Do you remember who lives on the continent of North America? We do!

Here's something interesting to see on this map. Your finger had to cross one big ocean, the Atlantic, to get to North America. Now keep moving your finger west across the continent of North America, and what happens? When you get to the edge of the land on the western side of the continent of North America, there is another ocean. It is called the Pacific Ocean.

Even though it is not as big as Asia or Africa, the continent of North America is still very big. North America has many different climates, which is a way of saying that the weather can be very different from one place to another. It has cool forests, with lots of trees; hot deserts, with lots of sand; and windy prairies, with lots of grass. North America also has steamy swamps where alligators live, tall mountains where mountain lions roam, farms where cows and horses live, big cities with tall buildings, and little towns with just a few stores.

The continent of North America has some amazing places where you can look for a long, long way and see no houses at all. This photograph shows one of those places, called the Grand Canyon. A long, long, long time ago—millions of years ago—a big river ran through here. All that water, rushing through these mountains, carved away the land.

People like to visit the Grand Canyon because it is so big and beautiful. Some of them stand at the top of the mountains and look from there, but others choose to go deep down into the canyon.

And when they do that, do you know how they get there? They don't walk. They don't drive in cars. They don't even ride bicycles. They ride on mules!

The United States shares the continent of North America with two other nations. They are Mexico and Canada.

Do It Yourself!

Sing the first verse of "America the Beautiful" together and talk about all the phrases that describe the geography of North America. Emphasize the last phrase, "from sea to shining sea," pointing first to one and then to the other ocean on the coastlines of North America. Remind your child that a "sea" is the same as an "ocean."

The Grand Canyon is in the state of Arizona.

A Mariachi singer playing guitar in Mexico

To get to Mexico from the United States, you travel south. Here is a picture of a Mariachi singer. Mariachi is a form of folk music from Mexico.

To get to Canada from the United States, you travel north. Here is a picture of police officers who work outdoors in Canada, called the Royal Canadian Mounted Police. They are called "mounted" because they sometimes ride on horses. They are known by a nickname: Mounties. They wear bright red jackets, and people say they "always get their man." So look out, bad guys!

Take a Look

Every photograph offers the opportunity to pause and talk about what it shows. For example, talk about the colorful house behind the man with the guitar. Have you ever seen a house painted with so many bright colors?

The Royal Canadian Mounted Police ride horses.

South America

Let's look at the map of all the continents in the world again. First let's find North America. Can you show me the two oceans on either side—the Atlantic on the east and the Pacific on the west?

There is another continent that stretches from the Atlantic to the Pacific. If you move your finger down—that's south—through Mexico and even farther, pretty soon you will come to that other continent. It is called South America.

So what does this map tell us about South America? Do you see mountains? Trace them with your finger.

These are the Andes Mountains, the longest mountain range in the world. The Andes run from north to south, along the western part of the continent of South America. Some of the people who live in the Andes Mountains raise big furry animals called llamas. Llamas are friendly and strong, but if you annoy them, they spit at you!

If we were to travel to South America and climb high into the Andes Mountains, we could go see the tumbled-down buildings of a famous old city called Machu Picchu [MAH-chew PEE-chew]. Long ago, people called the Incas built this city out of stone. No one lives there now, as you can see in the picture on page 166. Now the roofs have fallen down and there is grass growing on the floors. But imagine what it must have been like to live there, so high up in the clouds.

Machu Picchu is an Inca site located in Peru.

A big, long river flows through South America. The map uses a crooked line to show where the river flows. The line may look small on this map, but the river is very big and very long. It's called the Amazon River.

What does the map tell us about the Amazon? The Amazon River begins high up in the Andes Mountains. It flows to the east, all the way to the Atlantic Ocean. Along the way, the Amazon flows through a jungle called a rain forest. It's called a rain forest because it rains there almost all the time—not thunderstorms and hard rain, but hot, steamy rain coming down in little drips from the trees and vines high above. The Amazon rain forest has amazing animals, like anteaters and huge snakes called anacondas, jaguars and sloths, howler monkeys and colorful birds called toucans.

Talk and Think

The continent of South America gives you the opportunity to talk more about rivers. Help your child trace the line from one of the tributaries in central South America out toward the Atlantic. As she does, talk about how the water in a river flows to the ocean.

The toucan is a bird that lives in the South American rain forest.

Australia

Australia is the smallest of all the world's continents. It does not connect to any other continent. It is a big landmass, or piece of land, with water all around it, and so you could say that Australia is really a big island. There are also little islands around the coast of Australia. Can you find them on this map?

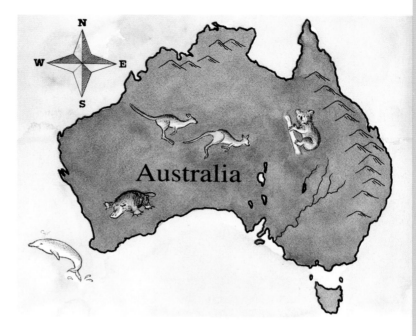

Australia

A baby kangaroo is called a joey.

People in Europe and North America sometimes call Australia "the land down under." That is because if you look at a world map or a globe, you will see the continent of Australia "down under" the continents of Asia and North America.

Australia is the home of some animals that don't live on any other continent. It's the home of koalas and kangaroos.

Koalas may look like teddy bears, but they're not bears at all. Koala babies and kangaroo babies ride inside the pouch of their mothers. So when a mother kangaroo hops along, and when a mother koala climbs a tree, looking for leaves to eat, their babies ride along.

Australia is also the home of a very unusual animal called a platypus. The platypus looks like a combination of parts from different animals. It has a furry brown body and a tail like a beaver, but it also has a bill like a duck. It has webbed feet so it can swim, and it lays eggs! Unless you see one in a zoo, you won't see a platypus anywhere in the world but on the continent of Australia.

A baby koala is also called a joey.

The platypus is one of only a few mammals that lay eggs.

Antarctica

We might call Australia "the land down under," but there is a continent even farther down under the globe. Far, far south, at the bottom of the world, lies the continent of Antarctica. Do you remember where the South Pole is on the globe? It is in the middle of the continent of Antarctica.

Here you will find only a few animals that can live in very cold weather, because Antarctica is blanketed by thick snow and ice that stays frozen all year round.

Hardly any people live on the continent of Antarctica. The only ones who stay there are scientists studying things such as animals or weather at this very cold place.

Every kind of animal found in Antarctica lives on the land and swims in the sea nearby. Penguins, for example, are birds that can be seen in Antarctica. They walk on the ice and they swim in the cold water, catching fish to eat.

Seals and whales live in the water near Antarctica, too, but they often swim over to the warmer islands that are around the continent of Antarctica.

These Adelie penguins live in Antarctica.

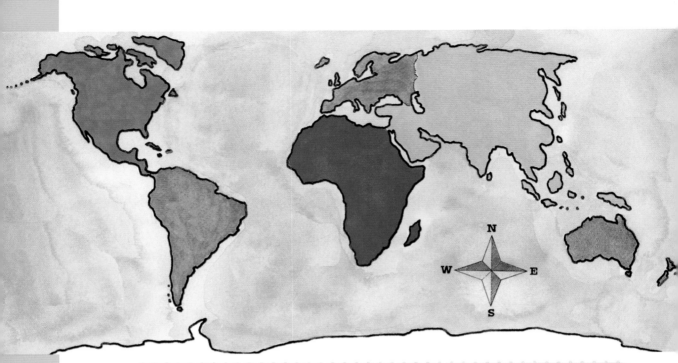

What Have You Learned?

PARENTS: Use this world map to ask your child these questions as a way to affirm her knowledge about the continents. She can answer by pointing to the continent, and you can say the name of the continent together if needed.

1. Which is the biggest continent?
2. On which continent will you find the Andes Mountains, the longest mountain range in the world?
3. Which continent would you visit to see the home of a lion or a zebra?
4. On which continent will you find the United States?
5. Koalas and kangaroos live on which continent?

American History and Geography

Do we live in the United States of America? Then that's our country.

Sometimes people use shorter names for the United States of America, such as "America," "the United States," or "the USA."

Your Country

The United States of America is part of a bigger piece of land, the continent called North America. Two other countries are found on the continent of North America as well. Canada is the country north of the United States. Mexico is the country south of the United States.

PARENTS: Be sure you have read the previous section on world geography with your child before you read this section on American geography. Certain concepts, such as a continent, were introduced earlier and are assumed to be understood here.

Most of the country of the United States can be found in the middle of the continent of North America. But two states of the United States lie farther from the middle. Do you know what states these are?

One of these states is very big. It would take a long time to travel from one end of this state, at the south, all the way out to this long piece of land stretching

> **Do It Yourself!**
> Show your child how to use a globe to find the United States. Then, continuing to use the globe, point with your child to the general location of your community, saying, "This is where we live in the United States." Name your town and help your child become comfortable associating your town name with a position on the globe.

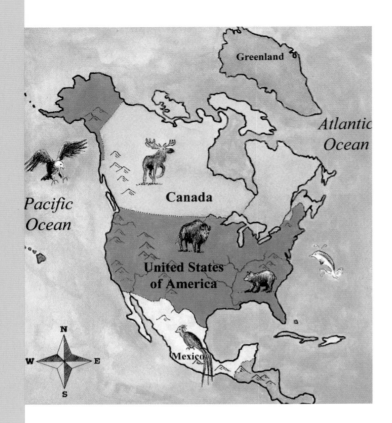

out into the ocean, called a peninsula. This state lies far north of the other united states. It can get very cold here. This place is called Alaska.

The other state far away from the continent of North America is a small group of islands called Hawaii. Your finger has to move across the map, south and west through the Pacific Ocean, to find this state. It stays nice and warm all year round in this state, and there are many beautiful beaches here.

The American Flag

Every country in the world has its own flag, with special colors and a special design that mean a lot to everyone who lives in that country. People hold their country flags high in a parade, or they salute their country's flag as it gets hoisted up the flagpole. We take care of flags because they stand for the country we love.

Have you ever seen the flag of the United States waving in the breeze? It's a glorious sight! Some people have even nicknamed our flag "Old Glory."

Flags in front of the United Nations building

What shapes do you see in it? What colors do you see in it?

There are other nicknames for the American flag, and you already know them. Sometimes it's named for its shapes, and people call our flag "the stars and stripes." And sometimes it's named for its colors, and people call it "the red, white, and blue."

The U.S. flag is sometimes called "Old Glory."

Our Country Long Ago

If we took a trip to visit many places in the United States today, we would come to roads and houses, big towns and cities, highways and tall buildings—and thousands and thousands of people. But a long time ago, in this same place, there were no big towns and cities. And there were not nearly as many people as you see today.

We can't really take a trip to see what life was like long ago, but we can read books, look at pictures, and use our imaginations to visit the America of long ago. Let's go way back, to the time before big towns and cities. Let's go back hundreds of years. All the school buildings, churches, banks, shopping centers, gas stations, skyscrapers—close your eyes and imagine them all fading away. As they disappear, thick forests and wide-open grasslands take their place in the landscape instead.

Now, let's follow a path through an imaginary forest. It winds into the cool shade of the trees. Let's pretend that this path is taking us back, back to the time of the first Americans.

Long ago, there were many more forests like this one.

Now there are many towns in the United States.

There were many grasslands called plains in the middle part of the country.

Cities and towns have replaced many grasslands and forests.

Running Dog Joins the Hunt

Running Dog woke up early. He pushed the deerskin blanket back, sat up, and looked around. Just a bit of daylight showed through the far opening of the long-house that he shared with his big family. He could see his mother and aunt standing outside, starting a fire. And then he remembered: today he was going to join the hunt.

It was chilly outside. Autumn was beginning. Soon his tribe, who called themselves the Clan of the Wolf, would celebrate the harvest. Children and adults from many tribes would get together for a feast that would last three days, with singing and dancing and races and games. All the people who joined in the harvest festival, even though they lived in different tribes, considered themselves to be members of one nation. They all called themselves the People of the Long-house.

All summer long, Running Dog and his younger sister, Shining Star, had spent most of their time with their aunts and mother, preparing the soil, planting the seeds, and tending the field where the crops grew. The stalks of corn were now standing tall. Bean vines twisted around them, long green beans dangling down. Below, squash plants stretched out their broad, fuzzy leaves. The Clan of the Wolf grew corn, beans, and squash, and they had ways of drying and storing those vegetables so they had some to eat even in winter.

The hunt was just as important for food in the winter, though. Today was the first day that Running Dog would join his father, older brother, and uncles in the hunt. They would walk through the forest, looking for deer, elk, and turkeys. The meat they brought home would hang over the fire, where the smoke cooked it. That way it lasted a long time and made good food to chew on in the winter.

Soon the hunters had gathered by the fire, eating corn cakes and berries without saying a word. When all was finished and they were ready to start the hunt, Running Dog's grandfather, the great chief of the tribe, called to his grandson. All the others, men and women, watched as the tall man with long white hair spoke to him.

"Running Dog, son of my daughter, today you join the hunt," said the chief. "Joining us, you take up a bow and arrow." As the old man spoke those words, Running Dog's mother stepped up and handed him a beautiful bow made of curved hickory wood. "With this bow, you become a hunter. We will all depend on you."

Running Dog understood the meaning of his grandfather's words, for every man in the tribe had to hunt for food, just as every woman had to gather herbs, nuts, and berries. He was no longer a child who sat and waited to be fed. He was becoming a man, and he had to share the work of bringing food to the longhouse.

> **Take a Look**
> Use this illustration to talk with your child about what she sees. "What has this young man been doing?" There are many details worth discussing in this illustration. See what interests your child.

The First Americans: Many Peoples and Many Places

The boy in the story, Running Dog, belonged to a group of people who called themselves the People of the Longhouse. Another name for their nation is Iroquois [EER-ah-kwoy]. The Iroquois people lived in the part of America long ago that was covered with forests where bears, elk, deer, and turkeys lived.

At the same time, long ago, other people lived in places where you didn't see any trees but you saw fields of tall grass stretching far, far away. Those fields are sometimes called plains. As you can imagine, the People of the Plains lived a different life from the People of the Longhouse. Because they lived in a different kind of place, or a different region, they had a different culture. They spoke a different language and they built their houses differently. They used logs and animal skins to make teepees.

Buffalo once roamed the American West.

The plains people hunted a big, shaggy animal called the buffalo. They got many things from the buffalo. They got meat, leather for shoes and clothing, and fur for blankets and rugs. When they wanted to make a painting, they used the juice from plants and berries and painted on buffalo hide. They didn't have any paper!

Make a Connection

The "Language and Literature" section of this book includes a legend from the Northern Plains Indians, "The Story of Jumping Mouse," on page 72. Reading it now is a good way to introduce another aspect of Native American life and culture into your child's understanding.

Homes in the Desert, Homes by the Sea

Think about how differently the People of the Longhouse lived compared with the People of the Plains. That was the way it was long ago in our country, and that is something important to learn. The first Americans did not all live in the same way. They were many different people, and they lived in many different regions throughout the continent of North America. They had different cultures and they lived in different ways.

There were the People of the Longhouse, who lived, hunted, and farmed in the eastern woodland forests. There were the People of the Plains, who hunted the buffalo. And far from them, there were other people who lived in a place with no tall trees or rich brown earth. They lived in the desert, where the land is dry and rocky.

To make homes in the desert, these people cut holes in hard rock cliffs. They made building blocks out of the rock, and they made bricks out of a special kind of mud, called adobe. Some of their cliff houses were two and three stories high, with wooden ladders inside to go from one floor to the other.

Hundreds of people made their homes in these cliffs! Their land was dry, and they had very little water, but the People of the Desert still were able to grow corn, beans, and squash. They became very skilled at using the earth not only to build their houses but also to make strong, beautiful clay pots for carrying water and storing seeds. It's amazing that people could live where there was so little water.

The Mesa Verde cliff dwellings are located in a national park in Colorado.

Native American pottery

Some other first Americans lived where there was lots and lots of water. As you can imagine, their culture was very different from the culture of the People of the Desert. They lived far north and west on the continent of North America, along the coast of the Pacific Ocean.

Because they lived in a region so close to the ocean, the People of the Pacific Northwest caught and ate many fish. One of their favorites was the strong-swimming salmon.

These people cut down trees and carved them into canoes. Some of them cut down trees and carved them into totem poles, too. They would carve amazing faces and figures into the wood, and they often painted them in bright colors. Often they were animal faces, such as a bear, an eagle, or a wolf. The totem poles were ways that the People of the Pacific Northwest told stories about their tribes and nations. The figures on the poles helped them remember stories of the great deeds of their families and their people.

PARENTS: We have many words that we use to name the people we here call the "first Americans," and it is fine to introduce them all to your child. Canadians call the original inhabitants of North America the "First Nations." Americans tend to call them "Native Americans," because they were "native"—born here. They are also called "Indians," which is a common name based on a big mistake, as you and your child will learn in this book's next section. As long as it is spoken with respect, any one of these names is acceptable.

Totem poles

Christopher Columbus

For a long time, only the first Americans, also called Native American people, lived on the continent of North America. But then other people came to North America. They came from Europe, and to get here they sailed all the way across the Atlantic Ocean.

One of the first Europeans to come here was a man named Christopher Columbus. Columbus was a sailor. He was also a dreamer with big ideas, and one of them was to take a long sailing voyage across the ocean.

Long ago, in Columbus's time, you had to be daring to make a long ocean voyage. Back then, people could not travel as easily as we do today. When you took a trip, it might take weeks or months or even years before you came home again. People walked, or they rode on animals such as horses or camels.

People also rode in boats. But no matter whether they were canoes or rowboats or sailing ships, boats long ago had no motors. Sailing ships relied on the wind blowing on their sails to make them move and get them where the people aboard wanted to go.

PARENTS: Use this opportunity to help your child reflect on how we travel today. We walk short distances, but for longer distances we rely on powered vehicles: cars, subways, trains, planes. Help your child imagine what it would be like if there were no powered vehicles to take your family where you usually go.

For the people in Europe long ago, sailing in a ship was the best way to travel to faraway places, including to the continent of Asia. Some people had come back to Europe after long, long trips to Asia. They told stories of palaces covered with gold and jewels, and they brought back wonderful things found only in Asia: delicious spices, such as pepper and cinnamon, and fine cloth, such as silk. The Europeans wanted more of these wonderful things, but they could only get spices and silk by going to faraway countries in Asia such as China, Japan, and India.

The Europeans called all those Asian countries "the Indies." They spent a lot of time trying to figure out the quickest way to get from Europe to the Indies. The voyage by sea was long, slow, and dangerous. You had to sail a long way south, around the continent of Africa, and then a long way north and east, in order to reach Asia. It took even longer, and it was even more dangerous, to go by land, through the mountains and deserts between Europe and Asia.

Make a Connection

Turn back to the map of the world and its continents on page 150 or, better yet, look together at a globe again. Help your child trace with a finger the two routes described here: the sea route from Europe down the west coast around Africa and up to India, China, and Japan; and the land route through Eastern Europe, Afghanistan, and Pakistan to India, China, and Japan. Keep the globe or map handy so that as you read about Columbus's westward route your child can trace that, too.

Christopher Columbus had a daring idea. He thought, "I want to find a better way to sail to the Indies. It takes too long to get to Asia by sailing around Africa. I believe that the world is round, and that my ships and crew are strong enough to be able to sail around the world in the other direction. I believe we can reach Asia by sailing west across the Atlantic Ocean. We will sail and sail, but then we will bump into the Indies coming from the other side!"

Let's look at a globe or map to see whether Christopher Columbus had a good idea. You can trace your finger from Europe, heading west, and get to Asia that way. But there were two things he did not know yet—though he soon learned!

First, the earth is a lot bigger than Columbus thought, which means that it took a lot longer to sail west to Asia than he could ever imagine. Second, he

didn't know about the big continent of North America lying right in his path as he sailed westward. It's not that Columbus was stupid, though. Hundreds of years ago, most of the people who lived in Europe had no idea that the continent of North America even existed!

When Columbus talked about his plan, lots of people laughed at him. They said he would never make it. He kept talking and believing, and finally he told his ideas to the king and queen of a country called Spain. King Ferdinand and Queen Isabella listened to Christopher Columbus and thought for a long time about what he wanted to do, and finally they said, "All right, Señor Columbus. Let's see if you are right. We will help you make your **voyage** if you promise to share all you find with us."

King Ferdinand and Queen Isabella helped by paying for Columbus's **voyage**. He needed ships and sailors and lots of supplies, including food and water. When you're on a long voyage across the ocean, you have to carry everything you need along with you.

> **New Word**
>
> Does your child know what a "voyage" is? A voyage is a long trip—usually on the sea.

Sailing with Christopher Columbus

Carlos was only eight years old when his father decided to take him with him on a long adventure. They joined 38 other men and boys aboard a ship named the *Santa Maria*, and set sail on the big ocean. Sailing alongside them were two other ships. All three ships headed west. The leader of the journey was a man named Christopher Columbus. "He believes he can find a way to sail to India," Carlos's father told him. "We will be with him when he does."

Talk and Think

Although kindergartners do not need to understand or manipulate numbers in the thousands, here is an opportunity to talk about what year it is as you read this book. Compare that date with the year that Columbus sailed, 1492, and tell them how many years back that was. Find ways to make that long period going back in time more real to them by finding a few time markers in the past that they can understand, such as how many years ago their parents or grandparents were born, and how short even that time is compared with the period between the present and 1492.

New Word

"Track" is a multi-meaning word. Does your child know what track means here? It means "count." Carlos lost count of the days.

It took a week for Carlos to get used to walking on the deck of the big wooden ship as it rocked through the ocean waves. He felt seasick, and he did not want to eat, because no food would stay down in his stomach. He lost **track** of the days.

All they could see around them was the big, wide ocean. After a week, though, Carlos grew more accustomed to the movement of the boat. He learned that the best way to keep from getting seasick was to go up onto the deck of the boat, breathe the sea air deeply, and work as hard as he could. Carlos was the smallest person among the entire crew, but he was given the most important job. Twice a day, once at sunrise and once just before sunset, he climbed up to the top of the tall wooden mast and stood inside a big basket that is called a "crow's nest" because it looks like a bird might live there. From the crow's nest, Carlos's job was to look all around, to see what he could see, in every direction—north, east, south, and especially toward the west, the direction in which the boat was sailing.

One day a little brown bird landed on the railing of the boat and sat there as if it was tired from flying and needed to rest. Carlos was used to seeing such little birds back home in Spain, but his father and the other sailors were so excited to see it. "Birds like that do not fly far from land," his father said. "We are approaching the Indies." Captain Columbus even called it a sign from God. The next day something else happened that excited the men aboard. The seas were so calm that the boat was hardly moving. All of a sudden one of the sailors called out, "See there! Floating on the water! A tree branch! And it has green leaves!" All the men aboard crowded onto the deck to see, talking with great happiness.

"Why does that matter, Father?" Carlos asked. "It's nothing but a broken tree branch."

"Where there are broken branches, there are growing trees not far away," his father answered. "And where do trees grow, my son, on land or on sea?"

That was an easy question to answer. "Trees must put their roots down into soil," said Carlos. "Trees grow on land." And then he began to see why the floating branch was so important. It was a sign that the three ships of Christopher Columbus were getting close to land.

That afternoon, Captain Columbus sent Carlos up the mast to the crow's nest earlier than usual. "Look very carefully along the horizon," he said. "There may be something for you to see." Step by step, as if he was climbing a ladder, Carlos went up the mast to the very top. He tied himself tightly into the crow's nest and focused on the line where the big ocean met the big sky. There, in fact, if he looked very closely, Carlos could see a distant shape, as if someone had taken a piece of charcoal and drawn a zigzag line on top of the straight, flat line where the sea met the sky. Carlos called out to say that he did see something. He pointed toward it. The entire crew, Captain Columbus among them, now turned their eyes in the direction he was pointing, and they all saw the same dark zigzag on the horizon.

"Land!" Captain Columbus cried out, and he dropped to his knees with his hands together, both praying that he had found what he was looking for and thanking God that the search might soon be over.

Carlos climbed down from the crow's nest and joined the crew in their celebrations. His father picked him up and hoisted him up onto his shoulders. All the men cheered. "Carlos was the first to see land!" cried one sailor.

"You are our hero!" shouted another.

And that is how a little boy helped Christopher Columbus find the way to the land that we still call the New World.

Reaching Land

After more than a month at sea, Columbus's three ships and all the crew had finally done it! They had sailed to the west and reached land. They probably first landed on a sandy beach on one of the islands that we now call the Bahamas. Soon after they went ashore, the Native Americans already living on that island came to meet them. Columbus was so sure he had reached the Indies that he called the native people Indians. Even though Columbus made a mistake—he had not reached Asia or the Indies—Native American people have been called Indians ever since.

When Columbus landed, he didn't find what he expected. There weren't many spices, and there was no silk to be found. It took years for people to understand that Columbus and his men had not landed in the Indies at all. They had not sailed to Asia. Instead, they had sailed to two huge continents that were unknown to Europeans back then. They called this place the New World. Later, it became known as America, and when other explorers realized there were two continents, they became known as North America and South America.

Pilgrims in the New World

Columbus first reached North America in the year 1492. In the years after that, more people sailed the Atlantic and explored the Americas, and pretty soon people in Europe began thinking about moving there to live. It was a long, hard sail from Europe to North America, but they thought they might be able to live a better life if they moved to this place that people were calling the New World.

One September, more than one hundred years after Columbus sailed to America, a group of people from the country called England decided to make that trip across the sea. They called themselves Puritans, and they wanted to pray and practice religion differently from most of the people in England.

The Puritans boarded a small ship called the *Mayflower*. There were sailors among them, of course, and lots of passengers—almost too many for the small ship! The passengers included thirty-four children with their mothers and fathers and some brave young men leaving their families behind. Because they knew they were going to North America and not returning to England, they took along their animals, too: two dogs, a big hungry cat, and some chickens, cows, and pigs.

The Puritans knew the ocean voyage would be hard and dangerous, and they were not sure what they would find in America. They were willing to go on such a difficult journey because they were very religious people. Because of their journey, they also called themselves Pilgrims. A pilgrim is a person who takes a trip because of what he or she believes.

A Hard Journey

The sail across the Atlantic Ocean was more difficult than the Pilgrims had expected. Their boat, the *Mayflower*, traveled through storms and terrible weather. Tall waves crashed all around, and fierce storms with thunder and lightning made it hard for the sailors to sail the boat smoothly. Most of the passengers got seasick and stayed in their bunks below. No matter how hard the journey was, though, the Pilgrims did not lose hope.

Then came the day when they saw land. It was a cold, rocky shore, not the warm sand beaches that Columbus had seen. The Pilgrims understood that their life together in the New World would be hard, and so they promised that they would work together. Every decision would be made for the good of everyone. They wrote this promise down and all the men signed their names at the bottom. The agreement is called the Mayflower Compact, and it's a promise that we still try to keep in the United States today.

After they had signed the Mayflower Compact, the Pilgrims stepped ashore and looked around at their new home. They saw a rocky beach stretching up to a hillside covered with trees and shrubs. There were no houses. They stood beside one big rock and said a prayer together. They named the place where they landed Plymouth, which was the name of the town in England where their journey had begun. Even today, people say that the Pilgrims landed at Plymouth Rock.

Do It Yourself!

Use the Mayflower Compact as a springboard to talk about a set of rules that your family can all agree on. You could even name it with your family name, the _____ Compact. Write the rules down in simple language and ask everyone to sign or make a mark at the bottom. Keep the compact in plain view and refer to it in your everyday conversations.

The Mayflower Compact, 1620

Meeting the Wampanoag

At first the Pilgrims saw nothing but rocks and dirt and trees, and they thought they were the only people in this part of the New World. Their ocean voyage was over, but their hard work had just begun. It was winter, and the air was damp and cold. They had to chop down trees to build their houses. They had to find rivers and streams with fresh water to drink. It was too late in the year to grow crops for food, so they searched for nuts and fruits growing in the forest. They had brought some food with them, but they were running out of supplies.

Soon they learned that they were not the only people living near Plymouth Rock. Native Americans, People of the Longhouse whose tribe name was Wampanoag (WAHM-puh-nog), came to see these newcomers who had arrived by sea. The Wampanoag helped the Pilgrims in many ways. They shared their food and helped them hunt for more. Still, it was a very hard winter. It was freezing cold and there was not enough food. That first winter, many of the Pilgrims died.

Plymouth Rock

But those who lived did not give up. They stayed in Plymouth and thanked God when the warm spring breezes came.

They thanked the Wampanoag Indians, too, for helping them find food to eat. The Indians showed the Pilgrims about plants they had never seen growing in Europe, such as wild rice and cranberries. They also helped the Pilgrims catch fish and hunt wild animals, such as deer and turkeys, for meat.

The First Thanksgiving, 1920

What a joy it was for the Pilgrims to see their crops growing through the summer months. When fall came, they felt so thankful for the harvest and for their lives in the New World that they held a celebration. They prepared platters heaped with corn, pumpkin, fish, and turkey. Some of their woodland Indian friends joined them for the feast.

And from that time on, every year at the end of the harvest, in the fall, the Pilgrims got together for a special feast. They had a good time and they ate plenty, but the most important thing they did was to give thanks for all that they had received throughout the year.

And that is why, here in the United States of America, we still have a holiday that we call Thanksgiving.

> **Do It Yourself!**
> Whether or not it's the season, your family can enjoy a Pilgrim-style Thanksgiving feast with a menu inspired by this story. Our traditional Thanksgiving fare is inspired by what the Pilgrims must have eaten—turkey, cranberries, pumpkin pie. Add to that wild rice or sweet corn. Make the meal together with your child and talk about what it would be like if those were the only foods you could choose from.

Happy Birthday, America!

The Pilgrims were not the only people who moved from Europe to America. Many other people made that long sea voyage across the Atlantic. Some came from the country called France and some came from the country called Spain, but to begin with, most of the people who moved to America came from England.

The people living in England had to follow the rules of their king. His name was King George. George's father had been king, and George knew that his son would become king. Even today, that is how a person usually becomes king—by being the son of the king before.

All the people of England were ruled by King George and had to obey his laws. Even the English people who lived far away were ruled by the king. They were called colonists, because their land was a colony of England—far away but still ruled by the king of England.

Make a Connection

As you read this passage, refer to a world map or globe and help your child trace the route from England, France, or Spain across to the east coast of today's United States. You can talk about how long it took the Pilgrims, more than a month, compared with how long it now takes us to make that journey by jet, just eight or nine hours.

The colonists did not agree with the Stamp Act, which required them to pay a tax on every piece of printed paper they used.

For many, many years, as the colonists built their houses and had their children, they followed the king's laws. But sometimes they disagreed with them. Sometimes they said, "The king is so far away, in a place that's so different from America. How does he know what's best for us? Should we always be ruled by a faraway king? Should we always let someone else make the rules that we have to obey? Maybe we should think about ruling ourselves!"

And that's just what happened. The people living in America got together and talked it over and decided to tell King George they weren't going to follow his rules anymore. They were going to make a new country, and that country would be free from the rule of England and England's king. The people in the new country could make their own choices about what they wanted to do, what laws they were going to follow, and how they would spend their money. They intended the new country to be a democracy, which means a place where ordinary people help make the rules on how to get along. They weren't going to obey a king anymore. They would choose their leaders. They would elect a president!

And so it happened on the fourth of July in the year 1776 that we Americans declared that we were free from England. Leaders among the colonists wrote an important letter to King George that said, "We are now independent. We aren't following your laws anymore. We are going to rule ourselves."

We had decided to become a new country, our own country, called the United States of America. That letter was called the Declaration of Independence, and it is still important today. Now, getting our independence wasn't quite as easy as just writing a letter—the Americans had to fight a war against England and King George. But the Declaration of Independence, dated July 4, 1776, was a very important first step. And that's why the Fourth of July is celebrated every year as the birthday of our nation.

Fun on the Fourth of July

It was the middle of the week, a Wednesday, but everyone in Caroline's family had slept late. "It's a holiday," said her mother. "Today is the Fourth of July. All day long we'll be celebrating the birthday of our nation, the United States of America."

Many communities celebrate the Fourth of July with a parade.

The Fourth of July—Caroline remembered from last year that there was a parade, sparklers, and fireworks. Maybe that would happen again this year.

She got to play all morning with her big sister, Julia. Her mother didn't go to work because it was a holiday. After lunch, her grandparents arrived. They lived in the country, and they liked to drive to Caroline's house for holidays.

Late in the afternoon, the whole family got into her grandpa's big car and drove downtown. They drove around searching for a parking place. There were already a lot of people walking toward Main Street and you could feel the excitement in the air.

As they walked along with the rest of the crowd, Caroline's grandpa picked her up and hoisted her onto his shoulders. Now she was taller than everyone else! They made their way to the sidewalk on Main Street. There were lots of people in front of them, but because she was on Grandpa's shoulders, she could look up and down the street and see just fine.

Then she heard a drumroll. It was the kind of sound that made you know something big was about to happen. All of a sudden, a band started playing. She could hear the music before she could see the band.

Marching in front of the musicians was a man dressed in a fancy uniform. He marched so hard, he leaned way back and his knees came up to his shoulders. Next to him marched a girl wearing the same uniform and carrying a great big flag with stars and stripes—the flag of the United States of America! She stood tall and carried it high, and the flag streamed out above her head. The people watching cheered.

The band marched by—lots of kids from her neighborhood, older even than Julia, playing instruments like horns and flutes and drums. The people all around her sang the song that the band played. "This song is 'The Star-Spangled Banner,'" her grandfather told her. "It's our national anthem. It's a song we all learn so we can sing along."

Caroline listened to the band and the people singing. "Oh, say, does that star-spangled banner yet wave / O'er the land of the free and the home of the brave?" When they finished that part of the song, everyone cheered, and the band kept marching past.

Next in the parade came clowns, riding in silly little cars, honking their horns, and throwing candy out to the crowd. Caroline's mother grabbed a piece and shared it with her.

Then came a big, beautiful **float** with three different groups of people in costumes.

On one side, people were dressed like Pilgrims and Indians. Some wore all black and others wore leather jackets and moccasins. On the other side, closer to Caroline and her grandfather, people were dressed like the colonists. The women wore bonnets and long dresses. The men wore wigs and knee socks. They waved to the crowd.

In the middle of the **float** stood a woman dressed in long green robes with a pointed crown on her head. She held something sparkly up in the air. It looked like she was holding a torch set on fire.

"Who is she supposed to be?" Caroline asked, looking at the robed woman.

"She is dressed up like the Statue of Liberty," Caroline's grandfather told her. "It is a statue that stands on an island near New York City. When people move to America, they feel as if the Statue of Liberty is welcoming them."

> **New Word**
> "Float" is a multi-meaning word. Here, **"float"** means a decorated scene on something that moves so it can take part in the parade.

After the parade was over, Caroline and her family walked over to the city park. They spread out a blanket and had a picnic dinner as the sun went down.

"Can't we have the sparklers now?" asked Julia.

"After dark," her mother said. So far, this was the best part of the Fourth of July, thought Caroline, because usually she and her sister had to come inside before dark.

The sun set. It was the middle of summer, and fireflies began blinking their little lights in the air.

"Now you can have your sparklers," said their mother. Caroline felt really grown-up as she held out the sparkler for her mother to light. "Be very careful and don't touch the part that is burning hot," said her mother.

Once it was lit, the sparkler started hissing and spitting out sparks. Caroline held it up high. "I'm the Statue of Liberty!" she said. "This is my welcome torch."

Just then, from far away, there was a big bang, then a loud whistle, and then it seemed like a million lights exploded high in the air. Everyone in the park said "Ooooooooh!" at the same time. Red and blue and white streamers exploded high above them with big noises and beautiful patterns, over and over again.

"Do you know why we have fireworks on the Fourth of July?" Caroline's grandfather whispered to her. She shook her head and looked to him for the answer. "Because many people have fought in wars, going all the way back to the colonists, to be sure that we have our freedom in the United States. The fireworks are a way for us to remember those people and to have fun, all at the same time."

Caroline smiled as another beautiful burst of color exploded in the air.

"The Fourth of July is my favorite holiday," she said.

Not Completely Free

The men who signed the Declaration of Independence on July 4, 1776, believed that their country should be free. But in fact, at that time there were many people in America who were not free, especially black people who worked as slaves on big farms. From sunrise to sunset, the slaves worked so hard in the fields. They cut tobacco and picked cotton under the hot sun. They planted seeds, hoed the dirt, and harvested the vegetables. If they grew tired, they could not stop to rest, because nearby there was a man—a white man—who held a whip in his hand and could beat them if they stopped working.

Other slaves did other kinds of work. Slaves did the laundry and cooked the meals. They cleaned the big houses for white people but they lived in little houses

of their own. They took care of the horses and, whenever the people in the big houses wanted to travel, they hitched the horses up to a carriage and drove them where they wanted to go. Slaves did whatever they were ordered to do. They weren't free, and they couldn't choose where to go or what to do on their own.

The people who lived in the big houses were called the masters. They owned the house, the horses, and the carriage—and the black slaves who did the work for them. Today we can't imagine the idea of owning another person. You own things, but you don't own people.

But back then, people had a different idea, and they thought they should be able to buy slaves to do work for them. Many black people were brought on big ships from the continent of Africa to be slaves in America. They didn't come because they wanted to, as the Pilgrims and other colonists had. They were forced to come. And when they got here, they were forced to work, and all their hard work was for their masters. They were not free.

Many years later, after a lot of arguing and a terrible war, new laws said you could not own people in America anymore, and slavery ended. It took a long time for people to realize that in the United States, freedom should be for everyone.

PARENTS: Slavery and the history of race relations in the United States are difficult subjects to broach with children, but it is worth the effort. Try to be honest and factual, not political. Answer the questions asked. Clearly state that slavery does not occur in the United States anymore, and that nowadays everyone in our country agrees it is wrong. One way into the subject is to read this book together: *To Be a Slave*, by Julius Lester.

Presidents of the United States

Do It Yourself!
Help your child learn to name the current president of the United States. Find a picture online or in the newspaper so she comes to recognize the president visually. If you find yourselves watching a news broadcast together, point out the president by name. It's a way to begin to engage your child in civics.

In the United States, we don't have a king or queen who makes decisions and laws for us. In our country, we choose the person we want to be our leader. Instead of a king or a queen, we choose a president.

The first president of the United States of America was George Washington. He became president soon after the United States declared its independence from England. Because Washington was the first, many people call him the father of our country.

People knew they could trust George Washington. He was a good soldier and an honest man. People said he was "first in war, first in peace, and first in the hearts of his countrymen."

There is a famous story about George Washington when he was a boy. It's a legend, which means that it probably didn't really happen, but people keep telling the story because it has something real at the heart of it.

The legend of George Washington and the cherry tree tells us how honest he was all his life. Here's the story.

George Washington and the Cherry Tree

When George Washington was a little boy, his father gave him a fine new hatchet. George was delighted. He tried his new hatchet on logs from the woodpile: *chop, chop, chop!*

Then a thought came to him: wouldn't it be exciting to cut down a real tree?

So he went into the nearby orchard. He saw a fine young tree and set to work with his new hatchet: *chop, chop, chop!* The tree fell—*bang!*—to the ground. George was pleased: how well his hatchet chopped! But then he looked at the tree lying on the ground. He remembered that it was a special cherry tree sent to his father from England. And now that he had chopped it down, it would never bear cherries again.

George began to worry.

Later that day, his father took a walk through the orchard. When he saw the cherry tree lying on the ground, he was angry. He had been looking forward to picking big, juicy cherries from the tree, but now look at it! It would never bear fruit.

George Washington's father asked one person after another who had done this deed. No one knew. Finally he came to his son, young George.

George knew that he had done something wrong. He felt ashamed, and he also felt scared. His father was very angry.

"George," said his father sternly, "do you know who cut down my cherry tree?"

George looked up into his father's

A 1911 vintage illustration, "First in war, first in peace, and first in the hearts of his countrymen."

angry eyes, but he did not turn away. He looked up and said, "Father, I cannot tell a lie. I cut down the cherry tree." He told his father he was sorry.

He worried that his father would punish him, but instead his father looked at him with love in his eyes. "I am sorry, too," he said, "but I would rather lose all the trees in my orchard than to have you tell a lie. Thank you for telling me the truth."

PARENTS: To emphasize how we still think Washington is an important person in our country's history, show his portrait to your child on the one-dollar bill and on the quarter. Compare those portraits to the one you see here and talk about how men dressed differently in those days.

Thomas Jefferson: The Idea Man

Thomas Jefferson was the third president of the United States. You can see his picture on a nickel. He had red hair, freckles, green eyes, and a huge appetite for . . . not candy, not ice cream, but books! He was full of curiosity, and he read as many books as he could get his hands on. He studied hard and wanted to understand everything in those books.

When young Tom Jefferson's friends would play games or go hunting, Tom would rather read a book. There were so many questions he wanted to answer. Who were the great heroes of history, and what made them so great? How do people speak and write in other languages? How should the leaders of a country make decisions? How many different kinds of violets grow in the woods? He even taught himself to play the violin by reading a book!

But don't get the idea that Thomas Jefferson was no fun. He liked horseback riding and dancing and exploring the woods near his home. But most of all he liked books. "I cannot live without books!" he once said.

As he read and thought about what he was reading, Jefferson got a lot of

Writing the Declaration of Independence, 1776. Benjamin Franklin, John Adams, and Thomas Jefferson review a draft of the Declaration of Independence, by J.L.G. Ferris. From a 1909 litho by Wolf & Co.

ideas. He wrote those ideas in books of his own. He was one of the people who wrote the Declaration of Independence. When he was an old man, even after he had been president of the United States, he said that writing the Declaration of Independence was one of the things he was most proud of doing.

The Declaration of Independence contained these words: "All men are created equal." It was an important new idea. No one had ever started a country with that idea before.

Abraham Lincoln

Abraham Lincoln: Honest Abe

Abraham Lincoln is another important president of the United States. He lived more than one hundred years after Thomas Jefferson—and he lived more than one hundred years ago, before you and I were born. If you want to see what he looked like, you can find him on a penny.

Abe Lincoln grew up in a little log cabin. His family lived on the frontier. There weren't many people nearby, but there were, as Abe once said, "many bears and other wild animals." His family was not rich. Their cabin had one door and one window.

Every day Abe helped his father with the farmwork. He was a strong boy—so strong that by the time he was only eight years old, he could swing an axe and chop trees almost as well as a full-grown man.

Abe helped clear the woods and plow the fields. At night, even though he was tired, he loved to read.

Now, this was in the days before electricity came into everyone's homes. So Abe Lincoln couldn't just switch on a light to read after dark. His only light came from the fireplace, so he would sit near the fire and read at night.

It was hard to find books in those days. There were no libraries on the frontier. Many families owned only one book: a Bible. Abe Lincoln sometimes walked for miles just to borrow a book to read.

There's a story people tell about young Abe Lincoln and a book that he borrowed. It was one of his favorites, and it told about George Washington. He would read it at night until it was time to go to sleep, and then, to keep the book safe, he stuck it between two logs in the wall of his family's cabin.

But one night it rained. The book got soaking wet. The very next morning Abe carried the book back to its owner. He held it out and looked down at his feet, ashamed. He admitted that he had ruined the book, and he offered to pay for it.

The man took the book in his hands and looked Abe in the eyes. "I'm not angry with you," he said. "I am proud of you because of your honesty. It's good that you told the truth."

Abraham Lincoln worked hard as a young man. He split wood into fence rails for his neighbors. He worked on a boat, and he worked as a postman and as a storekeeper. Once, when he was minding the store, a customer paid him six cents too much. When Abe Lincoln realized the mistake, he walked six miles to return the money to her.

When the people elected Abraham Lincoln president, he was nicknamed "Honest Abe." He was hardworking and honest when he was president, too, and he led our country through some of its most difficult times.

Theodore Roosevelt: The Teddy Bear President

Theodore Roosevelt was the twenty-sixth president of the United States. People called him Teddy, even though he wanted to be called Theodore.

He was not a healthy child. He had trouble breathing, and he couldn't see very well. He was smart and determined, though. He wanted to do something important with his life, but his sick body made that difficult. His father even said to him, "Theodore, you have the mind but not the body."

Young Theodore knew there were two things he had to do. He had to read and study to make his mind strong, and he had to exercise to make his body strong. He read many books. He wanted to learn everything he could about nature. He collected bugs, mice, birds, and other creatures and created his own little museum. His father built a gymnasium in their home, and Theodore exercised every day. He made sure his mind and his body be-

Teddy Roosevelt

came strong. When he grew up, he became a boxer, a hunter, a cowboy, a crime fighter, a writer—and the president of the United States.

Theodore Roosevelt loved to be outdoors, and he worked hard to be sure that across the United States there were parks where people could camp and hike. He encouraged other people to work on the conservation of nature, which means

Teddy Roosevelt as a young man.

protecting certain places so that wild animals and plants can grow there without anyone disturbing them.

Theodore Roosevelt was also a hunter, and he knew how important it was to follow the rules so you are a fair hunter.

Once, President Roosevelt went on a hunting trip with some friends. One of the other people fired his gun at a little bear—and he missed. The little bear just stood and stared. He was dizzy and confused and didn't even try to escape.

From where President Teddy Roosevelt stood, he had a perfect shot at the bear. But he knew it wouldn't be fair to shoot a little bear that was so dizzy and confused. He refused to shoot it, and the bear ran away.

The news got out that President Roosevelt had refused to shoot a little bear. The next thing you know, lots of newspapers printed a drawing of Teddy Roosevelt and a cute little bear. The newspaper reporters wrote about Roosevelt's sense of fair play. Then a toymaker got the idea to make little stuffed bears and call them "Teddy bears," after the president, Teddy Roosevelt.

Mount Rushmore

Honoring Our Presidents

Now you have learned a little bit about four important presidents: George Washington, Thomas Jefferson, Abraham Lincoln, and Theodore Roosevelt. While all presidents are important, many people would agree that these four presidents are special. And in fact, almost a hundred years ago, a man had an idea—a very big idea. He decided to carve the faces of these four great presidents in rock on the side of a mountain. He would make them so big that people could see them from miles away.

And so, with lots of people working on the project, the faces of Washington, Jefferson, Lincoln, and Roosevelt got carved on the side of Mount Rushmore in the state of South Dakota. It took fourteen years for people to finish this work.

Do It Yourself!

If you are lucky enough to be reading this passage about voting at a time when you can share the election process with your child, do so by showing her campaign posters, watching debates on television, and taking her with you into the polling booth. If the timing does not work out, you may want to reread this passage around election time, to help connect these ideas with the events of daily life.

They had to use dynamite and jackhammers and huge drills to carve those shapes in the hard granite rock. What a tremendous job! They turned a mountain into a monument, and now people come from far away just to see Mount Rushmore.

Choosing Our Presidents

There have been many more people who have served as president of the United States. Because the United States is a democracy, we have chosen every president who has been the leader of our country. Our presidents don't get the job just because they were born into a certain family, the way kings and queens do. Instead, every four years, grown-ups in the United States choose the person they want as president. They choose by voting. We vote for our president.

Suggested Resources

MAPS AND GLOBES

Me on the Map, by Joan Sweeney (Dragonfly Books, 1998)

The Seven Continents, by Wil Mara (Children's Press, 2005)

NATIVE AMERICANS

Fire Race: A Karuk Coyote Tale of How Fire Came to the People, retold by Jonathan London (Voyager, 1999)

Navajo ABC: A Diné Alphabet Book, by Luci Tapahonso and Eleanor Schick (Aladdin Library, 1999)

The Story of Jumping Mouse: A Native American Legend, retold by John Steptoe (Harper Trophy, 1989)

COLUMBUS AND THE PILGRIMS

Follow the Dream: The Story of Christopher Columbus, by Peter Sis (Knopf, 2003)

Sarah Morton's Day: A Day in the Life of a Pilgrim Girl, by Kate Waters (Scholastic, 1993)

Squanto and the Miracle of Thanksgiving, by Eric Metaxas (Thomas Nelson, 1999)

AMERICAN SYMBOLS

Betsy Ross, by Becky White (Holiday House, 1998)

Mount Rushmore: From Mountain to Monument, by Luke S. Gabriel (The Child's World, 2001)

The White House, by Lloyd G. Douglas (Children's Press, 2003)

PRESIDENTS

George Washington, by Philip Abraham (Children's Press, 2002)

A Picture Book of Thomas Jefferson, by David A. Adler (Holiday House, 1991)

Abe Lincoln: The Boy Who Loved Books, by Kay Winters (Simon and Schuster, 2003)

My Tour of Europe: By Teddy Roosevelt, Age 10, edited by Ellen Jackson (Millbrook Press, 2003)

III
Visual Arts

Introduction

For the kindergartner, it is best if art means doing: drawing, painting, cutting and pasting, working with clay and other materials. Children need lots of time and materials to draw, paint, cut, paste, work with clay, and so on. We can suggest many activities your child can do, sometimes with your help, and you can also find good art activities in some of the books recommended.

But the love of art also develops through seeing. Looking at works of art and talking about them can be a rewarding and enjoyable experience. By reading this section aloud together, you can help your child become comfortable talking about art at the same time that you introduce some legendary works of art. In this way, your child will come to understand that, while art is doing, it is also seeing and thinking. By looking closely at art and talking about it, your child will begin to develop a love of art and a habit of enjoying it in thoughtful, active ways. As your child looks, it will be helpful for him to touch the pictures, tracing lines or pointing out colors. We suggest some specific questions to direct your child's attention. Be positive in responding to your child's reactions and questions, and feel free to follow the path of your child's curiosity.

But always, especially at this age, help your child join the appreciation of art with the actual practice of art. You can do so by providing the materials, opportunities, fun, and encouragement it takes for him or her to experience the pleasure of being an artist.

What Do Artists Do?

Do you like to make things out of clay? Do you like to draw pictures? Do you like to build things with blocks? Every time you do any one of these things, you are making art.

Art is something designed and created by a human being. People have been making art since the earliest times. They use their imaginations, and they use clay, crayons, blocks, or other things to make something new. Even when you draw a circle in the sand or scribble on a piece of paper, you have made art. In fact, making art is one of the things that makes people different from animals. Can a cat draw? No, but you can!

People who create art are called artists. Some artists draw with pencil on paper. Some artists paint pictures. Maybe you've used brushes and watercolors to paint on paper. Some painters use watercolor paints, just like you, and other painters use oil paints to make pictures on a strong kind of material called canvas.

Which is your favorite?

Artists can use lots of other things to make art. Some artists cut paper or cloth into pieces, and then they glue those pieces onto a surface and produce something called a collage. You can make a collage, too.

Other artists use clay, wood, or stone and make statues. Some statues are small enough to hold in your hand, and other statues are so big and tall, you could climb on top of them. Artists who make statues, big or small, are called sculptors.

One thing that all artists need is imagination, which is something you probably have plenty of.

Art in Color

Artists pay attention to color. Let's look around for a minute and pay attention to color, too. What colors are the clothes you're wearing? What color is the sky today? What color is a banana? What color is a fire truck?

Everywhere we look, we see different colors. Let's see how many colors we can name. Which one is your favorite color?

Warm colors

Do It Yourself!

Have fun with color together by adding a few drops of food coloring to foods that have an expected color: blue into a glass of milk, green into a pat of butter, orange into mashed potatoes. Talk about how the food looks different but tastes the same.

Some things always come in the same color. When we think of the sky, we think of blue. What about grass? What color does grass come in?

How about ketchup? What color is ketchup? And it's always that color, isn't it? How would you like to put green ketchup on your french fries? Wouldn't it be funny to drink blue milk? What other silly colors for foods can you make up?

Artists think a lot about colors. They like to call some colors "warm," such as reds and oranges. This doesn't mean that you can actually touch a red picture and it feels warm, but it means that a red picture makes you feel warm in your imagination. Warm colors, including red, orange, and yellow, might make us think of fire, the sun, a bright day on a sandy beach, or even a lightbulb.

Artists call other colors "cool," such as blues and greens. They make us feel cool in our imagination, and they might make us think of the cool ocean or sitting in the shade of a tree. Paintings made up of mostly cool colors usually give us a different feeling from those made up of warm colors.

Cool colors

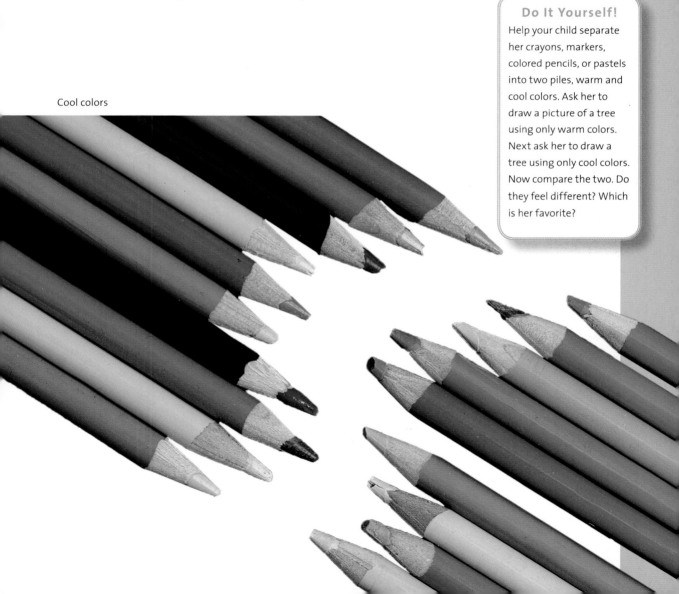

Hunters in the Snow, 1565   This painting uses cool colors.

Here are two paintings, one done with mostly cool colors and the other with mostly warm colors.

This first one is by an artist named Pieter Bruegel (**BROY**-ghel) the Elder. He called his painting *Hunters in the Snow*. Let's look at the picture together.

What colors do you see? The artist used mainly white, black, brown, and gray. Do these colors seem warm or cool to you?

Now let's look at what Bruegel wanted to show us in this picture. What season was he trying to paint? It's winter, because there is snow on the ground, and people are standing on the ice in the distance.

Bruegel chose cool colors in order to make you feel as if you are in that winter scene. The trees are bare and black. The frozen pond is icy gray-green, and the sky is that same gray-green color. The sun isn't shining at all. Brrr! Looking at this painting even makes you feel cold!

Bruegel lived in the north of Europe, where the winters are long and very

Tahitian Landscape, 1891

This painting uses warm colors.

cold. Many years after Bruegel, and far away from Europe, there lived an artist by the name of Paul Gauguin (go-GAN). He spent part of his life on an island called Tahiti, in the South Pacific Ocean, where palm trees grow all year long and it never gets cold.

Here is a painting by Gauguin called *Tahitian Landscape.* Let's look at the warm colors Gauguin used to make us feel as if we are in a hot place as we look at the painting. What are the warm colors that he chose to use? Red, yellow, orange. Even the color that he chooses to paint the brown hill is a warmer color than the cold brown trees in Bruegel's winter scene.

Blue Atmosphere, 1963

Sometimes artists make paintings of colors only. When you look at this kind of painting, you see shapes and colors without seeing a picture of a real place or person or thing. Here is a painting like that. What colors do you see? Do they seem to make a picture of a person or a thing?

This painting was made by an artist named Helen Frankenthaler. She called it *Blue Atmosphere*. "Atmosphere" is a word for the sky. Does this painting look like the sky to you? The colors do seem to float in the air because of the special way the artist put the paint on the canvas. There's a lot of red in the painting, though. It's not just blue. It's almost as if the hot red colors are pushing against the cool dark blue.

What name would you give this painting?

Lines and Patterns

Artists pay attention to colors. They also pay attention to lines. Look around, and you will see lines everywhere.

Lines frame every door and window. You make lines every time you write your name. Lines on the street tell cars what side to stay on. Sidewalks are filled with lines and cracks. Zebras are striped with lines. Bare tree branches make lines against the sky. Look at your hands: they're covered with thin lines.

Once you begin to look around, you see that we are surrounded by lines. Lines are all around us, in nature and in art. What lines can we see right now?

There are all kinds of lines: straight, curved, zigzag, and wavy.

Each kind of line has its own personality. Straight lines point us in a direction, like an arrow. Curved lines make us think of motion, like a ball rolling. Zigzag lines are full of energy, like a bolt of lightning. Wavy lines can be calm, like waves lapping on a beach.

Do It Yourself!

Hunt for lines where you live. Straight lines around doors and windows, curved lines around a clock face. Can you find any wavy lines? (Perhaps in the folds of curtains.) Any zigzags? (In the gables of a house.) As you find each in the world around you, ask your child to draw that kind of line as well. You can play a game in which you try to draw things using only one kind of line. Can you draw a dog with straight lines only? A person with curved lines only? A house with zigzags?

People and Dog in Front of the Sun, 1949

Just like you, artists use lines when they are making art. Here's a painting by Joan Miró (ZHU-ahn mih-ROW) in which the lines are easy to see. Can you trace the lines with your finger?

But what is it a painting of? At first, it's hard to see. I will tell you a secret, though: Miró liked to paint what he saw in his dreams, and as you know, the things you see in your dreams can be a little strange.

Let's look more closely at the lines in Miró's painting. Can you find some straight lines? Can you find some curved lines? Miró has painted some of the lines so that they come together to make shapes. What shapes do you see? What colors do you see?

Maybe the name Miró gave to his painting will help us figure out what it might be. He called his painting *People and Dog in Front of the Sun.*

Where is the sun?

Where are the people?

Can you see a dog?

You can even turn the painting upside down to see another one of the people.

Here is a picture drawn by an artist named Hokusai (HOE-coo-sye). The picture is made up completely of lines. Can you see what Hokusai made a drawing of? Do you see a person? A man or a woman? Do you see a musical instrument? It looks like a violin or a banjo.

Hokusai named this drawing *Tuning the Samisen*. "Samisen" is the name of this musical instrument, from a country in Asia called Japan. This picture shows the woman getting her instrument ready to play by tuning the strings.

When Hokusai made this drawing, he decided that some of the lines should be thick and some should be thin. Take a look.

Tuning the Samisen, 1615–1868

Can you point to thick lines in the drawing? Can you point to thin lines?

Do some things in the drawing look like they might be soft to touch? Does anything look hard and smooth?

A child used lines to draw this doll.

Do It Yourself!
Your child will enjoy being an artist, too. Suggest that he choose one of his favorite toys to draw. Look at the toy and first talk about its lines together. Is it made of any straight lines, or are they curved or zigzag? Point the lines out and trace them together with your fingers. Then encourage your child to draw those same lines. The point is not for your child to replicate the object perfectly but to begin to see lines in the world around him.

Let's look for lines now in another painting. This one was made by the artist named Henri Matisse (Hon-REE mah-TEECE). He called it *The Purple Robe*, and it's pretty easy to see why, isn't it?

The first thing you might notice about *The Purple Robe* is its bright, joyful colors, but let's focus on the lines instead. Matisse decided to paint many bold, thick lines in his painting. Take a look at how different these lines are from the sharp, thin black lines that Miró used in *People and Dog in Front of the Sun*.

Do you see lines in *The Purple Robe* that are side by side and look alike? Take a look at the wallpaper behind the woman, for example. On one side of the painting, the wall is painted with straight lines. On the other side of the painting, behind the woman, the wall is painted with curved lines.

These repeating lines are called patterns. You can trace the pattern on each side of the wall with the tip of your finger.

Where else did Matisse paint patterns in this picture? What about in the woman's purple robe? The vase? The floor?

Now see if you can find more patterns in your house or neighborhood.

Do It Yourself!

When children draw repeating patterns, they are practicing the small motor skills they will soon need as they learn to write. Providing them with a set of lines and patterns and encouraging them to use these to decorate favorite drawings or even to create drawings from them can be a fun exercise. See the lines on page 221.

Purple Robe and Anemones, 1937

Statues, Monuments, and More

Here are three pictures. Every one shows a sculpture, but you can see how different one sculpture can be from another.

The first sculpture is a statue of one of our presidents, Abraham Lincoln.

The second sculpture is a tall totem pole that was made by Native Americans who live near the Pacific Ocean.

The third sculpture is a little blue hippopotamus.

Abraham Lincoln

Even though these three sculptures look very different, they have something important in common. Sculptures come in all sizes, from figures as small as your thumb to works bigger than a full-grown tree. You can walk around a big sculpture such as the totem pole, and you can look at it from all sides. Or you can pick up a small sculpture such as the blue hippopotamus and hold it in your hands. A

Statuette of a Hippopotamus is an Egyptian statue

Totem pole

painting or a drawing is usually flat, but a sculpture isn't. That's what all sculptures have in common.

An artist who creates a sculpture is called a sculptor. Have you ever made your own sculpture out of clay? Then you have been a sculptor!

Sculptures can be made of many different things. They can be made out of clay, wood, metal, stone, or all sorts of other things.

Some artists start with a block of wood and use sharp tools to cut away wood to make it into a new shape. That kind of sculpture is called a carving. The totem pole is a carving. It started as a tree, and sculptors carved shapes into the wood and then painted them. Each carved face belongs to a different totem, or creature, with important meaning to the Native Americans who carved it. What animal faces do you see on this totem pole?

Sometimes a sculptor makes a work of art that is big and sturdy enough to stay outside. Do you have any sculptures outside where you live?

The Statue of Liberty

Sometimes sculptures have special meaning. Here is a very big statue that stands on an island near New York City. It is probably the most famous sculpture in the United States. Do you know the name of this sculpture? It is called the Statue of Liberty.

- Do you see a woman? Many people call this sculpture "Miss Liberty."
- What is she wearing? What does she have on her head?
- What is she holding? She has something different in each hand, doesn't she?

This sculpture was designed as a lighthouse—a building that has a strong light in it, so strong that its beams shine through the fog or darkness to show ships the way to New York. Where do you bet the light was? It was high up in the top of the torch that Miss Liberty is holding, so that when the lights went on, it looked like she was holding a torch that was burning. Today the torch is covered in gold, which makes it gleam in the sun.

The Statue of Liberty is very tall, taller than many buildings. In fact, this sculpture was designed so that people could walk around inside and climb up stairs inside. It is made up of hundreds of sheets of a metal called copper, stretched over a strong framework of iron. It is one of the largest sculptures in the world, and for many people, it stands for the United States of America.

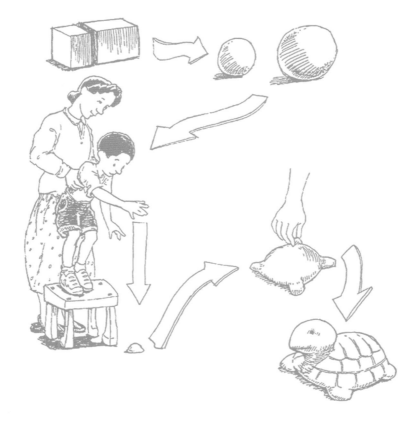

PARENTS: Here are easy instructions on how to make a sculpture of a turtle. Start with about a cup of modeling clay or play dough along with a plastic knife or a pencil. Divide the clay into two parts, one twice as big as the other, and make two balls. The big ball will be the turtle's body; the little ball will be the head. Stand on your tiptoes and drop the big ball on a smooth floor. Now the ball of clay should have a flattened side. Make legs by pinching four corners of the flattened side. Stick the smaller ball onto the front of the larger ball, smoothing them together. Now make a design on the turtle's back with a plastic knife or a pencil. You can help your child sign his sculpture by writing his initials on the underside of the turtle.

Lobster Trap and Fish Tail, 1930

Mobiles

Some artists make sculptures that can move. An American artist named Alexander Calder loved to make sculptures that move, especially ones that hung from the ceiling and were balanced perfectly. Those sculptures are called mobiles.

Here is a picture of one of Calder's mobiles. He called it *Lobster Trap and Fish Tail.*

- Which part do you think is meant to be the trap, and which the fish tail?
- What do the dark shapes at the bottom look like? Maybe they are plants swaying under the water, or fish down deep.

To make a mobile, Calder carefully designed every piece. Even a slight breeze will push its shapes around. Every part moves, but none of the parts hits another when they move around. Mobiles are fun to watch! If there isn't any wind, you can blow lightly and watch the parts move around each other.

PARENTS: Making a mobile can be a satisfying art project. Here are simple instructions that you can follow with your child. You'll need two plastic drinking straws, about four feet of string or fishing line, some cardboard or heavy construction paper, and a pair of scissors. Begin by helping your child make four similarly sized cut-outs: a crescent moon and three stars, or four favorite animals, or four simple shapes, for example. Cut out the shapes and decorate them on both sides. Punch a hole in the top of each shape. Cut the string into five equal lengths. Cross the straws and lash them with one piece, leaving some as the hanger. Thread a string through each shape and tie the other end to one of the ends of the crossed straws. Adjust the straw lengths for best balance. Hang your mobile where there's a breeze, and watch it move!

Let's Talk About Art

Sometimes, when you look at a work of art, you have the most fun finding lines, patterns, and colors. And sometimes you have the most fun looking at the picture and talking about what you see. Both are good ways of talking about art. Here are a few paintings that we can look at together. Let's talk about each work of art.

Snap the Whip

An American artist, Winslow Homer, painted this picture, called *Snap the Whip*, more than one hundred years ago. It shows boys playing a game at recess. Do you see the little red schoolhouse in the background? Does it look like your school?

In the foreground, boys are playing the game called Snap the Whip. In that game, children hold hands in a line and then they run behind a leader, who runs fast and makes quick turns—so quick that children at the end might get thrown out of line! Have you ever played this game?

Now let's look at the painting and talk about it, so that we see what Winslow Homer painted and understand it even better.

- How can you tell the boys are moving?
- Name some of the colors in the painting. Do they seem mostly like cool colors or warm colors to you?
- If you were going to be one of the children in the painting, which one would you be? Why?
- If you were to paint a picture of children playing a game, what would your picture look like? What game would you like to paint? How many children? Boys or girls? What other decisions would you make?

Just think, when Winslow Homer painted this picture, he made the same kinds of decisions. I wonder if he went to a school that looked like this one.

Snap the Whip, 1872

Children's Games, 1560

Children's Games

Here is another painting that is fun to look at and talk about. It is called *Children's Games*, and it was painted by Pieter Bruegel, the same artist who made *Hunters in the Snow* (page 218).

Bruegel lived in a time when many people were peasants. They lived in the country, they worked hard, and they did not have much money—but, Bruegel's paintings show us, they knew how to have fun! Somebody counted the number of different games that the children are playing in this picture—more than ninety!

Pieter Bruegel, who lived in Europe, painted *Children's Games* more than four hundred years ago. Maybe that's so far away and so long ago, no one plays these games anymore. Let's take a look. Do you see anyone playing games you have played yourself?

If you have a magnifying glass, it may help you see the tiny figures. There are so many of them! Of course, what you're looking at in this book is just a small copy of the painting. The real painting that Bruegel made is a lot bigger than this copy. Bruegel's original measures five feet from side to side and four feet from top to bottom. That means it might be taller than you are!

- Do you see someone wearing a mask? Have you ever done that for fun?
- Do you see children playing tug-of-war? Leapfrog? Have you ever played either of those games? Are these children playing them the same way you do?
- Some of these children are doing acrobatics. What can you see? A child standing on his head? Someone walking on stilts? Another one spinning around and around?
- What colors did Bruegel use to paint the children's clothing? Do these children dress differently from the way you and your friends dress today?

Here's one more interesting thing about this painting for us to talk about. To see all of these games going on at once, where would you have to be standing? Maybe on top of a tall building or high up in a tree. What is it about this picture that makes you feel as if you can see a long, long way? You can see lots and lots of children, and you can see a tall building all the way down at the end of the road. Bruegel may not have been standing on a rooftop to paint this picture, but he used his imagination to make it look as if he was.

Talk and Think

When asking a child a question, be patient in the silence that follows. Listen for answers, and if they do not come, ask your question a different way, leaving room for your child to offer her thoughts rather than offering your own set of answers right away. Use the artworks in this chapter to provide an opportunity for conversation.

Le Gourmet

This painting is by a famous Spanish artist named Pablo Picasso. He named his painting *Le Gourmet*, which are words in the French language. Even in English, we use the word "gourmet" (goor-MAY) to mean a person who knows and cares a lot about good food. Let's talk about this painting by answering a few questions.

- What is this child doing in the painting?
- What might be in her bowl? Does she seem to like it? Do you think she is a gourmet?
- What colors did Picasso decide to use in this painting? Are they warm or cool colors? What color did he use most?
- If you were going to make a painting using a lot of one color, what color would you use?

Le Gourmet, 1901

The Banjo Lesson, 1893

The Banjo Lesson

Here is a painting by the African American artist Henry O. Tanner. He named his painting *The Banjo Lesson*— why do you think that might be?

- Tell me a little about the two people you see in Tanner's painting. What are they looking at? What are they doing?
- How do you think the man feels about the boy?

Now let's talk about some of the decisions that the artist made when he painted this picture. Remember, artists often think a lot about the colors they are using as they make their paintings.

- What part of the painting seems to have the most light? How do you know that?

- If you imagine that you are there in the room with these two people, where do you think the light might be coming from? Is there one part of the room we are in right now that has more light than another?

- By making the wall and table behind them bright white and yellow, Tanner made it easier for us to see the man and the boy on his knee. The light even helps us see their faces. Do you see how Tanner has made the two people stand out by painting colors that look like light around them?

The Bath

The artist who painted this picture, Mary Cassatt (kah-SAHT), was an American woman, although she lived most of her life in Paris, a big city in the country of France. She loved to paint portraits of her friends, and she especially liked to paint women and children together.

When Cassatt painted this picture, which is called *The Child's Bath*, more than one hundred years ago, many people did not have running water in their homes. They couldn't just turn on the faucet and fill a big bathtub full of water. They had to carry water in buckets and pitchers and wash themselves by pouring water in a basin like the one you see here.

The Child's Bath, 1893

- How do you think this basin got filled with water? Is there something in the picture that someone used to fill the basin?
- Who do you think these two people might be? How does the woman seem to feel about the child? How do you think the child feels about getting a bath?

Remember that artists often use lines and patterns to create their paintings. Can you use your finger and trace some lines that Cassatt used here? What about patterns? Did she make patterns in this painting?

- These two paintings, *The Child's Bath* and *The Banjo Lesson*, sort of look alike. What makes them similar? What makes them different? In which part of her painting did Cassatt put the brightest light?

Really Looking

It's fun to look at and talk about art. Whether you see a painting in a museum, in a store, in a house, or reproduced in a book—and even if you are looking at something you painted yourself—here are some things to think and talk about that will help you look carefully.

- Does the painting have one color that seems to stand out most?
- Pick out three colors and see how many places the artist has repeated them.
- Describe some of the lines in the painting. Are they straight, curved, zigzag, or wavy? Are they thick or thin, clear or blurry? Do any of the lines make a pattern?
- If there are people in the painting, what do the positions of their bodies or the expressions on their faces tell you about them? What might they be thinking or saying?
- Can you imagine a story about this painting? Would it be happy, scary, funny, serious, mysterious—or something else?

Suggested Resources

LEARNING TO LOOK
The I Spy series, by Lucy Micklethwait (Cartwheel, 1992 on)
When a Line Bends . . . A Shape Begins, by Rhonda Gowler Greene (Sandpiper, 2001)

COLORING BOOKS
Start Exploring: Masterpieces: A Fact-Filled Coloring Book, by Steven Zorn (Running Press, 2011)
The Color-Play Coloring Book (Museum of Modern Art, 2012)

Colors, by Philip Yenawine (Museum of Modern Art, 2006)

The Come Look with Me series, by Gladys Blizzard (Charlesbridge Publishing, 1996 on)

Lines, by Philip Yenawine (Museum of Modern Art, 2006)

Shapes, by Philip Yenawine (Museum of Modern Art, 2006)

MAKING ART

Discovering Great Artists: Hands-On Art for Children in the Styles of the Great Masters, by MaryAnn F. Kohl and Kim Solga (Bright Ideas for Learning, 1997)

Ecoart! Earth-Friendly Art and Craft Experiences for 3- to 9-Year-Olds, by Laurie Carlson (Williamson Publishing, 1992)

Kids Create! Art and Craft Experiences for 3- to 9-Year-Olds, by Laurie Carlson (Williamson Publishing, 1990)

Mudworks: Creative Clay, Dough, and Modeling Experiences, by MaryAnn F. Kohl (Bright Ring Publishing, 1989)

Scribble Art: Independent Creative Art Experiences for Children, by MaryAnn F. Kohl (Bright Ring Publishing, 1994)

Something to Do (When There's Nothing to Do): A Coloring and Activity Book, by Mary Englebreit (Andrews and McMeel, 1995)

IV
Music

Introduction

There are many enjoyable ways to share a wide range of musical experiences with your child—singing songs, listening to all kinds of music, dancing around at home, attending local musical performances.

Singing with your child has all kinds of pleasures and benefits. In this chapter, we suggest some old favorite songs to sing together (see pages 258–271). Don't worry if you don't feel confident about your own singing voice. In your own home, you're the star! It's fine to play recorded music for your child (see the Suggested Resources at the end of the chapter), but the more you sing together, the more comfortable you will feel, the more fun you both will have, and the more you'll enjoy music together.

Some families will choose to arrange music lessons that will take their children to a level of musical competence beyond what we describe in the following pages. Different children will develop musical appreciation and skills at different rates and to different degrees. What's important is for you and your child to enjoy music and have fun with it.

You can help develop your child's knowledge and appreciation of music through the activities suggested in this section. Some of the activities ask your child to make sounds along with the basic elements of music, such as rhythm, pitch, and tempo. Others involve moving and listening to music. Repetition is fine: children love to hear, sing, or dance to the same song over and over again.

Have fun and enjoy these activities and songs with your child.

Making Music

Do you like music? Do you like to sing and dance? Do you have a favorite song or a favorite kind of music?

Violin

People make vocal music by singing. People make instrumental music by playing instruments. But you don't need a special musical instrument to be a musician. You can make music by drumming on a pot, humming through a paper-towel tube, shaking a plastic container half full of dry beans, or plucking rubber bands stretched over a small open box. With a little imagination, you can be a one-man band, with all sorts of homemade instruments!

Guitar

You can make sounds with all these homemade instruments, but maybe someday you will decide to make music with an instrument. Would you enjoy doing that? You will have to practice in order to be able to make beautiful music. Here are some of the instruments that people like to play.

Many people who play the guitar sing along with the music. They can hold the guitar, strum its strings, and sing at the same time.

The violin is another instrument with strings. Most of the time the violinist draws a bow over the strings to make beautiful sounds come from the violin.

A piano is a great big instrument. Inside, it has many strings, many more than on a guitar or a violin. The pianist never touches the strings, though. She sits on a bench and presses the keys on a keyboard, and then the strings make beautiful sounds.

A trumpet is a kind of horn. To play music on a horn like this one, the musician holds it to his mouth and blows in a special way. Horns can make loud noises that can be heard from far away, but a good trumpeter can make quiet sounds as well.

Trumpet

Flute

A flute is another kind of instrument that a musican holds to her mouth. But to make music, she has to blow *across* the hole, not into it. Have you ever heard someone make sound by blowing over the top of an empty bottle? Flutists make beautiful sounds that same way.

A drum is the instrument that keeps the beat. Drums can be big and loud, or they can be smaller and make a snappy sound. Sometimes a drummer uses drumsticks, and sometimes he uses his hands.

Drum

Once you get to know each one of these instruments and how it sounds, you can hear a piece of music that they are all playing together, and you can listen for the sounds of each instrument.

Piano

What instrument is this boy playing?

Do It Yourself!

Introducing musical instruments works best when the child hears them as well as sees them. Or, better yet, when the child can make sound on them! So if you have any of these instruments, or know someone who does, perhaps you can share with your child. Alternatively, if you have a recording that features the instrument you are talking about with your child, play it and point out the specific sound of that instrument.

Let's Listen to Music

Moving to Music

Everyone loves to move to music. When you hear some good music, it's hard to keep from dancing! Do you like to dance? Are there special times when you have danced with friends or family? Dancing is a wonderful way to enjoy music.

PARENTS: To get ready to move to music, choose the right place, where you have room to move and where you have equipment on which to play music. Here are some suggestions of instrumental music that is easy to find and sure to inspire dancing: Tchaikovsky's *The Nutcracker* ballet; "The March of the Siamese Children" from the Rodgers and Hammerstein musical *The King and I;* and "The March of the Toys" from Victor Herbert's *Babes in Toyland.*

From *The Nutcracker*, you can play music from different scenes and move differently for each: from Act I, "March"; from Act II, "Tea (Chinese Dance)," "Trepak (Russian Dance)," and "Dance of the Sugar Plum Fairy."

You may have developed some embarrassment or reserve about dancing over the years, but chances are good your child has not yet, so let go and enjoy dancing together. Most important, let yourselves feel comfortable being creative. There is no right or wrong way to move to the music. Lose your inhibitions and have fun!

Sometimes, instead of dancing to music, it's a good idea to listen carefully and even talk about the music you hear. Music can remind you of so many different things—different places, different feelings, and even different animals.

A famous composer—a person who writes music—named Camille Saint-Saëns wrote a piece called *The Carnival of the Animals*. In this piece, different instruments of the orchestra play music that is meant to remind us of animals. It is fun to listen carefully, to see if you can imagine the animal, and to dance along, pretending to be the animal—a donkey, an elephant, a crocodile, a swan!

PARENTS: Many recordings of *The Carnival of the Animals* are available, and some include a narrator identifying the animals and reading amusing poems written by Ogden Nash to go along with the music. This section of the recording is greatly enriched by listening together to the entire piece.

Follow the Beat

Can you think of some sounds that are steady—sounds that you hear again and again, very, very regularly? Let's think of some and make those sounds.

What about the ticking of a clock? What does that sound like? *Tick-tick-tick-tick*, in rhythm.

What about the sound that the windshield wipers on the car make? *Swish-swosh, swish-swosh, swish-swosh*, with a regular beat.

If we stop and listen, we can hear a lot of steady sounds in our world. It's fun to listen and hear them, and then to make that same sound, following the beat.

You have some steady sounds inside your own body, too. Put your right hand on your chest and see if you can feel a steady *beat, beat, beat.* That is the steady rhythm of your heart beating inside your body.

Sometimes the words that we say out loud have a steady beat, too. Listen to this rhyme. Does it have a steady beat?

> Clap your hands
> On the beat.
> Steady sounds
> Are so sweet!

Do It Yourself!

Here is an experiment that emphasizes the rhythm of a heartbeat and also teaches something about how the heart works inside your child's body. Help your child sense his own heartbeat and count the beats—*one, two, three, four; one, two, three, four*—so that you both have a sense of the pace. Now ask your child to jump up and down ten times (count it with him) and sense the pace of his heart again. Can you count along? An exercising body requires a faster heartbeat, but it still beats in a regular rhythm.

Let's say this rhyme together and clap our hands when a word makes a strong beat.

> Cláp your hánds
> Ón the béat.
> Stéa-dy sóunds
> Áre so swéet!

That rhyme has a rhythm, doesn't it? Let's say it again, but this time, let's clap hands when the beat is strong and stomp our feet when the beat is soft.

> Cláp your hánds
> *clap, stomp, clap*
> Ón the béat.
> *clap, stomp, clap*
> Stéa-dy sóunds
> *clap, stomp, clap*
> Áre so swéet!
> *clap, stomp, clap*

Let's keep playing Follow the Beat until we both have it right.

We can play this game with all kinds of rhymes. Listen to this one.

Three little kittens lost their mittens
And they began to cry,
"Oh, mother dear,
We very much fear
That we have lost our mittens."

Can we do this one with claps for the strong beat and stomps for the quiet beat? It's a lot more difficult!

The three lit-tle kit-tens lost their mit-tens
stomp, clap, stomp, stomp, clap, stomp, clap, stomp, clap, stomp
And they be-gan to cry,
stomp, clap, stomp, clap, stomp, clap
"Oh, moth-er dear,
stomp, clap, stomp, clap
We ve-ry much fear
stomp, clap, stomp, stomp, clap
That we have lost our mit-tens."
stomp, clap, stomp, clap, stomp, clap, stomp

Following the beat gets harder with lots of words, but it's still a fun game to play and a good way to hear the rhythm of the words we say.

Make Up the Beat

We can make up our own patterns of steady beats, too. It's like playing the drums and making up music.

Listen to the rhythm that I make with claps and stomps. I'll say the words "clap" and "stomp" as we do them, just to begin.

clap, stomp, clap, stomp

Now you join in, doing the same thing. Let's make it a very regular rhythm. Can we keep up the rhythm without saying the words?

PARENTS: Have fun making the sounds of different rhythmic patterns. Start simple at first, just a few beats at a time. Say the words out loud at first as you clap and stomp, but once your child seems to have the beat, continue it together without the words.

- clap, clap, clap, stomp; clap, clap, clap, stomp
- stomp, stomp, clap; stomp, stomp, clap
- stomp, clap, clap; stomp, clap, clap

When your child catches on, ask her to make up rhythms for you to follow.

Loud and Quiet

We hear sound all the time, through the day and even sometimes through the night. Some sounds are loud and some are quiet, and you already know the difference. Let's say the word "loud" really loudly! LOUD! And now let's say the word "quiet" very quietly. [quiet]

What is the loudest thing you can hear right now? It might be the radio playing, or it might be the refrigerator running, or it might even be a dog barking outside. Or maybe it's so quiet all around us that the loudest thing is us talking to each other. Let's whisper to make it very, very quiet.

Can you think of anything you have heard that is even louder than what we can hear right now? Have you heard a siren on an ambulance or a fire engine? Have you heard the sound of a train or a bus starting up the engine? What else have you heard that is really loud?

Now let's think of things that make sounds that are very quiet. What about the sound when you breathe in and out? You do make a sound, but it's very quiet, isn't it? Have you ever heard a cat purr? A purring cat can be very quiet. What about when a baby sleeps? Is that quiet? What about when a baby wakes up and wants something? Then the baby can get very loud!

Which baby is loud? Which baby is quiet?

Loud Songs, Quiet Songs

Music can be loud and quiet. Even in one song, we can sing some parts loudly and other parts quietly.

Here is a song that is fun to sing, and as you sing it, one part gets louder and louder.

John Jacob Jingleheimer Schmidt,

His name is my name too,

Whenever we go out,

The people always shout,

John Jacob Jingleheimer Schmidt!

Let's sing this song three times. We will sing the beginning of the song very quietly, more quietly every time we sing it. But when we get to the last words, when he shouts out his name—John Jacob Jingleheimer Schmidt—let's sing it more and more loudly every time.

Loud Drum, Quiet Drum

Musicians who play the drums think a lot about rhythm, but they also think about making sounds that are loud or sounds that are quiet.

Let's find a drum. If we don't have a toy drum, there are things in the house that will work just fine. How about an old kitchen pot, turned upside down? How about a bucket? Or even an empty oatmeal container! Lots of things in our house can serve as drums.

Drums are sometimes played with hands and sometimes with a drumstick. If you have a toy drumstick, great! But if you don't, that's fine, too, because there are lots of things in our house that can serve as a drumstick. How about a wooden spoon? How about a bamboo chopstick? Even a pencil, as long as it doesn't have a sharp point on the end.

Now you have a drum and a drumstick. Let's practice Loud Drum, Quiet Drum. Can you practice playing loudly and then quietly along with those words?

LOUD DRUM! LOUD DRUM!

[quiet drum] [quiet drum]

Now we'll play a game. I'll say "loud drum" or "quiet drum" and you respond by playing one or the other, whichever one I said.

Musicians playing all sorts of musical instruments think a lot about whether they want the sounds they are making to be loud or quiet. Let's listen to some of your favorite music and see if we can find places where the music is especially quiet.

When you sing, do you like to sing loudly or quietly? Let's hear you sing both ways!

When it's time for bed and a lullaby, should we sing the song loudly or quietly? There are times for loud music, and there are times for quiet music.

Talk and Think

Talk with your child about how the loud and quiet sounds in a song or a piece of music change the way the music feels. What kinds of movements go along with the loud parts? The quiet parts? He will probably find, instinctively, that he makes smaller, more careful movements to quiet music and more sweeping, dynamic movements along with louder music.

A favorite work that builds dramatically from quiet to loud (and is easy to find as a recording) is Edvard Grieg's "In the Hall of the Mountain King" from the music for the play *Peer Gynt*. It is one that your child will enjoy dancing to, changing her movements as the volume increases.

Fast and Slow

Think of all the different ways that animals move. Some move fast and some move slowly, don't they?

What animals can you think of that move very slowly? Turtles move slowly. Cows walk slowly, too.

What animals can you think of that move very quickly? Rabbits run quickly, don't they? Birds can fly fast. Mice scurry fast.

What about cats? A cat's way of moving can be either fast or slow. When it's stalking a mouse in the grass, a cat takes slow steps, one by one. But when it runs away from a dog and scampers up a tree, it moves very fast.

The rhythm of music can be fast or slow as well. We can sing the same song fast or slow—let's try it with "Old MacDonald." Let's make up new verses for slow animals, such as a turtle and a cow, and then let's make up verses for fast animals, such as a mouse and a rabbit. We'll sing the verses slow or fast, depending on how the animal moves.

Let's start with a turtle:

Old . . . Mac . . . Don . . . ald . . . had . . . a . . . farm . . .
E . . . I . . . E . . . I . . . O.
And . . . on . . . this . . . farm . . . he . . . had . . . a . . . turtle . . .
E . . . I . . . E . . . I . . . O.
With . . . a . . . ho . . . hum . . . here
and . . . a . . . ho . . . hum . . . there, . . .
etc.

Now let's sing about a rabbit. Will it be fast or slow? Let's sing it fast!

Old MacDonald had a farm, E-I-E-I-O.
And on this farm he had a rabbit, E-I-E-I-O.
With a zip-zip here and a zip-zip there, . . . etc.

> **Talk and Think**
> The same piece of music suggested as an example of loud and quiet ("In the Hall of the Mountain King" from Grieg's *Peer Gynt*) is good to use in a conversation about how music can be slow or fast. The piece starts out with a moderately slow pace and turns furiously fast by the end. Use it as an opportunity for your child to dance along, feeling the slow pace and then the fast pace by moving her body. If you feel like it, join in!

High and Low

Musical sounds—even just our voices when we speak—can sound high or low. I'll say those words in the pitch they name: HIGH and low. Do you hear the difference?

You try it, too. Say your name, but say it as high as your voice will go. Your voice sounds high, like a little bird or a mosquito.

Now say your name again, and make your voice go as low as you can. You sound like a big bear or a bullfrog.

PARENTS: You'll need a simple instrument for the next activity—a toy xylophone is the easiest. Orient the xylophone so the low notes (the longest keys) are closest to your child. Prop up the other end (with the shortest keys) to reinforce the ideas of "low" and "high."

You can also use a piano, toy or real, or an electronic keyboard. An African finger piano can work as well, although be sure to know which notes are high and which are low, because they are not in order, left to right, low to high, as they are on a keyboard. If you do not have any such instrument at home, save this part of the chapter for a time when you can sit together at a xylophone or keyboard.

> **Talk and Think**
> Bells of different sizes also illustrate high and low. With two bells, one big and one small, you can also talk about how big things make low sounds, and little things make high sounds.

Let's make some sounds that are low and some sounds that are high. First let's just listen. Tap the longest bar on the xylophone, over here. Now tap the shortest bar, up here. Why don't you tap them, back and forth, and listen to how different the sounds are.

Now tap the short bar—that sounds high. And tap the long bar—that sounds low. We can even use our voices to remember what those two words mean: HIGH and low.

Now let me ask you a question. I'm tapping a long bar—let's listen—and now I'm tapping a short bar. Which sound was higher—the first or the second?

Now let me tap two more bars, and you tell me which sound is lower—the first or the second.

Now it's your turn. Tap two different bars on the xylophone. I will listen and tell you which one is higher and which one is lower.

Favorite Songs

At home, in the car, in the bathtub, walking along: there are many good times and places for singing, and many wonderful songs to sing. Here are some to share with your child. (See also page 271 for recorded versions of favorite songs that we recommend.)

Bingo

There was a farmer had a dog,
And Bingo was his name-o.
B-I-N-G-O, B-I-N-G-O, B-I-N-G-O,
And Bingo was his name-o.

Go In and Out the Window

Go in and out the window,
Go in and out the window,
Go in and out the window
As we have done before.

[You can also sing the last line as "As fast as you can go."]

Hush, Little Baby

Hush, little baby, don't say a word,
Papa's gonna buy you a mockingbird.
And if that mockingbird won't sing,
Papa's gonna buy you a diamond ring.
And if that diamond ring turns brass,
Papa's gonna buy you a looking glass.
And if that looking glass gets broke,
Papa's gonna buy you a billy goat.
And if that billy goat won't pull,
Papa's gonna buy you a cart and bull.
And if that cart and bull turn over,
Papa's gonna buy you a dog named Rover.
And if that dog named Rover won't bark,
Papa's gonna buy you a horse and cart.
And if that horse and cart fall down,
You'll still be the sweetest little baby in town.

London Bridge Is Falling Down

London Bridge is falling down,
Falling down, falling down,
London Bridge is falling down,
My fair lady.

How shall we build it up again,
Up again, up again,
How shall we build it up again,
My fair lady?

Build it up with iron bars,
Iron bars, iron bars,
Build it up with iron bars,
My fair lady.

Iron bars will bend and bow,
Bend and bow, bend and bow,
Iron bars will bend and bow,
My fair lady.

Build it up with wood and clay . . .
Wood and clay will wash away . . .

Build it up with silver and gold . . .
Silver and gold will be stolen away . . .

[Repeat first verse]

Here We Go Round the Mulberry Bush

Here we go round the mulberry bush,
The mulberry bush, the mulberry bush,
Here we go round the mulberry bush,
So early in the morning.

This is the way we wash our face . . .

This is the way we brush our teeth . . .

This is the way we put
on our clothes . . .

This is the way we clap
our hands . . .

[Sing other verses about
other things you do.]

My Bonnie Lies over the Ocean

My bonnie lies over the
ocean,
My bonnie lies over the
sea,
My bonnie lies over the ocean,
Please bring back my bonnie to me.

Bring back, bring back,
Oh, bring back my bonnie to me, to me.
Bring back, bring back,
Oh, bring back my bonnie to me.

Old MacDonald

Old MacDonald had a farm, E-I-E-I-O.
And on this farm he had some chicks, E-I-E-I-O.
With a chick-chick here and a chick-chick there,
Here a chick, there a chick, everywhere a chick-chick,

Old MacDonald had a farm, E-I-E-I-O.
And on this farm he had some ducks, E-I-E-I-O.
With a quack-quack here and a quack-quack there,
Here a quack, there a quack, everywhere a quack-quack . . .

[Continue in the same manner with:
cow: moo-moo
sheep: baa-baa
pig: oink-oink, etc.]

Twinkle, Twinkle, Little Star

Twinkle, twinkle, little star,
How I wonder what you are.
Up above the world so high
Like a diamond in the sky.
Twinkle, twinkle, little star,
How I wonder what you are!

Pop! Goes the Weasel

All around the cobbler's bench,
The monkey chased the weasel,
The monkey thought 'twas all in fun,
Pop! goes the weasel.

A penny for a spool of thread,
A penny for a needle,
That's the way the money goes,
Pop! goes the weasel!

I've no time to sit and sigh,
No patience to wait till bye and bye,
Kiss me quick, I'm off, good-bye,
Pop! goes the weasel.

Go Tell Aunt Rhody

Go tell Aunt Rhody,
Go tell Aunt Rhody,
Go tell Aunt Rhody,
The old gray goose is dead.

The one she's been saving
The one she's been saving
The one she's been saving
To make a feather bed.

She died in the mill pond
She died in the mill pond
She died in the mill pond
Standing on her head.

[Repeat first verse]

The Bear Went over the Mountain

The bear went over the mountain,
The bear went over the mountain,
The bear went over the mountain,
To see what he could see.
And all that he could see,
And all that he could see,
And all that he could see.
Was the other side of the mountain,
The other side of the mountain,
The other side of the mountain,
Was all that he could see!

Jingle Bells

Dashing through the snow,
In a one-horse open sleigh,
O'er the fields we go,
Laughing all the way.
Bells on bobtail ring,
Making spirits bright,
What fun it is to ride and sing a sleighing song tonight!

Jingle bells, jingle bells, jingle all the way,
Oh, what fun it is to ride in a one-horse open sleigh!
Jingle bells, jingle bells, jingle all the way,
Oh, what fun it is to ride in a one-horse open sleigh!

The Farmer in the Dell

The farmer in the dell,
The farmer in the dell,
Heigh-ho, the derry-o,
The farmer in the dell.

The farmer takes a wife . . .

The wife takes a child . . .

The child takes a nurse . . .

The nurse takes a dog . . .

The dog takes a cat . . .

The cat takes a rat . . .

The rat takes the cheese . . .

The cheese stands alone . . .

The Hokey Pokey

You put your right foot in,
You put your right foot out,
You put your right foot in,
And you shake it all about,
You do the Hokey Pokey,
And you turn yourself around,
That's what it's all about.
You put your left foot in . . .
You put your right hand in . . .
You put your left hand in . . .
You put your head in . . .
You put your whole self in . . .

If You're Happy and You Know It

If you're happy and you know it, clap your hands. [*clap, clap*]
If you're happy and you know it, clap your hands. [*clap, clap*]
If you're happy and you know it,
And you really want to show it,
If you're happy and you know it, clap your hands. [*clap, clap*] . . .

If you're happy and you know it, stomp your feet. [*stomp, stomp*] . . .

If you're happy and you know it, shout hooray. [*hooray!*] . . .

If you're happy and you know it, do all three. [*clap, clap; stomp, stomp; hooray!*] . . .

Kookaburra

Kookaburra sits in the old gum tree,
Merry, merry king of the bush is he;
Laugh, kookaburra, laugh, kookaburra,
Gay your life must be.

Kum Ba Yah

Chorus:
Kum ba yah, my lord, kum ba yah,
Kum ba yah, my lord, kum ba yah,
Kum ba yah, my lord, kum ba yah,
O, lord, kum ba yah
Verse:
Someone's sleeping, lord, kum ba yah,
Someone's sleeping, lord, kum ba yah,
Someone's sleeping, lord, kum ba yah,
O lord, kum ba yah.

[Sing other verses with "laughing," "dreaming," "crying," "singing"; then repeat chorus.]

Row, Row, Row Your Boat

Row, row, row your boat
Gently down the stream,
Merrily, merrily, merrily, merrily,
Life is but a dream.

The Wheels on the Bus

The wheels on the bus go round and round,
Round and round, round and round,
The wheels on the bus go round and round,
All through the town.
The wipers on the bus go swish, swish, swish . . .
The doors on the bus go open and close . . .
The driver on the bus says, "Move on back!" . . .
The babies on the bus say, "Waa, waa, waa" . . .
The mommies on the bus say, "Shhh, shhh, shhh" . . .
The kids on the bus go up and down . . .

[Repeat first verse]

This Old Man

PARENTS: "This Old Man" is full of rhymes, and it's a song for which children can have fun making new rhymes. After your child knows the song well, start making up new verses for each number: "He played one on my tum," "He played two on my kazoo," and so on.

This old man, he played one,
He played knick-knack on my thumb,
With a knick-knack, paddywhack, give a dog a bone,
This old man came rolling home.

This old man, he played two,
He played knick-knack on my shoe . . .

This old man, he played three,
He played knick-knack on my knee . . .

This old man, he played four,
He played knick-knack on my door . . .

This old man, he played five,
He played knick-knack on my hive . . .

This old man, he played six,
He played knick-knack on my sticks . . .

This old man, he played seven,
He played knick-knack up in heaven . . .

This old man, he played eight,
He played knick-knack on my gate . . .

This old man, he played nine,
He played knick-knack on my spine . . .

This old man, he played ten,
He played knick-knack over again . . .

Suggested Resources

The Carnival of the Animals (including CD), by Jack Prelutsky (Knopf, 2010)

Core Knowledge Music Collection: Preschool and Kindergarten, various artists (Core Knowledge Foundation)

Cumbayah, illustrated by Floyd Cooper (HarperCollins, 1998)

Kids Make Music! by Avery Hart and Paul Mantell (Williamson, 1993)

My First Classical Music Book (including CD), by Genevieve Helsby (Naxos, 2009)

The Farmer in the Dell, illustrated by John O'Brien (Boyds Mills Press, 2000)

From Sea to Shining Sea, edited by Amy L. Cohn (Scholastic, 1993)

I Hear America Singing! (including CD), by Kathleen Krull (Knopf, 2003)

Jane Yolen's Mother Goose Songbook, edited by Jane Yolen (Boyds Mills Press, 1992)

Knick Knack Paddywhack, by Paul Zelinsky (Dutton, 2002)

The Seals on the Bus, by Lenny Hort (Henry Holt, 2008)

Story of the Orchestra (including CD), by Robert Levine (Black Dog and Leventhal, 2000)

Wee Sing Nursery Rhymes and Lullabies, by Pamela Conn Beall (Price Stern Sloan, 2005)

Wheels on the Bus, by Paul Zelinsky (Dutton, 1990)

V
Mathematics

Introduction

We hope that parents will place a special emphasis on the activities in this section. The most effective kindergarten programs provide youngsters with lively and almost daily exposure to age-appropriate math concepts and operations, thus giving the children a comfortable familiarity with the elements of math, as well as a firm foundation for later mastery.

Among grown-ups, mastery of math has been shown to be a reliable road to getting a good job in the modern world. Yet the greatest barrier to mastery, math anxiety, usually arises in the early grades, because children have not been made to feel at home with the conventions and procedures of math. The only good way for them to gain the needed familiarity and avoid the widespread symptoms of math anxiety is to provide them with a lot of lively exposure and practice at an early age.

Practice does not mean mindless repetition but, rather, varied practice, including the use of countable objects (often called "manipulatives" in schools) and also some paper-and-pencil work. Regular practice and review in the early grades will make the basic ideas and operations of math interesting and familiar, and eventually lead children to the effortless, automatic performance of basic operations upon which later problem solving depends.

If we adults have math anxiety ourselves, our duty is to avoid conveying to our children the idea that we "don't like math" or "aren't good at math." By engaging our children in the kinds of activities suggested in this section, we can let them know that math is important and interesting to us. Keep in mind, however, that the activities suggested here are supplemental ways for parents to reinforce their children's learning at home. They are not sufficient for teaching math in school, where children need more extensive opportunities for practice and review.

Patterns and Classifications

PARENTS: When you recall your earliest experiences with math, you may think of counting on your fingers, or perhaps adding and subtracting: 2 + 2 = 4, 3 - 1 = 2. Besides such familiar operations, early math also involves some fundamental concepts and ways of thinking.

Children need to learn how to sort and classify, and many start to learn these skills well before kindergarten. By their kindergarten years, they are ready to recognize likeness and difference, to see patterns, and to sort objects according to specific attributes, such as size, color, or function. You can help your child reinforce these concepts through some activities.

Activity 1: Collecting Things by Likeness

Get Ready

Tell your child you're going on a "likeness hunt." Get a paper bag and tell your child that you're going to collect objects that are alike in some way and put them in the bag. Talk about what sorts of things you will collect and how they will be alike. You may want to collect things that are all one color or things that are all used in the same way (things to eat with, things to draw with, etc.).

Go

With your child, label the bag with the attribute or characteristic you've selected, such as "red things" or "things used to eat with." Now it's time to collect. Together look for objects in and around where you live. If necessary, you can model the selection of the first object or two by finding an object and saying, "Look, here's a red crayon. We can put it in our bag because it's red."

Activity 2: Sorting Everyday Objects

Get Ready

You will need an assortment of familiar items from around the house. Choose items that can be sorted into two groups according to a specific attribute, such as size, color, or function. For example, collect a bunch of socks, some white and some with designs. Or gather some books, some big and some small.

Go

With the pile of mixed-up items in front of you, tell your child you're going to separate the objects into two groups. Ask her to guess the rule you're using to separate the objects. Then start to put items into two groups: for example, the white socks in one pile, the socks with designs in another.

Go a Little Further

Give your child an item that doesn't belong in either group—for example, if you're sorting big and small books, give her a spoon. Then talk about why the item is different and why it can't be sorted into either group.

Talk and Think

Guide your child to comment on each object as it goes in the bag, by asking:

- "Why does this go in the bag?" (If he says, "It's red," you can reinforce the idea of likeness by saying, "Yes, like all the other things.")
- "What else can you find that's red [or used for eating, etc.]?"

On another day, repeat this activity beginning in the morning because you'll find that as you go through your day, you and your child will find objects for your collection even when you aren't thinking about the game.

Talk and Think

To help your child focus on the concepts of likeness and difference, ask:

- "How are all the items in each group alike?"
- "How are the items in these two groups different?"
- "Here's one more item. Where would you put it? Why?"
- "What do you think is the rule for sorting these items?"

Activity 3: Alike and Different

Get Ready

Put a variety of different objects in a bag. Choose items that can be grouped in different ways, such as by color, shape, texture, or function—for example, crayons, buttons, or blocks in different colors and shapes. Be sure to include at least one set of items that share the same function, such as three different drinking cups.

It's easier to see some qualities of things than others, so it may help to examine some of the objects with your child in order to help him see both the obvious characteristics of an object, such as color, and the less obvious qualities, such as function. For example, if you examine a common pencil, you can ask such questions as: "What color is it?" (*yellow*) "What do we use it for?" (*to write with*)

Go

Dump the objects on the floor and spread them around if necessary. To model the activity for your child, pick up two items that are alike in some way and tell your child how they are alike and how they are different. For example: "Here are two cups. They are alike in the way we use them; we use them both to drink with. They are different in their color: one is red, but the other is blue." Then tell your child to pick two other items that are alike in some way. Discuss the items by asking:

- "How are the items alike?"
- "How are they different?"
- "Can you find another item that belongs with these?"
- "How is it like the other items?"

As your child answers the questions, occasionally give him the words that help him categorize. For example, if your child picks two red blocks and says that they are alike because "they're both red," you might say, "Yes, they're both red;

the way they're alike is their color." With two writing implements—for example, a pen and a pencil—if your child says they're alike because "they're both long," you might add, "Yes, and another way they're alike is the way we use them: we use them both to write with."

Activity 4: Shape Sort

Get Ready

To do this activity, your child needs to be familiar with the six basic shapes pictured here and with their names. If she is not yet familiar with these shapes and their names, we suggest that first you do Activities 1 and 2 in the Geometry section of this chapter (see pages 323–325).

You will need:

Sturdy paper such as poster board

Crayons

Scissors

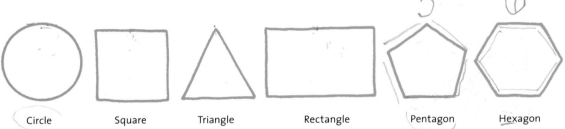

| Circle | Square | Triangle | Rectangle | Pentagon | Hexagon |

Review with your child the shapes pictured here and tell her their names several times. You might want to have her touch each shape and say or sing its name. You can point out that a square and a rectangle are alike: they both have four sides. But in a square, the sides are all the same length.

Draw some circles, squares, triangles, and rectangles of different sizes on sturdy paper. As you draw, talk with your child about the shape names. Let her join in the preparation by coloring the shapes before you cut them. Once your child has mastered the four basic shapes, introduce the pentagon and the hexagon.

Go

Spread the cutouts on a flat surface. Ask your child to pick one and help her examine the shape by asking:

- "How many sides does this shape have?"
- "Are the sides straight or round?"
- "Does the shape look the same if I turn it this way? How does it change?"
- "Can you tell me the name of this shape?" (If your child correctly names the shape, you can reinforce the name by repeating it: "That's right, it's a [name of shape].")

Go a Little Further

Have a scavenger hunt for shapes. For example, your child may compare a rectangle and a tabletop; an ice cream cone and a triangle; or a tire and a circle. The hunt can take place at home, in the park, in the car, or anywhere else that shapes exist—that's everywhere!

Activity 5: Shape Train

Get Ready

This activity will help your child learn how to identify and describe patterns of alternating shapes.

You will need a bunch of blocks. Make sure there are at least eight blocks of two different shapes, such as four blocks with square faces and four blocks with triangular faces.

After you collect the blocks, discuss the names of the block faces with your child and give him some time to examine and touch the two kinds of shapes.

Talk and Think

Pick another shape that's different from the first one. To help your child focus on the differences, put the shapes side by side and ask:

- "How are the shapes different from each other?"
- "Do both shapes have sides?"
- "Does each shape have the same number of sides?"
- "If we turn the shapes this way, do they still look different?"

Then ask her to sort the rest of the shapes and tell which shapes belong together and why.

Go

Tell your child that you're going to build a "shape train." To get started, lay six blocks in a row, alternating the shapes. To help your child understand the pattern, point to each block face and ask:

- "What shape is the first car? And the next? And the next?"

Talk about the pattern with your child—for example, "Do you see the pattern? There is a triangle car, then a square car, then a triangle car, then a square car." Then tell your child that you want to continue the pattern, and ask him to add another car.
    Ask:

- "What shape should the next car be? Why?"

Talk and Think

To help your child focus on different patterns, use the same blocks to form a different pattern, such as two squares and two triangles. Ask:

- "How many squares are there?"
- "How many triangles?"
- "What pattern can you see in this shape train?"

Ask your child to add more blocks to the train and describe the pattern.

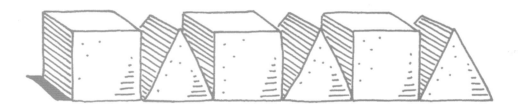

A shape train

Go a Little Further

Introduce another shape, such as a rectangle. Work with your child to make and describe other shape trains. Encourage him to name the shapes he uses to build the train and then describe the pattern he has made.

Activity 6: Potato Prints

Get Ready

You will need:

> 2 large potatoes
>
> Paring knife
>
> Newspaper
>
> Tempera paint in several colors
>
> Big sheets of paper
>
> Paper towels

Warning: The adult must do all the cutting in this activity.

Explain that you are going to cut the potatoes so that they can be used to print shapes: a square, a rectangle, a circle, and a triangle. First, cut the potatoes in half and draw an outline of one shape on each half. Next, cut down around each outline, which will leave a raised shape that you can use to print with.

Cover your work surface with newspaper; this activity can get messy! Put about two tablespoons of tempera paint on a small plate or in a shallow plastic lid. Show your child how to dip the potato stamp into the paint to coat only the raised shape. Then show your child how to make a print by pushing the potato stamp firmly and evenly on a piece of paper.

Go

To get started, let your child make any prints he wants on a big sheet of paper. Children love to print and will enjoy just printing before you begin to work on patterns. (You'll need to rinse the potato stamp and dry it on a paper towel if your child wants to dip the same potato stamp into different colors.)

When your child is ready, get a new piece of paper and stamp out a pattern on it. Begin with a pattern of two shapes, for example, a triangle and a circle. Alternate the shapes but use only one color. Repeat the pattern three times. Ask your child to copy the pattern. It's okay if your child makes mistakes doing this—it's part of learning. While your child is stamping the pattern, ask:

- "What are the names of the two shapes we're using?"
- "Which shape comes first?"
- "Which shape comes next?"
- "Which shape comes after that?"
- "What pattern do you see?"

Ask your child to continue the pattern.

Go a Little Further

Add another shape to the pattern so that you're using three different shapes: for example, a triangle, a circle, and a square.

Activity 7: More Play with Patterns

Get Ready

You will need:

    Colored construction paper

    Scissors

Using three different colors of paper, cut out 18 of each shape (circle, triangle, rectangle, square), each about three by three inches. In other words, when you're finished you'll have, for example, 18 triangles: 6 blue, 6 yellow, and 6 red.

Go

To help your child focus on color patterns, choose one shape and create a color pattern, such as blue triangle, red triangle, yellow triangle. Repeat the pattern several times. Then point to the pattern and ask:

- "What is the name of this shape?"
- "What is the color of this shape?"
- "Are the colors of the shapes alike or different?"
- "What pattern do you see?"

Ask your child to continue the pattern. Then have him explain his choices.

Go a Little Further

Ask your child to make up his own pattern. To make the activity more challenging, guide him in creating a pattern that repeats both shape and color, such as blue square, yellow triangle, blue square, yellow triangle.

Numbers and Number Sense

PARENTS: We encourage you to read this introduction, which is addressed to you, before proceeding with the activities for your child that begin on page 288.

You may already have shared with your child some familiar counting rhymes, such as "One, Two, Buckle My Shoe" (page 34) or:

One, two, three, four, five,
I caught a fish alive;
Six, seven, eight, nine, ten,
I let it go again.

Through such counting rhymes and games, many children, even before kindergarten, learn to recite numbers aloud ("one, two, three, four, five . . .") in the same way they sometimes recite the alphabet song, without really understanding what the numbers (or letters) represent, except that they are said in a certain order. Reciting the numbers aloud in order, quickly and without missing a number, is an important first step toward using numbers in a meaningful way.

Next, children can begin to combine their recitation of the number sequence with the act of counting objects. Counting aloud a group of objects then becomes the foundation for learning addition, subtraction, and place value in first grade.

Children also need to become aware that written numerals (1, 2, 3 . . .) correspond to what they have been saying when they recite the number sequence aloud. They need to learn to put these written numerals in order as well.

With practice, kindergartners can learn to write the numerals. You can help at home by having your child practice writing one numeral at a time. You can use workbooks available at bookstores and toy stores,

or you can provide paper with broadly spaced lines, on which (as illustrated) you lightly write the numeral a few times for your child to trace over, to be followed by writing the numeral several times without tracing it.

Your child should write the numerals as directed by the arrows in the following chart. Early in the kindergarten year, your child should practice until he can write all of the numerals from 1 through 10 without help. Later, as your child works with quantities greater than 10, he can practice writing the numerals for those quantities. You might want to pay special attention to the differences between potentially confusing numerals, such as 6 and 9, 1 and 7, 12 and 21, 13 and 31, and so on.

To summarize, early in the kindergarten year, your child should learn to count from 1 to 10 fast without making any mistakes, and to write the numbers up to 10. He may need to review the numbers many times in order to learn them. By the end of the kindergarten year, your child should be comfortable counting to higher numbers (a reasonable goal is counting by ones up to 31, and counting by fives and tens up to 50), as well as writing the corresponding numerals.

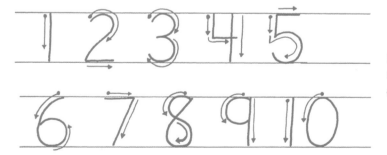

Handwriting chart for numerals. Start at the dot.

Here are some excellent counting books that can make learning about numbers enjoyable for both you and your child:

Anno's Counting Book, by Mitsumasa Anno (Harper, 1975)

Numbears: A Counting Book, by Kathleen Hague (Scholastic, 1986)

One Bear at Bedtime, by Mick Inkpen (Little Brown, 1987)

One Hungry Monster: A Counting Book in Rhyme, by Susan Heyboer O'Keefe (Joy Street Books, 1989)

Seven Blind Mice, by Ed Young (Scholastic, 1992)

Activity 1: Numbers from 1 to 10

PARENTS: Read the following aloud with your child:

Numbers tell how many of something there are.

There is 1 bird.

There are 2 kittens.

There are 3 boats.

There are 4 pigs.

There are 5 balls.

There are 6 robots.

Here are the numbers from 1 to 10. Let's point to each number as we say it aloud in order.

1 2 3 4 5 6 7 8 9 10

Can you put your finger on the number that shows

- How many years old you are?
- How many feet you have?
- How many fingers you have?
- How many noses you have?

Activity 2: Loading the Train: Counting Objects to 10

Get Ready

In this activity your child will count objects while picking them up and moving them from one pile to another. When children start counting the number of things in a group, it helps if they can touch and manipulate the things they are counting.

You will need:

At least 55 dried beans (or buttons or other small objects for counting)

Bowl

Egg carton

Scissors

Tape

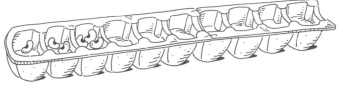

Go

Put 55 beans in a bowl. Set this aside as you prepare the egg carton as follows: cut the top off the egg carton and set it aside. Now cut the bottom of the carton in half down the middle of the long dimension. Then tape these two sections together, end to end, so that you have a single line of little cups. Cut the line so that you end up with ten cups. This is the "train," and now it's time to load the "cars."

Tell your child that you're going to play a counting game in which you "load the railroad cars," but that each car must have a different amount put in it. Point to the cup on the left and say, "The first car gets one bean." (If you want to pretend that the beans are lumps of coal, or gold, or whatever, that's fine.) Model the activity for him so that he sees how to say "one" as he picks up one bean and puts it in the first cup. Model the activity again for the next cup: as you pick up the first bean, say "one" and put it in the cup; as you pick up a second bean, say "two" and put it in the cup.

Have your child start from the beginning. Tell him he is to put 1 bean in the first car, 2 in the next car, 3 in the next car, and so on up to 10 beans in the last car. Remind him to continue saying the number as he picks up each bean, each time. Your child may need some coaching in order to time the action of picking up a bean with saying a number: the picking up and the counting aloud need to be simultaneous (some children will tend to say the numbers aloud faster than they pick up the objects).

Activity 3: The Size of 10

Get Ready

You will need:

15 small objects, such as buttons, raisins, macaronis, or pieces of O-shaped cereal

2 small clear plastic bags

Go

Put 5 of the small objects you have selected in one of the plastic bags and 10 in the other. Put the bag with 5 items on a table in front of your child. Ask her to guess, without counting, if the bag has 5 or 10 items. Then ask:

- "How can you tell?"
- "How can you find out if there are that many in the bag?"

Have her count to find out how many there are in the bag.

> **Talk and Think**
>
> To help your child think about the size of 10, put the bag with 10 items in front of her and ask:
> - "What about this bag? Do you think there are 5 buttons or 10 buttons?"
> - "How can you tell?"
>
> Then have your child count to find out how many are in the bag.

Go a Little Further

Later, when your child is comfortable with counting larger quantities, you can put 20 buttons in a clear plastic bag. Ask her to guess if there are 20 or 50 buttons in the bag. Then she can count to find how many are in the bag.

Activity 4: Counting Game

Get Ready

You will need:

  Paper

  Markers, pencils, or crayons

  Small objects to be used as markers, such as buttons or pebbles

Tell your child you're going to play a number game. Make up a game board like the one above, with a path of squares numbered in order. Have your child help you write the numbers in the squares.

Go

Tell your child to put a button (or pebble) on square 1. Then tell her to say each number as she moves the button from one space to the next. When she gets to the last number on the board, have her turn around and move the button back to number 1, saying the numbers backward. Then ask:

- "What is the first number on the board?"
- "What is the last?"
- "Can you say every number that you put your button on?"
- "Can you say the numbers backward?"

> **Talk and Think**
>
> To help your child focus on counting numbers, place her button on a number on the board. Then ask:
>
> - "Which number is the button on?"
> - "Which number comes before it? After it?"
> - "Can you count forward from where the button is to 10?"
> - "Can you count backward from where the button is to 1?"

You can have fun counting backward by singing this favorite song with your child:

Ten Little Monkeys
Ten little monkeys jumping on the bed,
One fell off and bumped his head,
Mama called the doctor, and the doctor said,
"No more monkeys jumping on the bed."
Nine little monkeys jumping on the bed,
One fell off and bumped his head,
Mama called the doctor, and the doctor said,
"No more monkeys jumping on the bed."
Eight little monkeys jumping on the bed,
One fell off and bumped his head . . .

Go a Little Further

You can challenge your child by extending the game board to higher numbers. A reasonable goal for kindergartners is gradually to build up to counting by ones to 31. As for when to introduce the higher numbers, you may want to ask your child's kindergarten teacher when the class will begin working with numbers greater than 10, so that you can reinforce the classroom learning at home.

Your child may need a little extra help when he first works with numbers greater than 10, since the English names for numbers do not always give a clue to the actual quantity. That is, in some languages, the numbers after 10 are logically called "ten-one," ten-two," and "ten-three," but in English we say "eleven," "twelve," and "thirteen." This may cause some initial confusion for your child, but encouragement and gentle review will lead to understanding.

Activity 5: How Many?

Talk and Think

For more practice with number sense, arrange five pennies in a row and five in a stack. Point to the stack and ask:

- "Do you think this group has more pennies?"
- "How can you find out?"

Get Ready

This activity helps children develop number sense. You will need at least 30 pennies.

Go

Arrange 6 pennies in a row and another 6 pennies in a cluster. Ask your child which group has more pennies. Then take the cluster of pennies and line them up, coin for coin, under the row of pennies. Have your child count along with you as you point to the pennies in each line. Ask:

- "How many pennies are in this group?"
- "How many are in the other group?"
- "Are there the same number of pennies? How do you know?"

Go a Little Further

Make three groups of pennies of equal amounts up to 10. Arrange one group in a row. Put the second group in a cluster, and stack the third group. Talk with your kindergartner about which group she thinks has the most pennies. Then ask her to arrange the other two groups coin for coin under the row of pennies.

Activity 6: Number Match

Get Ready

You will need:

    20 three-by-five-inch unlined index cards

    Crayons, markers, or pencils

Tell your child that you are going to prepare some cards so you can play a kind of matching game.

On ten of the index cards, draw large dots for the numbers 1 to 10. Your child can color in the dots. Next, have your child count the dots on each card and draw a numeral on a blank card to match the number of dots. When he's finished, you'll have one set of ten dot cards and one set of ten numeral cards.

Talk and Think

As you play, ask:
- "How many dots are on this card? What number does the other card show?"
- "Do they match? How can you tell?"

Go

Tell your child to mix up each pile of cards and place the piles face-down on a table. Then take turns turning up a card in each pile until someone finds a dot card and a numeral card that match. Keep playing by reshuffling the unmatched cards and putting them back into two piles until you've matched all the pairs.

Go a Little Further

Ask your child to put the number cards in order, laying them flat on a table from left to right. You might need to help by putting the first two or three cards on the table to show him what you mean. Then ask him to put the matching dot cards in order under the number cards.

Activity 7: One More, One Less

Get Ready

To give your child practice with the concepts of more and less, you will need:

At least 10 blocks or 10 large beads

String or shoelace

Talk and Think

Continue choosing new numbers for your child to show. For the fourth or fifth number that you choose, have him predict without counting what will be one more and one less. Then have him make one more or one less and count to be sure. Ask:

- "How can you tell what is one more [or one less]?"
- "Can you tell without counting the blocks?"

Tell him that you're going to play a game in which you say a number and he shows that number by lining up that many blocks or putting that many beads on the string or the shoelace.

Go

Say any number between 1 and 10, such as 5, and ask your child to show that number of blocks. To focus on the concept of one more, say:

- "Now show me one more than five."
- "How many is that?"

Then start over and have your child show a different number. This time, ask him to show one less and to tell how many that is.

Activity 8: Most and Fewest

Get Ready

Tell your child that you're going to play a counting game together using the names of family members. If your family is small, include the names of family friends or pets.

You will need:

Sheet of paper

Marker or pencil

Rusty
Joe
Heather
Chloe
Nick

Talk and Think

To focus on the concept of fewest, ask her which name has the fewest letters.

- "How can you tell this name has the fewest letters?"
- "How many letters does it have?"

Have your child count to find out.

Go

Ask your child to name four or five family members. As she names each person, use the marker to write the names in big letters on a sheet of paper. When you complete each name, point to the name and read it with your child. Then ask:

- "Which name has the most letters?"
- "Why do you think this name has the most letters?"
- "How can you tell?"
- "How many letters does it have?"

Then ask your child to count to find out how many letters there are.

Activity 9: Counting More Than 10 Objects

Get Ready

Children find it easier to count objects when they can touch objects that are lined up in an organized way. With practice, your kindergartner will find it easier to keep track of items that aren't organized or touchable. To start out, let your child help you gather between 10 and 31 small items, such as paper clips, macaronis, or small toys.

Go

Arrange the items in a row and ask your child to count them. Ask:

- "How many [paper clips, macaronis, etc.] are there?"

Then spread the items around and ask your child to count them. Ask:

- "How many did you count this time?"
- "Which way that you counted is easier?"
- "Is there a way you can organize these to make them easier to count?"

Go a Little Further

Go outside and ask your child to count something that cannot be touched, such as a row of windows. Again, ask how many he counted to be sure he understands that the last number counted is how many there are.

Activity 10: Things That Come in Pairs

Get Ready

To get started, have your child look at a stuffed animal or doll. Ask her to name parts of the stuffed animal or doll that come in twos:

- "What do you see that your animal [or doll] has two of?"

Then tell your child that "a pair is two of something that go together," and that the animal (or doll) has a pair of eyes, a pair of arms, and so on.

Go

Arrange several groups of like objects, including some pairs of objects, such as a pair of shoes, a pair of forks or spoons, and so on. Other groups should contain three objects. Say:

- "Here is a pair of shoes; there are two shoes, and they go together. Can you show me some other pairs of things here?"
- "How do you know this is a pair?"
- "Why isn't this group a pair?"

Activity 11: Counting by Twos

Get Ready

Tell your child you're going on a shoe hunt. Try to find at least five pairs of shoes and line them up in pairs next to each other. Then tell your child that you're going to find out how many shoes there are by counting them two ways.

Go

First, ask your child to count the shoes one by one. Tell him he is "counting by ones." Then, tell him there is another way to count the shoes, called "counting by twos." Ask him to listen as you point to and count the shoes. Put the emphasis on every second number. For example, you could whisper the numbers 1, 3, 5, 7, 9 and say the numbers 2, 4, 6, 8, 10 in a loud voice. After this, count the shoes by twos: 2, 4, 6, 8, 10. Repeat and then ask your child to follow along. Then give him an opportunity to count the shoes by twos on his own. Ask:

- "How many shoes are there? Can you count them by twos?"

Go a Little Further

Use other items, such as spoons or crayons, and gradually use more than ten items. Start with a review of counting by twos up to 10, then ask:

- "What number comes next if we keep counting by twos?"

Activity 12: Counting by Fives and Tens

Get Ready

You will need:

    Big sheet of sturdy paper

    Finger paints

Tell your child that you are going to make a handprint poster. You're using finger paints, so do this where it's okay to make a mess! (*Note:* Your child should already have practiced counting by ones to 30 before you do this activity.)

Go

Use the finger paints to make colorful handprints all over the paper. If possible, have family members or friends make handprints, too. At first, start with six handprints; later, you can work up to ten hand-prints. When the poster is finished, point to it and ask:

- "How many fingers are there?"
- "How could you find out?"

Point to one handprint, and ask:

- "How many fingers are on this one hand?"

Point to the next handprint and ask your child to continue to count. Continue until your child has counted all the fingers on the poster. Ask:

- "How many fingers are there in all?"

Talk and Think

Explain to your child that there is a faster way to count. This fast way is called "skip counting," and explain that you're going to "skip-count by fives." Say:

- "We're going to count five fingers at a time, like this: 5, 10, 15, 20 . . ." (As you count, move your finger from one hand on the poster to another.)

Have your child listen as you skip-count by fives. After repeating the pattern, ask her to join in. Repeat the same procedure as you skip-count by tens. Then ask:

- "Did you end up with the same number when you counted by ones? How about fives?"
- "Which way is faster?"

Go a Little Further

The next time the family is having dinner, ask how many toes are under the table.

Activity 13: Half and Half

Get Ready

You will need:

> 10 items of one kind that are of particular interest to your child, such as stickers, cookies, or small toy cars
>
> 8 pennies
>
> Slice of bread

Go

Spread the 10 items on a table. Ask your child to show a fair way to share the items between the two of you.

When your child has made two equal shares of the 10 items, explain that each share is half of the whole group of items: you have one half, and he has the other half.

Now, show your child the eight pennies; allow him to count them. Then put all eight pennies in a pile between you. Give two pennies to your child. Ask:

- "Do you have half?"
- "Can you show me how to share them fairly, half for you and half for me?"

Go a Little Further

Put the piece of bread on the table and ask your child to show a fair way to break it into

Talk and Think

Many kindergartners don't yet understand that halves are equal in size. To focus on the concept of halves as equal shares, ask:

- "Do we each have the same number of toy cars [or other items]?"
- "How could you find out?"

two pieces to share, half for you and half for him. After he has broken it (in two roughly equal pieces), ask:

- "Is my half of the bread the same size as yours, or is it a different size?"

Reinforce what he has done by saying, "You have half of the whole piece of bread, and I have half of the whole piece of bread, and both halves are equal."

Activity 14: A Good-Job Graph

Get Ready
You will need:
    Sheet of paper
    Crayons or markers

Tell your child that the two of you are going to make a Good-Job Graph, which will show some of the good things she does in a week. You can talk together about what sort of jobs to include: picking up toys, brushing teeth, washing hands before dinner, helping Mom or Dad, and so on.

Write the days of the week along the bottom of a sheet of paper and numbers up to 5 along the side edge. Post this chart in an easy-to-reach spot and explain that every day she can color a square on the graph for each of the "good jobs" she does. Try to help her record from one to five "good jobs" a day.

Go
At the end of the first day, look at the graph with your child. Point to the name of the day and ask:

- "How many 'good jobs' did you do today?"
- "How do you know?"

At the end of each day, look at the graph together and make some comparisons by asking:

- "How many squares did you color today?"
- "Was that more or less than yesterday?"

Go a Little Further
Ask your child:

- "This week, how many good jobs did you do in all?"

To help her answer this question, ask her how she could find the answer to that question. You might need to coach her that one way to find out would be to count all the squares on the graph. Then ask her to count all the squares.

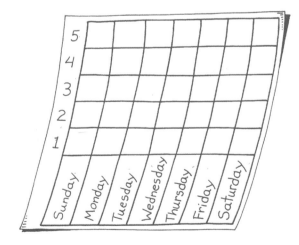

Activity 15: Block Train

Get Ready

This activity provides practice with order words—"first," "second," "third," and so on. Let your child help you gather:

    6 blocks
    6 different small objects (such as a button, a piece of macaroni, a pebble, etc.)

Go

Tell your child to build a block train by arranging the blocks in a row. Then have her put one of the small objects on top of each block. Identify one car for your child by using an order word such as "first" or "second" in a sentence, like this: "The button is on the second block." Then have your child identify the other cars, using an order word. Ask:

- "Which block is carrying the macaroni?"
- "Which block is carrying the pebble?"

Continue until you and your child have identified all the blocks by their order words.

If your child has trouble using these words, say them all aloud in order as you point to each car. Have her repeat them as you point to blocks first in order and then at random. Then repeat the questioning activity.

Money

PARENTS: Even before children know what money is for, they are fascinated by the shape and appearance of coins and bills. By kindergarten, your child probably also realizes that money is important.

Kindergartners need to know that money is used to buy things, and that different kinds of coins and bills have different values. The following activities will help children start to recognize coins and the $1 bill and to understand what each is worth. At this point, don't expect your child to be able to trade coins for other coin combinations of the same value. Exchanging money is a skill that will come later.

Activity 1: Identifying Money

Get Ready

You will need:

    4 small containers such as a margarine tub
    A way to label your containers (masking tape and pen or marker)
    Coins: at least 2 of each type of coin

Label the containers "1¢," "5¢," "10¢," and "25¢." Pile the coins in front of the containers. Tell your child that together you are going to separate the coins into different groups.

Go

Spread out the coins. To get started, pick up one of each kind of coin and tell your child what it is: penny, nickel, dime, or quarter. Give him an opportunity to look at the coins and say their names to you. Ask him to watch as you put one coin of each type in a container. Then ask him to sort the rest of the coins. Depending on your child's experience with money, you can explain what each coin is worth as you sort, or simply have him tell you in which container to put the coins.

Go a Little Further

The next time you go shopping, give your child a change purse with some coins. Ask for his help in picking out coins to give the cashier. For example, you can ask for three pennies, one dime, or other coins, and your child can supply them. (But don't expect him to know which coins add up to a certain amount. That skill comes later.)

Activity 2: Money Bingo

Get Ready

Tell your child that you are going to play Money Bingo. Before you begin, remind your child of what a penny, a nickel, a dime, and a quarter are worth. Also be sure she knows that a dollar is worth 100 cents. Show her the cents sign and the dollar sign, and show how these denominations are written: 1¢, 5¢, 10¢, 25¢, $1.00.

You will need:
Stiff paper or poster board
Scissors
Ruler
Crayons or markers
Buttons or other small items for markers

Coins and $1 bills

Box or hat

Make at least two bingo cards. Each card should have five squares across and five squares down. Instead of numbers, use these labels: 1¢, 5¢, 10¢, 25¢, $1.00 in the squares. Let your child help you write the numbers and dollars and cents signs on each card.

If your child has never played bingo, explain that you are going to cover the rows on the cards with markers and that the first person to cover a whole row—across, up and down, or diagonally—calls out "Bingo!"

Go

Put the coins and dollar bills in the box or hat, then give each player a bingo card and about a dozen markers. To play the game, choose a coin or bill and hold it up. As you hold up each denomination of money, ask these questions:

- "What am I holding up?"
- "How much is it worth?"

Then each player puts a marker in every box on the card that says the amount just held up. When one of you calls out "Bingo!" ask your child to remove each marker and read out the money values underneath. Now you're ready to play again.

1¢	5¢	10¢	25¢	$1.00
25¢	$1.00	1¢	5¢	10¢
5¢	10¢	25¢	$1.00	1¢
$1.00	1¢	5¢	10¢	25¢
10¢	25¢	$1.00	1¢	5¢

Computation

PARENTS: You probably don't remember a time when you didn't know that adding two groups of things gives you one larger group, while taking away something from one group leaves you with a smaller group. But these fundamental mathematical concepts may be new to your kindergartner.

The activities that follow use real objects to help your child understand what happens when groups of things are added together or taken away. By working with real objects, your child will learn that addition requires counting forward, while subtraction requires counting backward. The activities also introduce the + and – symbols. Some children can make an immediate connection between joining or separating groups and using symbols to describe what happens. Other children need a little more time to see this connection. Also, while some children might memorize specific addition and subtraction facts such as 2 + 2 = 4, don't expect or demand it of all kindergartners. That ability will come after your child understands the basic concepts.

Activity 1: Addition: Finding Totals

PARENTS: Before you begin this activity, it may help to read aloud the following introduction to addition with your child:

When two groups of things are put together, it's called addition.

There are three flowers in a vase. If you pick two more flowers and put them in the vase, how many flowers are in the vase now?

This is an addition problem, because you start with three flowers and add two more. After the flowers are added, there are five flowers. To show what happens, you can write

3 + 2 = 5

The sign + means "plus." It shows that you are adding.

The sign = means "equals." It shows that two amounts are the same:

3 + 2 is the same as 5

3 + 2 = 5

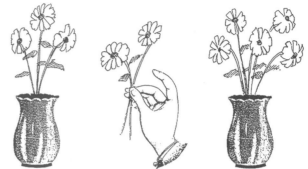

Get Ready

Gather 10 objects of the same kind, such as crayons, blocks, pebbles, or pennies. Put some of the objects in one pile and some in another pile. (When you start out, you do not have to use all 10 objects.) Draw a large plus sign on a slip of paper and place it between the two piles. Tell your child that the two of you are going to play an addition game.

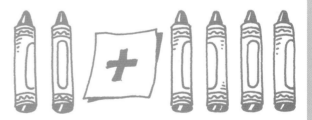

Go

Have your child count how many crayons are in each pile and tell you how many. Tell him that you are going to add the two piles to make one new pile. Point to the plus sign between the piles to show what you will do. Then put the piles together. Ask your child to count the crayons and tell how many there are now.

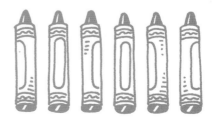

Talk and Think

After you make the new pile, ask:

- "How did we make the new pile?"
- "How many crayons are in the new pile?"
- "Were the other piles bigger than this pile?"
- "Is this the biggest pile?"

Repeat this activity several times with different-sized piles so your child can practice adding various combinations up to 10.

Go a Little Further

Here's how to have your child do some simple addition mentally. Display two groups that each contain just one or two items. Have your child count the items in each pile. Ask him to put both groups into a bag. Close the bag. Ask him to tell you how many objects are in the bag. Then he can open the bag and count the new group. Repeat this several times with different-sized piles.

Activity 2: Subtraction: The Take-Away Game

Get Ready

You will need:

> Small group of no more than 5 objects of the same kind, such as buttons or pebbles

Go

Tell your child that you're going to play a number game. Put the buttons on a table and ask your child to count them. While she watches, cover some of the buttons with your hand and slide them a few inches away (keeping them under your hand). Then ask:

- "How many buttons did you count before?"
- "How many buttons do you see now?"
- "Can you tell how many were taken away?"

Go a Little Further

As your child begins to understand subtraction, you can use more than five objects in the group. You can also try reversing roles and let her take away the items. For fun, you can occasionally "guess wrong" and have her tell you how many items she removed.

As your child repeats this activity, remind her that when you take away buttons, you are subtracting a number.

Activity 3: Addition and Subtraction Stories

Get Ready

You will need:

    5 to 10 index cards

    Pencil or marker

Write a plus sign on one of the index cards, a minus sign on one, and an equals sign on another.

Tell your kindergartner that you're going to tell some number stories. Show each sign to your child and remind him what each symbol means.

Go

As your child listens, tell a number story about a family event. For example, you might tell about the time that Uncle Ralph was a boy and ordered five hot dogs but could only eat four.

PARENTS: Put your hand over four of the hot dogs to show "taking away" the hot dogs that Uncle Ralph ate.

Use the plus, minus, and equals signs as you tell the story. Ask:

- "How many hot dogs did Uncle Ralph order?" (Put a 5 on one card.)
- "How many did he eat?" (Put a 4 on a card.)
- "How many were left?" (Put a 1 on a card.)
- "How could you use a plus sign [+] or a minus sign [−] to tell the story?"

Using the index cards, help your child write an addition or subtraction sentence that tells his story, for example, 5 − 4 = 1. Have him read the numbers and symbols aloud, "Five minus four equals one," as he points to each card.

Go a Little Further

Have your child tell another story using the same addition or subtraction sentence. The story can be about something that really happened or something he makes up.

Measurement

PARENTS: Your kindergartner probably uses words that describe size and degree, such as "big," "smaller," "long," "tall," and "taller." These words show that she recognizes size relationships. This important skill is fundamental not just to mathematics but to science, geography, and even storytelling.

Children need to learn that measuring is one way of describing something—for example, how big, how hot, how heavy, or how tall something is, or how long something takes to do. Children also need to learn that measuring is a way to compare objects in terms of such qualities as size, weight, and capacity.

Kindergartners generally have little trouble comparing things by placing them next to each other, but they are only beginning to understand measurement. The activities that follow will help your child recognize the standard measuring tools. Don't expect your child to be able to use the tools to measure. Your child should, however, be given opportunities to use arbitrary units, such as paper clips or footsteps, to measure length.

Activity 1: Measuring Tools

Get Ready

Let your child help you gather some household measurement tools such as a ruler, tape measure, thermometer, clock, and bathroom scale.

Talk and Think

To help her focus on how these tools are used, ask:

- "Which tool tells what time it is?"
- "Which tool tells us how hot or cold it is?"
- "Which tool tells how heavy something is?"
- "Which tool tells how long something is?"

Go

Tell her that these are all tools used to measure things. For each tool, ask:

- "Do you know the name of this one?"
- "Do you know what we use this for?"

Activity 2: Measuring with Paper Clips

PARENTS: When children first learn to measure, many of them have difficulty measuring with rulers that use standard units such as inches or centimeters. To help a child understand concepts of measurement and why we measure using units such as inches, it is generally helpful to begin by asking your child to use a set of identical objects, such as paper clips, to measure the length of an object.

Get Ready

Get together a few pairs of similar items to measure, such as two books, two cereal boxes, or two toy trucks. The items in each pair should be of different sizes. Also have ready a bunch of paper clips (all the same size) to use as measuring tools.

Go

Tell your child that the two of you are going to measure some items. Show him the pair of books and ask:

- "Which book looks bigger?"
- "How can you find out which is bigger?"

Your child may say that one book looks bigger, or he may hold the books next to each other to compare. Give your child some paper clips. Help him measure the book. Line up the clips one by one along the binding side of one book until you reach the end of the book. Do the same with the other book. Ask:

- "How many paper clips long is this book?"
- "How many paper clips long is that book?"
- "How can you tell which book is longer?"

Go a Little Further

Have your child hook the paper clips together after measuring each of several items. Then ask him to arrange the paper clip chains in order from shortest to longest.

You can also have your child make a paper ruler by tracing a paper clip several times, end to end. Have him use his new ruler to measure length. As he becomes familiar with using the paper ruler, provide an inch ruler and help him investigate how to measure small objects with this tool.

Activity 3: Measuring with Hands and Feet

Get Ready

Tell your child that you're going to measure some items using your hands.

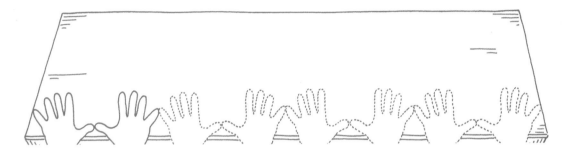

Go

Spread out your hand and have your child do the same. As your child watches, measure a table by alternating hands the length of the table. Ask her to count the number of hands it takes to measure the table. Ask:

- "How many hands long is the table?"
- "Will the table still be [number of] hands long if I measure it again?"
- "How long is the table if we use your hands?"
- "Why does it take more of your hands to measure the table than mine?"
- "What about our feet? Do you think it takes more hands or more feet to measure the table?"

Go a Little Further

Show your child how you can use your feet to measure an item, such as a small rug, by counting as you place one foot in front of the other. Then have your child use the length of her foot to measure the table by cutting out a paper foot length, using her foot as a model. Show her how to use this paper foot to measure the length of the table. She can also measure other furniture and spaces using this paper tool.

Activity 4: Full, Half Full, and Empty

Get Ready
You will need four identical glasses and a pitcher of water.

Go
Arrange the glasses in a row and fill up one glass with water. Fill another glass half full. After that, pour a small amount of water into the glass next to the half-full glass. This glass should be less than one-quarter full. The glasses should not be in order from full to empty.

Go a Little Further
Add another glass that is half full. Have your child decide which glass is "as full as" the new one.

Talk and Think
Have your child compare the water levels. Ask:
- "Which glass is full?"
- "Which glass is half full?"
- "Which glass is empty?"
- "Are the glasses in order from full to empty?"
- "Can you put them in order?"

Activity 5: Heavy and Light

Get Ready
Ask your child to help you pick out several different items of different weights, such as books, pebbles, and blocks. You can also use grocery items of different weights.

Go
Put all the items on a table. Ask her to pick something heavy from the group.

Which child is holding something light?
Which child is holding something heavy?

Talk and Think

To help your child recognize the difference between heavy and light, ask:

- "Why did you pick this [name of item]?"
- "Is it hard to lift? Can you find something that is harder to lift?"
- "Can you find something that is easier to lift?"
- "Can you find something that is light? Is it very easy to lift?"

If your child has difficulty understanding which object is light, you can pick up a light object and say, "This is not very heavy at all—it's light; it's very easy to lift." This will help her recognize that heavy things are hard to lift, while light things are easy to lift.

Then ask your child to choose two items. Ask:

- "Which item is heavier? Why?"

Go a Little Further

Choose three items of obviously different weights. Ask your child to arrange the three items in order of weight, from heavy to light.

Activity 6: Long and Short Events

Get Ready

Gather some photos or picture books that convey the idea of things that take a long time. For example, they might involve a car or train trip that takes all day, or the growth of a pet or plant.

Go

Ask your child to listen as you tell about something that takes a long time. Show pictures you've gathered as you tell your story. Then ask your child to tell about something that he thinks takes a long time. Next, give one or two examples of things that take a short time, such as snapping your fingers, clapping, or eating a cookie. Ask your child to tell about some other things that take a short time.

Talk and Think

To help him become more familiar with long and short events, you can ask questions such as:

- "Which would take longer: combing your hair or going from our home to school?"
- "Which would take longer: pouring a glass of water or reading a whole story?"
- "Which would take a shorter time: eating a raisin or eating dinner?"

Activity 7: Before and After: Morning, Afternoon, and Evening

Get Ready

A good time to begin this activity is in the evening, before your child's bedtime. Ask your child to tell about some of the things she did today.

- "Did you play today?"
- "Did you eat lunch?"
- "Did you brush your teeth?"

Go

Tell your child you want to talk about the parts of the day—morning, afternoon, and evening. Then ask:

- "What do we do in the morning?"
- "What do we do in the afternoon?"
- "What do we do in the evening?"

Talk and Think

To follow up, you can ask:

- "Did you eat breakfast in the morning, the afternoon, or the evening?"
- "Did you eat breakfast before or after you got dressed?"
- "Did you come home from school in the morning, the afternoon, or the evening?"
- "Did you eat supper before or after you came home from school?"
- "What part of the day is it now? Is this morning, afternoon, or evening?"

Activity 8: What Time Is It?

Get Ready

You will need:

Sheet of colored paper

Scissors

Paper plate

Marker or crayon

Brad

To make clock hands, cut two narrow strips from the colored paper; one strip should be longer than the other. Then have your child help you turn the paper plate into a clock face by numbering around the rim from 1 to 12. Finally, use the brad to attach the ends of both strips to the center of the clock face. Your child can use this homemade clock face to show different times.

Go

Put a real clock on the table. Use a clock with two hands and twelve numbers. Tell him that the short hand is the hour hand. It tells what hour it is. The long hand is the minute hand. It tells the minutes.

Set the clock to show four o'clock. Point out how the short hand points to the hour and the long hand points straight up, to the 12. Tell your child that you can tell what hour it is by looking at the short hand. Go over another example, such as five o'clock: point out that the long hand points straight up, to the 12, while the short hand points to the 5. Then ask:

- "Where is the short hand pointed?"
- "Where is the long hand pointed?"
- "Can you name the time?"
- "Can you show the same time on your clock?"

You can continue the activity by having him name the time shown as you move the short hand to other numerals on the clock. Show only whole hours. Don't expect your child to recognize parts of an hour, such as 5, 10, or 30 minutes before or after the hour.

Go a Little Further
Have your child help you keep track of the time until it's time for a snack or a story. About ten or twenty minutes before the hour of the activity, tell him that you will have a snack at (the next hour) o'clock. Several times before the hour, ask your child if it's time yet. You can also tell your child to let you know when it's time.

Activity 9: The Calendar

Get Ready
You will need a calendar, preferably one with big, easy-to-see numbers.

Go
Show your child the calendar. Remind her that a calendar is a way of keeping track of time and of showing what day today is. Explain that every day is part of a week and also part of a month. Have her touch the line of days that make up a week. With your help, have her point to and say the names of the week, starting with Sunday. Then have her touch all weeks that make up the month.

Show her today's date on the calendar. Identify today by the day of the week, the date, and the month; for example: "This is Wednesday, the fifth of October." Have her mark an X in the box for today's date on the calendar. Explain that tomorrow you will mark tomorrow's date. Set aside a regular time each morning to mark the calendar.

Most kindergartners don't have a good sense of long-term time, so ask about events that happen on a single day or on the same day every week.

Go a Little Further

As your child becomes familiar with the calendar, ask:

- "Can you name the days of the week in order, starting with Sunday?"
- "How many days are there in a week? How can you find out?"
- "How many days are in this month? How can you find out?"

Geometry

Kindergartners need to learn to recognize and name various shapes, and to use words of position and direction to tell where things are. The activities in this section will help you introduce basic shapes and words of position and direction to your child. Beyond these activities, you can use lots of everyday opportunities to give your child practice with shapes and words of position and direction. For example, when you are reading aloud, you can point to a picture and ask, "Can you tell me where the troll is? That's right, he's under the bridge."

Activity 1: What's That Shape?

Get Ready

You will need:

> Cardboard
>
> Scissors
>
> Markers or crayons
>
> Brown grocery bag

With your child, look at the pictures of the four basic shapes on the next page. Say their names aloud as you point to them and run your finger around their outlines.

You can point out that a square and a rectangle are alike because they both have four sides. But in a square, the sides are all the same.

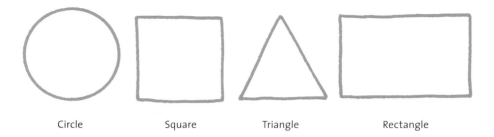

| Circle | Square | Triangle | Rectangle |

Now tell your child that you are going to make shapes like these and play a game. Cut from cardboard several of each of the four basic shapes. They should be about three inches by three inches. Your child can color or decorate the shapes as you cut them.

Talk and Think
After playing with all the shapes, ask your child, when he pulls out a correct shape, how he knew it was a [name of shape].

Go

Let your child put the shapes in the bag. Then hold the bag so your child cannot see into it. Ask him to reach into the bag (with one or both hands) and, without looking, to pull out a circle. If he brings out one of the other shapes, show him the picture of a circle and try again. Repeat this game with all the shapes.

Activity 2: Shape and Size

Get Ready

To make 16 shape cutouts, you will need:

Stiff paper, poster board, or cardboard

Scissors

Markers, crayons, or other decorations such as stamps or stickers

Cut out four of each shape. Two of the cutouts of each shape should be the same size, a third should be smaller than the others, and a fourth should be larger than the others. As you make the shapes, ask your child to tell you the name of each shape. Your child can color or decorate the shapes as you cut them.

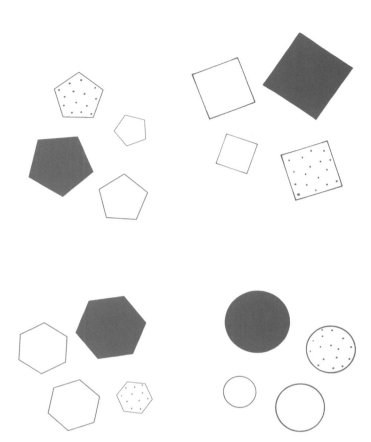

Talk and Think

To help her compare the shapes, ask:

- "Are the two shapes the same size?"
- "Is the shape you chose larger or smaller than the first one?"

Go

Put the shapes on a table and mix them up, turning some at different angles. Choose one and ask your child to find another cutout that has the same shape.

Go a Little Further

You can extend the game by picking up a shape and asking your child:

- "Can you find another piece that's the same shape and size as this?"
- "Can you find another piece that's the same shape as this but [bigger or smaller]?"
- "What is the name of this shape? Can you pick out all the other pieces that are the same shape?"

Activity 3: Where Is It? Using Words of Position and Direction

PARENTS: Direct your child's attention to the pictures below. Ask questions that will encourage your child to use position words in his answers. You can model the use of position words by answering the first two or three questions yourself.

- "Where is the lamp?"
  (*The lamp is on the table.*)
- "Where is the cat?"
  (*The cat is under the table.*)
- "Where is the balloon?"
  (*The balloon is over the table or next to the table.*)
- "Is the door open or closed?"
  (*The door is open.*)
- "Is the window open or closed?"
  (*The window is closed.*)

- "Is the girl in front of the house or behind the house?"
  (*The girl is in front of the house.*)
- "Is the boy in front of the girl, or is he behind the girl?"
  (*The boy is behind the girl.*)
- "Are the children inside the house, or are they outside the house?"
  (*The children are outside the house.*)
- "Do you see where the path goes?"
  (*It goes around the house.*)
- "Do you see the cow?"
  (*The cow is between the pig and the sheep.*)
- "Is the pig to the left of the cow, or is the pig to the right of the cow?"
  (*The pig is to the left of the cow.*)
- "Is the sheep to the left of the cow, or is the sheep to the right of the cow?"
  (*The sheep is to the right of the cow.*)
- "Is the rooster above the pig, or is the rooster below the pig?"
  (*The rooster is above the pig.*)
- "Is the pig below the rooster, or is the pig above the rooster?"
  (*The pig is below the rooster.*)
- "Does the tree look like it is near the animals or far from the animals?"
  (*The tree looks like it's far from the animals.*)
- "Is the pig near the fence, or is the pig far from the fence?"
  (*The pig is near the fence.*)

Activity 4: Simon Says

Get Ready

This game emphasizes right and left, but you can also use other directional words, such as "behind," "beside," "between," "above," "below," "under," "far from," "near," "inside," "here," and "there."

Go

Tell your child that you are going to play a game of Simon Says. If she does not know the game, explain that she is to do what you say only if you use the words "Simon says." If you tell her to do something without saying "Simon says," she should not do it.

Play the game by giving commands that use directional words, especially "left" and "right," such as:

- "Simon says: put your right hand on your hip."
- "Simon says: put your left hand on your chin."
- "Simon says: put your left hand on your tummy."

Occasionally give commands that do not begin with "Simon says."

Go a Little Further

If your child has no difficulty with left and right, make the commands harder by using more directional words. For example, instead of saying "Put your right hand on your neck," say "Put your right hand behind your neck," or "Put your right hand beside your left knee."

> **Talk and Think**
> To get your child to focus on directional words, after playing for a while, ask:
> - "Which commands were hard to follow?"
> - "Which were easy?"

Suggested Resources

....

12 Ways to Get to 11, by Eve Merriam (Aladdin, 1996)

Chicken Soup with Rice: A Book of Months, by Maurice Sendak (Harper Collins, 1962)

One Was Johnny, by Maurice Sendak (Harper Collins, 1962)

Monster Money, by Grace Maccarone (Cartwheel Books, 1998)

Patterns (Scholastic, 1998)

Ten, Nine, Eight, by Molly Bang (HarperCollins, 1991)

The Doorbell Rang, by Pat Hutchins (HarperCollins, 1989)

Today Is Monday, by Eric Carle (Scholastic, 1993)

Too Many Balloons, by Catherine Matthias (Children's Press, 1982)

VI
Science

Introduction

Children gain knowledge about the world around them in part from observation and experience. To understand the world of plants and animals, or of seasons and the weather, or of physical forces such as magnetism, a child needs firsthand experience with many opportunities to observe, experiment, and get her hands dirty. In the words of "Benchmarks for Science Literacy," a 1993 report from the American Association for the Advancement of Science: "From their very first day in school, students should be actively engaged in learning to view the world scientifically. That means encouraging them to ask questions about nature and to seek answers, collect things, count and measure things, make qualitative observations, organize collections and observations, discuss findings, etc."

While experience counts for much, book learning is also important, for it helps bring coherence and order to a child's scientific knowledge. Only when topics are presented systematically and clearly can children make steady and secure progress in their scientific learning. The child's development of scientific knowledge and understanding is in some ways a very disorderly and complex process, different for each child. But a systematic approach to the exploration of science, one that combines experience with book learning, can help provide essential building blocks for deeper understanding at a later time. It can also provide the kind of knowledge that one is not likely to gain from observation: consider, for example, how people long believed that the earth stands still while the sun orbits around it, a misconception that "direct experience" presented as fact.

In this section, we introduce kindergartners to a variety of scientific topics, consistent with the early study of science in countries that have had outstanding results in teaching science at the elementary level. The text is meant to be read aloud to your child, and it offers questions for you and your child to discuss, as well as activities for you to do together.

Plants and Plant Growth

Plants Are All Around Us

There are many different kinds of animals and plants that live in our world. You probably recognize many of the living things pictured on page 359. In some ways, animals and plants are alike—all animals and plants are alive. They produce young animals or plants. They need food, water, and air to grow and stay alive. But plants and animals are different in many other ways. Unlike animals and people, plants do not make sounds, and they do not leave one place and move to another.

Plants need a few basic things in order to live and grow: food, water, air, and light. If a plant has these things, then it can survive, even in a little crack in the sidewalk.

A few weeks ago, a tiny dandelion seed floated through the air and landed in this crack, where there was just enough soil for its new roots to take hold. The roots take up things the plant needs: water and nutrients. This dandelion gets plenty of sun here in the sidewalk, and it also gets plenty of air. As long as the plant does not get

The flowering plant in this picture is called a dandelion.

pulled up by a person or eaten by an animal, it will live in this crack until it dies.

All plants need food, water, air, and light. But, not every place in the world has exactly the same amount of food, water, air, or light.

Most plants on earth could not survive in the desert. Plants that grow here, such as this cactus, have adapted to a life beneath the blazing hot sun with very little rainfall and sandy soil. That tough little dandelion and the trees you saw earlier would wither and die if you tried to plant them here. And the cactus in this desert would not be able to live in either the sidewalk crack or the forest!

All the food that you eat comes from plants. Peas and potatoes, carrots and cucumbers, the wheat that gets ground into flour and baked into bread—they all come from plants. But wait a minute. What about meat, like a hamburger or sliced turkey? And what about fish? Cows, turkeys, and fish are not plants, they're animals! That's right—but all those animals eat plants.

And that's not all. Without plants we would have no paper for writing and drawing, no lumber for building houses, and no cotton cloth for clothes. We couldn't live without the plants in our world.

This is a desert, where it is hot and dry all year round.

Talk and Think

If you have a houseplant in your home, talk with your child about how your plants get food, water, air, and light. Is your plant by a window? Who waters your plant?

Plants have different parts.

Look at the pictures and put your finger on each part of the plant as you say the name of the part.

Flowers grow on plants. Flowers come in many different shapes and colors.

After the flower blooms, the plant makes seeds. Seeds can go into the ground and start new plants.

Leaves grow out from the stem. Green leaves use water and nutrients, together with light and air, to make food for the entire plant.

The stem grows up from the roots. It brings water to the leaves and flowers. It holds the plant up tall, toward the light.

Roots grow underground. They soak up water and nutrients from the soil. Water moves through the roots into the plant. Nutrients are good things the plant needs to grow.

Seeds Grow into Plants

Many plants grow from seeds. Have you ever seen the little seeds inside an apple? Or have you eaten a slice of watermelon and had to spit out a lot of seeds? Have you eaten a peach, which has one big seed in it? (Don't eat the seed!)

Many plants have flowers, and these flowers make seeds. Flowers bloom in all the colors of the rainbow: yellow tulips, orange marigolds, red roses, purple lilacs, blue forget-me-nots. A bouquet of colorful, sweet-smelling flowers is one of the nicest presents a person can give.

A little seed can turn into a giant plant. Even big trees start from little seeds. Have you ever found an acorn, then looked up to see the big oak tree that dropped it? That little acorn has all it needs to start growing another oak tree.

An acorn is the seed of an oak tree. Only an oak tree can grow from an acorn. Do you think a peach tree can grow from an apple seed? No—only an apple tree can grow from an apple seed. And only a sunflower can grow from a sunflower seed. What can grow from a pumpkin seed? That's right: only a pumpkin.

> **Make a Connection**
> Remind your child of the saying "Great oaks from little acorns grow." Show your child the acorn. Acorns are seeds for oak trees.

If you put a seed in dirt and water it, it will usually sprout into a baby plant. This bean is a seed. Let's look at what happens when it's planted and watered. After a little while, a small root pokes out and grows into the ground. Then a tiny shoot with leaves grows up in the other direction. Just like a human baby, a baby plant needs food. Where does the baby plant get its food? From the seed, which is like a little lunch box. As the baby plant grows, the seed gets smaller because the plant is using the food inside the seed.

Stages of a bean seed growing

Watch a Seed Grow in a "See-Through" Planter

PARENTS: Here's an activity you can do with your child that will let you see a seed grow into a plant. Tell your child that you're going to make a "see-through" planter. Have your child do as much as you and he are comfortable with. You'll need to be in charge of the first steps of making the planter, which require cutting a milk carton with strong scissors or a utility knife.

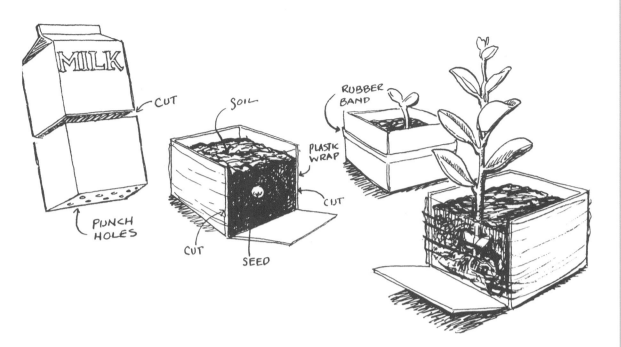

Get Ready

You will need:

- Half-gallon milk carton
- Scissors or utility knife
- Clear plastic wrap
- Masking tape or transparent tape
- Big rubber band
- Potting soil
- Bean seeds (not beans to cook and eat from the grocery store, but the kind that come in a sealed package for growing)

Go

First, cut the milk carton to about one-half of its height. Now you have a box with no top. Poke some holes in the bottom, for drainage.

Now cut straight down along two corners of the milk carton. This will allow one side of the carton to fold down, like a flap, while remaining hinged at the bottom.

Leave the flap down so that you have an open side. Cover this side with a sheet of clear plastic wrap. Pull the wrap taut and tape it securely to the outside of the milk carton. Now raise the flap and slide a big rubber band around the milk carton to hold the flap up in place.

Fill the carton about three-fourths full of soil. Now take some of the bean seeds and put them in the soil, next to the clear plastic wrap. Cover these seeds with just a little more soil (about a half inch).

Put the carton on a plate and sprinkle in just enough water to make the soil moist, not dripping wet.

Put the plate and carton in a warm place. Check the soil daily and add water as necessary to keep the soil moist. Every day, remove the rubber band and let down the flap. This will let you look through the window of clear plastic wrap and see how your seeds are growing "underground"! Pretty soon you should see roots poking down and sprouts growing up through the soil.

What Plants Need to Grow

What's the difference between a plant and a person like you? Well, both you and a plant start out small and then keep on growing. But you can walk around. Most plants stay put. As a plant grows, its roots sink deep down into the soil and hold on tight. A plant may sway in the wind, but it stays rooted, growing in one place for all its life.

Another big difference between you and a plant is how you eat your breakfast, lunch, and dinner. Have you ever seen a plant eat breakfast? Plants don't sit down for a meal, but they do need food. In fact, plants make their own food.

To make their food, plants need air, light, and water, and also minerals from the soil. The plant's leaves take in air and sunlight. The plant soaks up water and minerals through its roots. (These minerals are dissolved in the water, the way you can dissolve sugar in a cup of water.) The plant uses the air, light, water, and minerals to make its own food. Don't you wish you could do that when you're hungry?

You can grow a plant in a pot of soil if you give it enough water, air, and light. What do you think would happen to a plant if it didn't get enough water or light? Let's find out.

What Do Plants Need? An Experiment

. . . .

PARENTS: Here is a simple experiment you can do with your child to show what a plant needs to live. Have your child do as much as you and she are comfortable with.

Get Ready

You will need:

>3 paper cups
>Sharpened pencil
>Potting soil
>9 bean seeds (not beans to cook and eat from the grocery store, but the kind that come in a sealed packet for growing)
>Cookie sheet or tray

Go

Tell your child that you're going to do an experiment together that will take several days. In this experiment, you're going to plant some seeds and see what they need to grow.

Poke a tiny hole (you can use a sharp pencil point) in the bottom of each paper cup. Let your child fill each cup with potting soil to about a half-inch from the top. Then show her how to plant the seeds: have her use her finger to poke three holes in the soil in each cup, about half a finger deep. Then put one seed in each hole and cover them all with soil. (You need only three bean plants for this experiment, but you're planting more in case some of the seeds don't germinate.)

Put the cups, once planted, on the cookie sheet or tray. Water the plants sparingly, so that the soil is damp but not muddy. Take the tray to a spot near a sunny window. Help your child water the seeds (just a bit) every day until the seeds sprout and the first leaves begin to spread. If more than one plant has sprouted in a cup, then carefully pull out the other plants and leave only one plant per cup in order to proceed with the experiment.

When you have a plant growing well in each cup, write numbers on the cups: 1, 2, and 3. Now explain to your child that you're going to do something different with each of these plants.

Plant 1. Leave this plant where it is and continue to water it every day. Talk with your child so that she can see that this plant is getting everything it needs to live: water, air, light, and minerals from the soil.

Plant 2. Leave this plant where it is but do not water it anymore. Ask your child what this plant won't be getting. Help her see that it won't be getting water but that it will be getting air, light, and minerals.

Plant 3. Have your child put this plant in a dark place, such as a kitchen cabinet or a closet. Tell her to keep giving this plant a little water daily. Ask your child what this plant will not be getting. Help her see that the plant will be getting air, water, and minerals but no light.

Check the plants with your child every day. As changes in the plant become noticeable, you can ask your child:

- "What is happening to each plant?"
- "Which plant seems to be doing best?"
- "What does a plant need for healthy growing?"

Seeds to Eat

You've learned that a baby plant sprouts from a seed and then uses the seed for food as it grows. Did you know that you get food from seeds, too? Here are some seeds you might eat.

Corn is the seed of the corn plant that grows tall in the farmer's field. When you eat corn on the cob, you are eating rows of seeds.

Wheat is the seed of the wheat plant. Wheat seeds are so hard that if you tried to eat them, they would almost break your teeth. So we grind wheat seeds into flour to use for baking bread.

Peas are the seeds of the pea plant. Peas grow in long green pods.

Green beans are the seed pods of the bean plant. When you eat a green bean, you are eating a pod and a seed. If you pull one apart very carefully, you can see the little seeds inside.

Peanuts are the seeds of the peanut plant. Next time you eat a peanut, pull it apart very carefully. You can see the start of a tiny new peanut plant inside.

We Eat Many Plant Parts

Seeds aren't the only part of plants that we like to eat. We eat roots, such as radishes, onions, and carrots. We eat stems, such as celery. We eat leaves, such as lettuce and cabbage. We even eat some flowers. For example, when we eat broccoli, we're eating the flower of the broccoli plant just before it blooms.

And of course we eat the fruit of many plants. Apples, pears, and oranges are fruits. For us, these fruits are food. For a plant, the fruit protects the seeds that grow inside the fruit. In the plant world, by the way, tomatoes, green peppers, and pumpkins are also fruits, even though most of us call them vegetables. They are fruits because they hold seeds inside them as they grow.

Growing Food Plants

You may think that fruits and vegetables come from the grocery store. But that's just where we go to buy them. Somebody has to grow most of the fruits that we eat. Many of the fruits and vegetables at the grocery store grew on plants at farms and orchards.

The food you buy at grocery stores often comes from really big farms. There are different kinds of big farms. There are poultry farms, where they raise chickens. There are dairy farms, where they raise cattle and where your milk comes from. There are grain farms, where they grow big fields of wheat, corn, barley, and other grains. There are "truck farms," where they grow—no, not trucks!—lots of different vegetables, such as lettuce and broccoli.

Other farms grow important crops, but not for eating. For example, cotton comes from farms. You may be wearing something made of cotton.

LOOK AT WHAT PLANTS PROVIDE US!

Many of your favorite foods come from plants. Can you add to this list?

French fries	come from	Potatoes
Sugar	comes from	Sugarcane plants
Cereal	comes from	Wheat, oats, corn, and rice
Maple syrup	comes from	Maple trees
Chili beans	come from	Bean plants
Chocolate	comes from	Cacao trees
Bananas	come from	Banana trees

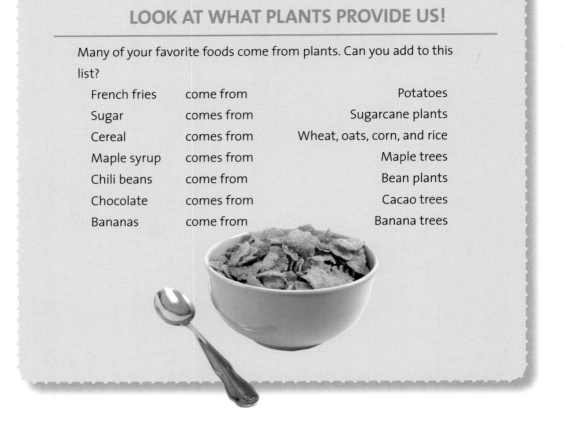

It takes a lot of work to grow all the plants we eat. Farmers work all year round to raise food. They plow the earth and plant the seeds. They try hard to keep weeds and animals away from their crops. Some farmers figure out ways to irrigate, or bring water to, their crops so that the plants will grow even if it doesn't rain.

Each farm or orchard packs its vegetables or fruits into crates and boxes so trucks can carry them to grocery stores across the country. Some trucks have refrigerators inside so the food stays fresh until it reaches the store. Some fruits or vegetables are cooked in factories, then canned or frozen to keep even longer.

Seasons and Weather

The Four Seasons

A year is divided into four parts, called the four seasons. Do you know the names of the seasons? They're spring, summer, fall, and winter. (Fall is also called autumn.)

What is each season like? That depends on where you live. In many places, spring is warm, and flowers bloom. Then comes a hot summer. Then comes a cool fall, when the days get shorter. Then comes a cold winter, and maybe lots of snow.

In other places, the seasons change in other ways. Some children live in places where it never snows. In some neighborhoods, the leaves stay green all year round.

But no matter what the weather does where you live, the year still cycles through four seasons—spring, summer, fall, winter—over and over, every year.

What are the seasons like where you live? When you think of each season, what do you hear or see or smell? What different things do you like to do during the different seasons?

TWO KINDS OF TREES

In many parts of our country, the leaves on many trees and bushes turn from green to red, gold, and brown, and then fall off. This happens in the season called—you guessed it—fall.

Trees and bushes whose leaves fall in the fall have a special name. It's a big word, so hold on: "deciduous" (dee-SIJ-oo-us). It's almost a tongue twister: try saying "deciduous" four times very fast! "Deciduous" means falling off. Even though deciduous plants lose their leaves in the fall, they grow new leaves in the spring. Maples, oaks, and apple trees are all deciduous trees.

But you may have noticed that some trees and bushes stay green all through the winter. They lose some of their leaves every year, but because they seem to stay green forever, we call this kind of plant evergreen. Pine trees and holly bushes are evergreens.

Spring

Summer

Fall

Winter

Evergreen trees stay green even in winter.

Talking About the Weather

I'm going to ask you the same question in two different ways. Here's the first way: "What's it like outside?" Here's the second way: "What's the weather?"

The weather is what it's like outside. Did you think about the weather today? Maybe you did without even realizing it. What kind of clothes did you wear today? The weather had a lot to do with your choice.

No matter where people live, they talk about the weather. It's something everybody shares. When it's cold outside, we shiver. When it's pouring rain, we need raincoats or umbrellas. When it's hot and humid ("humid" means the air is moist and sticky), we sweat and want a cold, icy drink.

What do we talk about when we talk about the weather?

Temperature. Is it hot or cold, cool or warm? The temperature goes up and down. When the sun comes up, it warms the air and the temperature goes up. When the sun goes down, the air gets cooler and the temperature goes down.

The temperature changes with the seasons. In many places, summer days are usually warm or hot. In most places, the temperature in summer is much higher than in the winter. Winter days are usually cool or cold.

To tell what the temperature is, people use a thermometer. Many thermometers, like the ones in the picture here, have a colored liquid inside a tube. As the temperature goes higher, the liquid rises in the tube. As the temperature goes lower, the liquid goes down in the tube.

Clear or cloudy? Look up in the sky. Is it a clear day? On a clear day, the sun shines in a bright blue sky. Or is it a cloudy day? Or a partly cloudy day—which means some clouds but also some blue sky?

Clouds are made of very tiny drops of water or tiny bits of ice. Clouds come in different shapes, sizes, and colors. Are there any clouds in the sky now? Are they big, white, and puffy? Or are they white streaks or dark gray stripes? Or is the sky covered over with a blanket of gray clouds so thick that you can't see through to the sun? A thick blanket of gray clouds sometimes means that rain is coming.

A partly cloudy sky

The wind.

Is the air calm and still, or is the wind blowing? The wind is moving air. You can't see the wind, but you can see the way the wind moves the branches of trees, carries a kite higher and higher, or blows your hat off your head. Sometimes the wind blows gently and feels good. Sometimes the wind blows hard and brings stormy weather.

I DO NOT MIND YOU, WINTER WIND

by Jack Prelutsky

I do not mind you, Winter Wind
when you come whirling by,
to tickle me with snowflakes
drifting softly from the sky.

I do not even mind you
when you nibble at my skin,
scrambling over all of me
attempting to get in.

But when you bowl me over
and I land on my behind,
then I must tell you, Winter Wind,
I mind . . . I really mind!

The Wind Blows in Many Directions

· ·

PARENTS: This activity can help your child see which way the wind is blowing and understand that the wind blows in different directions. The activity requires some cutting and stapling. Have your child do as much as you and she are comfortable with.

Get Ready

Tell your child that together you are going to make a weather vane that she can use to see which way the wind is blowing.

You will need:

Empty plastic milk container

Scissors and stapler

Plastic straw

Pen or marker

Pin

Pencil with eraser

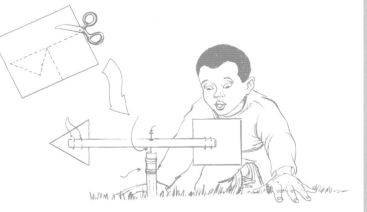

Go

The weather vane will look like an arrow. Cut two small squares out of a side of the plastic milk container. Staple one square to one end of the straw. Cut a triangle out of the other square, then staple the triangle to the other end of the straw.

Hold out your index finger and put the straw across it. Move it until it balances on your finger. With a pen or marker, mark this balancing point. Push a pin through the straw just at the balancing point.

Now, take the straw with the pin through it and carefully push the pin into the eraser of the pencil. Push the pencil into the ground, straight up and down.

The weather vane will point in the direction the wind is blowing from. Check your weather vane every day for a few days or more. Does the wind change directions?

Rain can pour down hard.

RAIN

by Robert Louis Stevenson

The rain is raining all around,
It falls on field and tree,
It rains on the umbrellas here,
And on the ships at sea.

Rain. Rain falls from clouds and soaks into the earth, filling up the lakes and streams and helping the plants grow. Sometimes you may not welcome the rain: you know the poem "Rain, rain, go away, come again another day." But without enough rain, the ground becomes dry and hard. When that happens, then the roots of plants cannot soak up enough water and the plants can die.

Rain can fall in fine, tickly droplets, called mist or drizzle. It can come down in a short, friendly shower. Or it can pour down hard. Have you ever

Have you ever seen a rainbow?

heard the funny expression people sometimes use to describe a really heavy rain? They say, "It's raining cats and dogs!" If it rains too much for a long time, then that can cause a flood.

If you're lucky, then sometimes when it's raining, or just after a rain, you'll see a rainbow. Rainbows look like magic, but they appear naturally, when sunlight shines through raindrops in the sky. Have you ever held a prism up to sunlight and seen how it breaks the light coming through it into bands of color? Raindrops do the same thing to sunlight—they break it into bands of color—and that's why you see a rainbow.

Snow. In winter, if the temperature drops low enough, then instead of rain we get snow. When just a little snow falls, we call it a snow flurry. If a big snowstorm dumps lots and lots of snow, we call it a blizzard.

It has snowed!

When snowflakes fall, they may look like little bits of white, all of them the same.

But did you know that every snowflake is different? Each snowflake is its own beautiful design of tiny ice crystals.

These are snowflakes. Every snowflake is different, but they're all six-sided. Can you count the sides?

Make a Snowflake

· ·

PARENTS: Children like the lovely snowflake designs they can cut out of folded paper. The folding is a bit complicated, and some cutting is required.

Get Ready

You will need:

    White paper

    Scissors

Go

Tell your child that, though almost every snowflake has a different design, all snowflakes have six sides, and that you're going to cut some six-sided snowflake designs out of white paper. Proceed as follows:

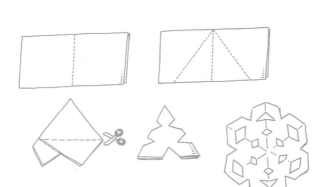

1. Begin with a square sheet of paper.
2. To fold this sheet into six parts, first fold it in half.
3. Then fold it in half again, but just crease that fold lightly.
4. Open the fold you just made.
5. Folding from the point where the two fold marks meet, make three overlapping pie slices. You might have to try this part a couple of times to make sure the two outer pie slices match up.
6. Cut off the edges as indicated.
7. Now, each time you clip through your folded piece of paper, you are making six cuts. Snip here, snip there.
8. Open it up—you've got a six-sided snowflake!

Storms

On any day, the weather can change quickly. You might be playing outside on a sunny day, and then suddenly a storm will blow in.

What's the sound of a thunderstorm? *Rumble! Boom! Snap! Crack! Boom!* You hear the thunder roaring. You see the bright, jagged streaks of lightning in the sky. Thunder and lightning might scare you, but they're part of nature during a thunderstorm.

You don't have to be scared of lightning if you follow some simple rules. If you're outside when you hear thunder and see lightning, go inside quickly. Never stand under a tree during a lightning storm. Never stay in a swimming pool or lake during a lightning storm. Find your way to a dry shelter and wait for the storm to pass. Lightning storms usually don't last long.

During a thunderstorm, rain can fall fiercely. Sometimes the rain can even freeze before it comes down. Then it becomes hail—balls of ice that can be as small as peas or as big as golf balls!

Bolts of lightning light up the sky.

Animals and Their Needs

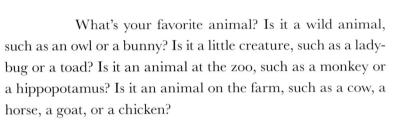

What's your favorite animal? Is it a wild animal, such as an owl or a bunny? Is it a little creature, such as a ladybug or a toad? Is it an animal at the zoo, such as a monkey or a hippopotamus? Is it an animal on the farm, such as a cow, a horse, a goat, or a chicken?

Or maybe your favorite animal is one that lives at home—a pet dog or cat, a goldfish, or a hamster.

We share the world with many different animals. Some are wild, such as lions and wolves and bears. Can you name some wild animals that live near you? Have you seen squirrels in the park or the woods? Have you seen robins or bluejays in the trees? Some animals are tame, like pet dogs and cats.

Whether animals are wild or tame, they need certain things to live. They need water to drink and food to eat. Do you remember that plants can make their own food (from water, minerals, air, and sunshine)? But animals can't do that. Some animals, like rabbits, eat plants. Some animals, like lions, eat meat. Some animals, like bears, eat both plants and meat.

Animals also need safe homes. Wild animals find or make their own homes. Some rabbits make their homes in holes in the ground. Bald eagles build their nests way up high, on mountain ridges or in the tops of tall trees.

This is a fox. Is he wild or tame?

Taking Care of Pets

Wild animals can take care of themselves. But pets need special care. You can learn a lot about animals by taking care of a pet. Owning a pet is almost like being a parent. Think about what your pet needs. You provide food and water and a safe home. You teach your pet and you love your pet. If you do all these things well, you'll have a healthy pet.

Some people like dogs best. They give them food and water and a place to sleep. Dogs love to take walks. Some dogs can learn tricks such as fetching a ball, rolling over, or catching a Frisbee in midair!

Some people like cats best. They give them food and water and a place to sleep. Cats curl up on the sofa or at the foot of the bed. When cats feel content, they purr. When they're frightened they arch their backs, their hair stands on end, and their tails puff out like a big brush!

Some people like birds best. They give them food and water and a clean, dry cage. Some birds sing. Some birds even "talk." People teach parrots to say funny things such as "Hello, sugar!" and "What's up, doc?"

Some people like to keep more unusual animals as pets, such as tropical fish, snakes, iguanas, ferrets, or monkeys. No matter what kind of pet a person chooses, the animal will always need food, water, a safe home, and loving care.

Animals Care for Their Babies

This mother robin is feeding her babies a worm. Yum!

Have you ever held a kitten? It's so tiny, it fits inside your hands. It's soft and furry, just like its mother. It has two ears and two eyes, four paws, and one tail, just like its mother.

How is a kitten different from its mother? Well, it's smaller. It may have the same color and markings as its mother, or it may have very different color and markings. An orange-striped mother cat could have a kitten with gray stripes or black and white spots. Or she could have orange-striped kittens. Even though the kittens may not have the same color or markings as their mother, the kittens are definitely cats! Can a mother cat have a puppy? No way!

If you've ever seen a mother cat with kittens, you know how much attention she pays to her babies. She washes them by licking them clean. (Imagine if you took your baths that way!) She plays with them. She makes sure they get enough food, by letting them drink her milk. She even teaches them how to hunt when they get bigger.

> **Make a Connection**
> Discuss the saying "The early bird gets the worm" with your child. Read more sayings and phrases on pages 140–143.

Many animal parents take special care of their babies. Mother robins bring bugs and worms back to the nest, and then they help their babies learn to fly. Mother whales help their babies learn to swim down deep and come up for air above the water. Baby animals need these special lessons because one day they will have to take care of themselves.

Just like baby animals, human babies also need special care and attention from their parents. Think of all the ways adults help a newborn baby. Babies can't feed themselves. Babies can't dress themselves. Babies can't clean themselves. Babies need adults to help them learn how to walk and talk. Sometimes you still need help from adults, right? But you're not a baby any longer, and there's a lot you can do for yourself.

The Human Body

Your Five Senses

Look up. Look down. What part of your body do you use? Your eyes.

Listen very carefully. What part of your body do you use? Your ears.

Sniff. What do you smell? What part of your body do you use? Your nose.

Lick your lips. Can you taste anything? What part of your body do you use? Your tongue.

Rub the top of your head. Use your fingertips to feel your hair.

Your body can sense, using your five senses.

| Sight | Hearing | Smell | Taste | Touch |

You see with your eyes. With your eyes you can see how big things are, and what colors things are. Did you know that some animals can't see colors? Cats, for example, can't see colors. But their eyes can see better in the dark than your eyes can.

You hear with your ears. You hear pleasant sounds, such as a bird singing or someone reading to you. You hear loud sounds, such as the siren of a fire engine. You hear quiet sounds, such as a whisper. You can hear a lot, though some animals can hear more than you: a dog, for example, can hear a special whistle that puts out a very high-pitched squealing sound that you may not be able to hear. Some animals can't hear at all: you may hear a bee buzz, but the bees never hear their own buzzing, because they don't hear anything.

You smell with your nose. Smells can be pleasant, such as the scent of a rose or the aroma of bread baking in the oven. What smells good to you? Smells can be unpleasant, such as the smoke from a car's exhaust or the odor of a rotten piece of fruit. What smells bad to you? You can smell a lot, but dogs can smell even more. Have you noticed how dogs like to sniff, sniff, sniff around almost everything? Have you ever heard of dogs who can help find people who've gotten lost in the woods or the snow? The dogs do this by using their sense of smell.

Your sense of smell also helps you taste things. Have you noticed that it's hard to taste things when you have a bad cold? Why do you think that happens? What's your nose like when you have a bad cold?

You taste with your tongue. Look in a mirror and stick out your tongue. See how it's covered with little bumps? Those little bumps have tiny parts that tell you what things taste like. They tell you whether things are sweet, like ice cream; sour, like a lemon; salty, like potato chips; or bitter, like some medicine you might have to take when you're sick.

You touch things and feel them. What do you feel if you pick up an ice cube? If you pet a cat or dog? If you rub a piece of sandpaper? If you step barefoot on the grass? You feel by touching with your hands, and with the skin all over the rest of your body.

Taking Care of Your Body

Okay, get ready to use your body. Ready? Then . . .

Put your arms over your head and reach way up to the sky. Stretch!

Jump up and down!

Bend at your waist and touch your toes.

Curl up in a little tiny ball.

Lie down and be absolutely still. Close your eyes. Shh! Don't move!

Your body can do so many things. It can bend and jump and run and sleep. It can see and hear and smell and taste and touch. It can talk and sing. It can draw and paint.

It's important to take good care of your body. Your body needs special care. You need to keep clean by washing your hands before eating and after going to the bathroom, by taking baths regularly, and by brushing your teeth. You need to help your body grow stronger by eating good foods, by getting plenty of exercise, and by getting a good sleep every night.

Taking Care of the Earth

The Forests and the Trees

Imagine that you're climbing a high tower. When you reach the top, you look out over a great forest. You see trees stretching for miles, like a big blanket of green—so many trees that it might seem as though we could never run out of them.

Think about forests and trees. Why are they important? If you were an animal in the forest— a bear, raccoon, owl, or deer—the forest would be important to you because it's your home! Many people like to hike through forests and camp out in the woods, where the air is fresh and clean. Those are some reasons why forests are important: because they are homes for many animals, because people enjoy hiking and camping in the woods, because the trees help keep the air we breathe fresh and clean.

But people cut down trees. Think how many ways we use the wood from trees. We burn wood in fireplaces. We use wood to build houses. We use it to build furniture: chairs, tables, dressers, and more. Pencils are made from wood. Paper comes from wood. It takes a whole forest—almost half a million trees—just to make the paper that goes into the newspapers that Americans read every Sunday.

These toys are made of wood.

Think of all the other paper we use: paper towels, cardboard, the paper you use for writing and drawing, the paper that makes up the pages of this book.

So, trees are important to us when we cut them down and use them to make things we need: houses, furniture, paper, and more. But trees are also important to us when they're standing tall in the forests. We have to be very careful not to cut down too many trees. And we should grow new trees to take the place of the ones we've cut down. Some logging companies—companies that cut down trees—are careful to plant new trees after they have cut down the old ones.

Conservation: Saving and Protecting the Earth

It's not just trees that we have to be careful about. We have to be careful about how we use other riches of the earth, too.

For example, the earth has only so much fresh water for us to drink and use. So it's important not to waste water. You can help save water if you don't let the water run in the sink when you're not using it, and if you turn off the faucet firmly whenever you're finished.

When you don't let the faucet run and you make sure to turn it off firmly, you're helping to conserve water. To "conserve" means to use something carefully. It means to save and not to waste. There's an old saying that people use: "Waste not, want not." That means if we're careful not to waste what nature gives us, then we will have enough of what we need. But if we waste what nature gives us, then someday we may want something—such as trees or fresh water—but be unable to find what we need.

You can recycle, too.

It's Smart to Recycle

One good way to waste less is to recycle. Recycling means using things over and over instead of throwing them away. Lots of families already recycle clothing: when one child grows up and gets too big for a shirt or pair of pants, then the clothes are passed on to a smaller child—maybe a brother or sister, or cousin or neighbor—to be worn again.

By using things over again instead of throwing them away, we help conserve what the earth gives us. Waste not, want not!

Many cities and towns have recycling centers to collect materials that can be used over and over. Is there a recycling center in your town or city? Do you know where it is? Here are some things that you shouldn't throw away; instead, take them to a recycling center.

> **Make a Connection**
> Now is a good time to review the saying "A place for everything and everything in its place." Talk about how we use recycling bins to put everything in its place when we recycle.

Cans.
Factories can recycle most metal cans. They clean them, melt them, and use them to make new cans. Recycling centers will usually ask you to separate two different kinds of cans. One kind is made of aluminum, like the cans that soda comes in. The other cans are often called tin cans: these cans hold fruits and vegetables, dog food and cat food, beans and spaghetti with sauce, and lots more.

Paper.
Factories can recycle newspapers and lots of other kinds of paper with writing on it. They grind it up and make it into new paper. You can recycle paper, too. How? You can take a piece of paper that you or someone else has already used, turn it over, and draw or write on the back.

Plastic.
Factories recycle plastic, such as milk jugs and soda bottles. They melt the plastic and reshape it into other things, such as chairs and picnic tables. You can recycle plastic jugs at home or at school. You can use them for all kinds of things: as paint jars, as pots to grow plants in, even as musical instruments.

Cardboard.
Factories recycle cardboard. They grind it up and make it into new paper or cardboard.

Glass can be recycled, too.

Keep Our Earth Clean

It's hard to live without making a mess. When you paint a picture, you make a mess. When you cook dinner, you make a mess. When people work in factories, making cars or clothes or televisions, they make a mess, too. But we all have to learn to clean up our messes.

People who work in factories today are studying the problem. They are trying to figure out how to make the things we need without making messes. They are trying to keep unhealthy smoke from polluting the air. They are trying to keep dangerous chemicals from going into the streams and polluting the water.

We can help, too. There's a place to put our garbage. Not on the floor. Not on the sidewalk. Not in the street. Not in the woods.

You know where garbage belongs, right? Garbage goes in the garbage container. People who throw garbage wherever they want are littering. "Litterbugs" are thoughtless, lazy people. Don't litter: that's one way to help clean up the earth.

THREE THINGS YOU CAN DO TO HELP CONSERVE

Can you add to this list?

1. Turn off water faucets firmly.
2. Recycle paper, metal cans, glass, and plastic.
3. Turn off the lights when you don't need them.

An Invisible Force: Magnetism

PARENTS: We recommend that you obtain a simple magnet and some paper clips to use with your child as you read this section. (But keep magnets away from computers and credit cards.)

This is a paper clip. It's made of metal. Can you pick it up without touching it? Don't use tweezers or pliers—you're not allowed to touch it with anything. So, can you pick it up?

Yes! How? With a magnet. If you hold a magnet close to the paper clip—which is made of metal—the clip will come flying up to the magnet.

Now, if you slowly pull the paper clip off the magnet, what do you feel? You feel the magnet pull back. Hold your magnet close to a refrigerator door: can you feel the pull? Let the magnet touch the refrigerator and it won't fall. It sticks to the door. Put a pencil or shoe up against the refrigerator, and what happens? It just drops to the ground. But the magnet sticks.

It seems almost like magic, but it's not. Magnetism is what pulls the paper clip to the magnet and makes the magnet stick to the refrigerator door.

We cannot see magnetism, but we can see what magnetism does. We can see the magnetic force attract a paper clip. We can see how a magnet holds a note or picture on the refrigerator door. In some cabinets, you can see how little magnets keep the cabinet doors closed. And if you were to visit a junkyard, you could see how huge magnets pick up things as big as a whole car!

Can Magnetic Force Pass Through an Object?

PARENTS: Here is an experiment you can do with your child to find out whether the invisible force of magnetism can pass through another object.

Get Ready

You will need:

    Piece of writing paper

    Paper clip

    Magnet

    Piece of construction paper

    Book

Go

Have your child start with the piece of writing paper. Show him how to hold it flat in front of him, with one hand. Put the paper clip on top. Now have your child put the magnet under the piece of paper. Tell him to move the magnet under the paper clip, and to keep moving the magnet while he watches the paper clip move.

Talk with your child about what's happening. The magnetic force is passing right through the piece of paper. See if it will pass through thicker objects. Try the same experiment with a piece of construction paper and with a book.

What Do Magnets Attract?

A magnet is made of metal. It feels cold and hard, like a doorknob or a spoon. A doorknob and spoon are also made of metal, but they're not magnets. Only magnets have that special magnetic attraction.

What do magnets attract? Let's do an experiment.

Get Ready

You will need:

    Crayon or marker

    2 boxes

    Magnet

    A variety of objects and materials, such as a sheet of paper, a piece of wood, a safety pin, a plastic toy, a key chain, an apple, a ruler, a staple, a pencil, an aluminum soda can, a penny, a thumbtack, a small rubber ball, a nail, a feather

Go

Use your crayon or marker to label the two boxes. On one write "Yes"—this means, "Yes, a magnet attracts these materials." On the other write "No"—this means, "No, a magnet does not attract these materials."

Now have your child hold the magnet close to a variety of materials. Does it attract? Does she feel a pull? As she tries each material, have her put it in the appropriate box. (Be careful with sharp objects, such as the thumbtack and staple.)

You can also have your child try the magnet on some objects too large to put in one of the boxes. Does the magnet attract a car door? A tree trunk? A tabletop?

So, what has your scientific experiment shown? Do magnets attract paper, wood, or plastic? No. But magnets do attract safety pins, thumbtacks, staples, nails, paper clips, the car door, and the refrigerator door. What are all these different things made of? They're made of metal. Magnets attract things made of metal.

But magnets don't attract everything made of metal. If you try to make your magnet stick to a soda can, it won't. Soda cans are made of a metal called alumi-

Hold the paper
thumb-up like this.

num. Try to pick up a penny with a magnet: it won't work. Pennies are made of a metal called copper. Magnets attract some metals, but not aluminum and copper. The most common metal that magnets do attract is called iron. All the things your magnet picked up before—the paper clip, safety pin, nail, and other things—all have some iron in them.

Stories About Scientists

George Washington Carver

George Washington Carver was born in a small cabin near Diamond, Missouri, in 1865. This cabin was owned by a man and woman named Moses and Susan Carver. George, his brother Jim, and their mother, Mary, lived with the Carver family because his mother was a slave who helped the Carvers take care of their family farm. At the time George was born, many people, particularly in the southern United States, owned slaves who were not free to do what they wanted; they were required to work for their owners with no pay, usually on large farms.

When George was just a baby, he and his mother were kidnapped. Luckily, George was found again by Moses and Susan Carver, who decided to raise George and his brother as if they were their own children.

As George grew up, he was often sick and not very strong. As a result, George often stayed at home, helping his adoptive mother, Susan, with simple chores around the cabin, such as washing clothes and cooking. George used his free time to explore the forests that were part of the Carver farm. He spent many hours roaming the woods discovering all sorts of wonderful things. George liked to collect things that caught his eye.

George was especially curious about the different kinds of plants that he noticed during his explorations. He wanted to study these plants further, but he knew that if he pulled them out of the ground and took them back to the cabin, they would die. So when George found an interesting plant, he would carefully

dig it up and remove it from the place it was growing, roots and all, so that he could plant it in a special garden close to the cabin.

George transplanted plant after plant to this special garden, where he looked after each and every plant, watering and caring for them all to be sure they continued to grow. As an adult, George later wrote, "I literally lived in the woods. I wanted to know every strange stone, flower, insect, bird, or beast. Day after day I spent time in the woods alone in order to collect my floral beauties and put them in my little garden I had hidden in the brush not far from the house."

Fascinated by the plants in his garden, George spent hours tending, observing, and studying them. In time, he came to learn about the special needs of each plant—how much water each needed, whether it grew best in full sunlight or with some shade. George also took a special interest in caring for plants that were not growing well. He became so skillful at caring for these sick plants that people throughout the neighborhood began to call him the "plant doctor."

George's passion for plants led him to develop another talent, that of an artist. Of course, his favorite subjects to paint were his beloved plants! Though he did not have a proper canvas or paints, he improvised with what he could find. Like the Native Americans, George made his first paints from different plant parts. He mashed bark, roots, and wild berries and used them to paint on old boards or even flat rocks. George continued to paint his entire life.

George was truly a remarkable and talented person. As a young boy, his adoptive mother, Susan, taught him to read and write at home. At the time when

George was growing up, most African Americans were not permitted to attend school, as strange and unfair as that may seem. When George turned twelve, he moved away from home so that he could attend a school for African Americans. There were no schools for African American boys near George's home with the Carvers. George proved to be an excellent student who learned quickly. He went on to study at college, eventually becoming an expert in botany, the study of plants. After he finished college, George became a professor at a famous university for African Americans called the Tuskegee Institute in Alabama.

There, he spent the rest of his life continuing to study plants and experiment with ways to make them grow better. He discovered many ways to help poor farmers improve how they grew plants and crops on their farms. George encouraged farmers to grow crops other than cotton—especially peanuts and sweet potatoes. He also found many ways to use peanuts in all different types of products, such as dyes, oils, and makeup. He even came up with a number of recipes for foods that used peanuts.

George Washington Carver is especially remembered today for these discoveries.

Jane Goodall

Did you ever try to sit very, very still and watch an animal? Maybe you looked out the window and saw a bluejay at a bird feeder, or you watched a mother dog lick her puppies clean. Or maybe you sat very quietly and looked at a fly as it landed on your arm. You can learn a lot about animals by watching closely, especially if you take care not to scare them.

When she was a little girl, Jane Goodall loved watching animals. She crouched in a henhouse quietly for hours, hoping to see how a chicken lays eggs.

She brought earthworms into her bed to watch them. When she read *The Story of Dr. Dolittle* and the Tarzan books, she decided, "I want to go to Africa, study animals, and write about them."

When she grew up, Jane Goodall went to Africa. She was sent to study chimpanzees in the wild by a very famous scientist named Dr. Louis Leakey. He wanted her to watch chimpanzees to learn more about how they behave in nature.

Jane Goodall went to what is today the African country of Tanzania (tan-zuh-NEE-uh) to a forest where several groups of chimpanzees made their home. Every morning, she would climb to the top of the highest hill and look through her binoculars, trying to see the chimpanzees. She was very patient.

At first, the chimpanzees were scared of her, but they slowly came to trust her. After four months, she was able to get close enough to watch one chimpanzee make and use a tool. She learned that red chimpanzees know how to make tools to catch termites—small wood-eating insects—a favorite chimpanzee snack. They break off long, thin twigs or pieces of grass and poke them down into the holes where the termites live. The termites climb onto the twigs or grass. Then the chimpanzees pull the twigs or grass out of the holes and lick off the termites. The chimps make sort of a fishing pole for termites! Before Jane Goodall saw this, no one believed that chimpanzees made or used tools. This was a really big discovery!

The more the chimpanzees trusted Jane Goodall, the more she saw how they really lived. She learned a lot about chimpanzees that people didn't know before she began her study. She saw chimpanzees holding hands, hugging, and kissing. She also learned the sounds and facial expressions they used to communicate with one another, as well as the way they sometimes fight.

Jane Goodall has now spent more than 50 years working in Africa and watching the chimpanzees. She recognizes many of the chimpanzees and even calls many by name, including Frodo, Glitter, and Google!

Do It Yourself!
The Jane Goodall Institute has an international environmental and humanitarian program, Jane Goodall's Roots and Shoots, for youth of all ages. Visit the website at www.rootsandshoots.org.

Wilbur and Orville Wright

Nowadays, thousands of airplanes and jets fly across the country and around the world every day. But it wasn't very long ago that people thought that human beings would never fly. They thought that flying was something that birds, bats, and some insects could do—but people? No, they said, that won't happen. But it has happened; and it took two brothers, Wilbur and Orville Wright, to prove that human beings could build a machine to fly.

When they were young, Wilbur and Orville Wright were known by their friends as boys who could build and fix things. Together they opened a bicycle shop. They built, sold, and rented bicycles. In the 1890s many people wanted one of those new two-wheeled traveling machines.

At night the Wright brothers used their brains and tools to study the possibilities of flying. They heard about a German engineer who had built a glider. A

The Wright brothers making their first powered flight

glider is a plane with no engine; it's carried by the wind, like a kite. Even when the Wright brothers heard the sad news that the German engineer had been killed when his glider crashed, they kept on trying to find a way to fly.

They built their own glider. It had two big wings, one on top and one on the bottom, and a place for a person to lie down in the middle. They found a special place to test it, on the windy sand dunes near the Atlantic Ocean at Kitty Hawk, North Carolina.

That first glider flew low to the ground, but then it crashed. Wilbur was discouraged. "Man will not fly in a thousand years," he said.

But he was wrong. He and his brother kept working and kept coming up with new ideas. Soon they had built another plane, but not a glider—this plane had an engine, to turn the propellers.

On December 17, 1903, the Wright brothers stood on the Kitty Hawk sand dunes and tossed a coin to see which one of them would fly their new plane first.

Orville won. Wilbur helped him climb into *Flyer I*, as they had named their new machine. The engine started. The plane rolled along the dune. Then it lifted into the air! Orville flew *Flyer I* a total of 120 feet, staying in the air 12 seconds.

That doesn't sound like a very long flight to us today, but to the Wright brothers, 12 seconds meant success! They flew *Flyer I* three more times that day, and on the fourth flight the plane stayed in the air 59 seconds (almost a minute) and flew 852 feet (almost the length of three football fields). The Wright brothers had proven it: human beings could fly in a flying machine!

Only five other people saw them fly that December day at Kitty Hawk. Only a few newspapers even wrote about it. No one seemed to understand how important the airplane would be. But the Wright brothers kept on flying. They built new airplanes and flew them for audiences in France and the United States. Once Orville flew circles around the Statue of Liberty.

In five years of practice flying, they had only one accident, but it was a bad one. Orville was hurt, and a friend flying with him died. It reminded the Wright brothers how dangerous flying could be, but it didn't stop them from continuing to build and fly airplanes. By 1908 they were famous around the world for their flying machines.

Suggested Resources

PLANTS AND PLANT GROWTH

A Tree Is Nice, by Janice May Udry (HarperTrophy, 1987)

From Seed to Plant, by Gail Gibbons (Holiday House, 1991)

Growing Vegetable Soup, by Lois Ehlert (Voyager Books, 1990)

Jack's Garden, by Henry Cole (HarperTrophy, 1997)

SEASONS AND WEATHER

Snowflake Bentley, by Jacqueline Briggs Martin (Houghton Mifflin, 1998)

On the Same Day in March: A Tour of the World's Weather, by Marilyn Singer (HarperTrophy, 2001)

The Cloud Book, by Tomie dePaola (Scholastic, 1975)

What Will the Weather Be Like Today?, by Paul Rogers (Greenwillow, 1990)

ANIMALS AND THEIR NEEDS

How Much Is That Doggie in the Window?, retold by Iza Trapani (Whispering Coyote Press, 2001)

Can You See It?, by Wiley Blevins (Compass Point Books, 2003)

Animals Born Alive and Well, by Ruth Heller (Grosset and Dunlap, 1982)

Chickens Aren't the Only Ones, by Ruth Heller (Grosset and Dunlap, 1981)

Night of the Pufflings, by Bruce McMillan (Houghton Mifflin/Walter Lorraine, 1997)

THE HUMAN BODY

Me and My Body, by David Evans and Claudette Williams (Dorling Kindersley, 1992)

My Five Senses, by Aliki (HarperCollins, 1989)

TAKING CARE OF THE EARTH

I Am Water, by Jean Marzollo (BT Bound, 1999)

The Lorax, by Dr. Seuss (Random House, 1971)

Recycle That!, by Fay Robinson (Children's Press, 1995)

AN INVISIBLE FORCE: MAGNETISM

Science with Magnets (EDC Publications, 1992)

What Magnets Can Do, by Allan Fowler (Children's Book Press, 1995)

What Makes a Magnet?, by Franklyn M. Branley (HarperTrophy, 1996)

STORIES ABOUT SCIENTISTS

George Washington Carver, by Martha E. H. Rustad (Capstone Press, 2002)

First Flight: The Story of Tom Tate and the Wright Brothers, by George Shea (Scott Foresman, 1997)

Illustration and Photo Credits

© Adisa 350(b)

© africa924 161

© Elena Aliaga 346

The Art Archive at Art Resource, NY 218

© Art-Hunters 216

© Silvano Audisio 247(b)

The Baltimore Museum of Art: The Cone Collection formed by Dr. Claribel Cone and Miss Etta Cone of Baltimore, MD, BMA 1950. 225

© Marilyn Barbone 174(a), 348(a)

© O. Bellini 368

© Bike Rider London 173

© Blend Images 360

© Bokstaz 159(a)

© Tommy Brison 175(b)

© Ralf Broskvar 207

© Lukasz Burkowski 179

Jesse Bushnell 189

© 2013 Calder Foundation, New York/Artists Rights Society (ARS), New York 230

© Jakub Cejpek 344(a)

© Jacek Chabraszewski 364

Lina Chesak-Liberace 248, 249, 254, 258, 259, 261, 262, 263, 264, 268(a, b), 269

© debr22pics 217

© Marc Dietrich 344(d)

© Zhu Difeng 157

Digital Image © The Museum of Modern Art/Licensed by SCALA/Art Resource, NY 230

© Dionisvera 142(a)

© Le Do 140

© dragon-fang 247(a)

© Jaimie Duploss 214(b)

Jennifer Eichelberger 66, 67

The Julius C. Eliel Memorial Fund, Minneapolis Museum of Art, MN, USA 219

© Elena Elisseeva 337(b)

© 2013 Estate of Helen Frankenthaler/Artists Rights Society (ARS), New York 220

© 2013 Estate of Pablo Picasso/Artists Rights Society (ARS), New York 237

© Fotokostic 355

Freer Gallery of Art, Smithsonian Institution, Washington, D.C.: Gift of Charles Lang Freers F 1904.241 223(a)

© g215 344(e)

© Gelpi 142(b)

Barbara L. Gibson 135, 336

The Granger Collection, New York 185, 192 (a), 194, 205, 206(b)

© Pawel Grebenkin 344(c)

Shari Griffiths 91, 94, 96, 178, 376, 377(a, b)

© Tom Grundy 181(a)

Scott Hammond 199, 206(a)

Hampton University 238

Amy Nichole Harris 166(a)

© Joshua Haviv 228

Jared Henry 60, 62

Steve Henry 153(a), 221, 245, 253, 256, 257, 265, 277, 279, 281 (a, b), 282, 283, 284, 287 (a, b), 288, 289, 290, 291, 292, 293(a, b), 294, 295, 296, 297, 298, 299, 301, 303, 305, 207, 309 (a, b, c), 310, 311, 314(a, b), 316, 317(a, b), 318, 321, 324, 325, 326(a, b), 327, 341, 350(a), 357, 371

© Holbox 164(a)

Hannah Holdren 223(b)

Image Copyright © The Metropolitan Museum of Art, Image Source: Art Resource, NY 233

© IRC 359(a)

© Eric Isselée 141(b), 359 (d)

© Jakelv7500 372

© johnfotol8 215

© jun.su. 352

© Christian Jung 343(e)

© Evgeny Karandaev 366

© Kemeo 343(a)

© Kichigin 356

Bob Kirchman 150(a, b), 152, 153(b), 155, 156, 158, 160(a), 162, 165, 167(a), 169(a), 170, 172(a)

© Charles Knowles 354

© K. L. Kohn 226

© Devin Koob 141(a)

© Nici Kuehl 166(b)

Kristen Kwan 33(a), 33(b), 107,111, 112, 114

Alvina Kwong 49

© Lalito 246(c)

Amanda Larsen 32

© Jason Lee 348 (b)

© Katrina Leigh 338

Erich Lessing/Art Resources, NY 218, 234

© Keith Levit 154

© Joshua Lewis 359(c)

© lgorXIII 152(a)

© lwka 337(c)

Dustin MacKay 31, 183, 184, 187

© Marafona 365

Richard McGuire 164(b)

Gail McIntosh iii, 1, 37, 38(b), 48, 52(a, b), 53(a, b), 54, 55, 56, 57, 64, 70, 71, 81, 87, 89, 125, 132, 139, 145, 148, 201, 211, 213, 229, 231, 243, 270, 273, 276, 312, 319, 331, 339, 347, 349, 351, 353(a, b), 362, 373

© The Metropolitan Museum of Art, Image Source: Art Resource, NY 227(b)

Rebecca Miller 34(a), 97, 100

© Caitlin Mirra 175(a)

© Stuart Monk 247(d)

© Monkey Business Images 143

© Anna Morgan 163

© Morgan Lane Photography 367

Steve Morrison 34(b), 39(b), 41(b), 47, 182 (a,b), 188

Frank J. Murphy 63

© Maks Narodenko 337(a)

NASA 149

A new science is born, 17th December, 1903 (photogravure), American Photographer (20th Century)/Private Collection/The Stapleton Collection/The Bridgeman Art Library 380

© Orientaly 345

Gianni Dagli Orti/The Art Archive at Art Resource, NY 222

© Reigien Paassen 181(b)

Julia Parker 45(b)

Mary Parker 58, 176

Michael Parker 75, 76, 79, 101, 104, 116

© Edyta Pawlowska 151

Charles Peale 38(a), 39(a)

© Photoline 343(d)

© Pixachi 227(a)

© pjmorley 343(c)

© Tatiana Popova 246(a)

© Stu Porter 160(b)

© Matt Ragen 196

© Dennis Albert Richardson 167(b)

© Rigamondis 246(b)

© Robyn vg 359(b)

© Armin Rose 169

Brooke Sadler 190(a)

© Elena Schweitzer 247(b)

E. H. Shepard from "Pooh Goes Visiting and Gets into a Tight Place" by A. A. Milne, from *Winnie the Pooh* by A. A. Milne, illustrated by E. H. Shepard 120, 121, 124

© Ljupco Smokovski 344(b)

© Kenneth Sponslor 174(b)

While every care has been taken to trace and acknowledge copyright, the editors tender their apologies for any accidental infringement where copyright has proved untraceable. They would be pleased to insert the appropriate acknowledgment in any subsequent edition of this publication.

Text Credits and Sources

Poetry

"April Rain Song" from *The Collected Poems of Langston Hughes* by Langston Hughes, edited by Arnold Rampersad with David Roessel, Associate Editor, copyright © 1994 by the Estate of Langston Hughes. Used by permission of Alfred A. Knopf, a division of Random House, Inc. Any third party use of this material, outside of this publication, is prohibited. Interested parties must apply directly to Random House, Inc., for permission.

"I Do Not Mind You, Winter Wind" from *It's Snowing! It's Snowing!* by Jack Prelutsky, Text Copyright © 1984 by Jack Prelutsky. By permission of Greenwillow Books, a division of William Morrow and Company, Inc.

"The More It Snows" from *The House at Pooh Corner* by A. A. Milne. Illustrations by E. H. Shepard. Copyright 1928 by E. P. Dutton, renewed © 1956 by A. A. Milne. Used by permission of Dutton Children's Books, a division of Penguin Books USA Inc.

"My Nose" by Dorothy Aldis, reprinted by permission of G. P. Putnam's Sons from *All Together*, copyright 1925–1928, 1934, 1939, 1952, © renewed 1953–1956, 1962, 1967 by Dorothy Aldis.

"Tommy" from *Bronzeville Boys and Girls* by Gwendolyn Brooks. Copyright © 1956 by Gwendolyn Brooks Blakely. Reprinted by permission of HarperCollins Publishers.

Stories

All Aesop's Fables in this text adapted from *The Fables of Aesop*, retold by Joseph Jacobs (c. 1900); our version of "The Grasshopper and the Ants" also draws upon the retelling in *Everyday Classics: Third Reader* by F. Baker and A. Thorndike (1917) and *The Natural Method Readers: A Second Reader* by H. McManus and J. Warren (1915).

"The Bremen Town Musicians" adapted from versions in *Everyday Classics: Third Reader* by F. Baker and A. Thorndike (1920) and *The Progressive Road to Reading: Book Two* by G. Burchill et al. (1909).

"Casey Jones" is an original retelling by John Holdren, copyright © 1996 Core Knowledge Foundation.

"Chicken Little" adapted from versions in *The Merrill Readers: First Reader* by F. Dyer and M. Brady (1915); *The Progressive Road to Reading: Book One* by G. Burchill et al. (1909); and *New American Readers: Book One* by L. Baugh and P. Horn (1918).

"Cinderella" is primarily based on the version by Charles Perrault, in *The Blue Fairy Book*, edited by A. Lang (1889), and incorporates elements of the Brothers Grimm version (translated by L. Crane, 1886), as well as details from the retelling by F. Baker and A. Thorndike in *Everyday Classics: Third Reader* (1920).

"Goldilocks and the Three Bears" adapted from versions in *The Natural Readers: A First Reader* by H. McManus and J. Haaren (1914) and *Story Hour Readers Revised: Book Two* by I. Coe and A. Dillon (1914).

"How Many Spots Does a Leopard Have?" from *How Many Spots Does a Leopard Have and Other Stories* by Julius Lester. Copyright © 1989 by Julius Lester. Reprinted by permission of Scholastic, Inc.

"Johnny Appleseed" condensed and adapted from "Johnny Appleseed, Planter of Orchards on the Frontier," in *Tall Tale America: A Legendary History of Our Humorous Heroes* by Walter Blair (Coward, McCann & Geoghegan, Inc., 1944).

"King Midas and the Golden Touch" condensed and adapted from "The Golden Touch," in *A Wonder-Book for Boys and Girls* by Nathaniel Hawthorne (1852).

"Little Red Riding Hood" adapted from "Little Red-Cap" in *Household Stories from the Brothers Grimm* (translated by L. Crane, 1886) and from "Little Red Riding Hood" in *Everyday Classics: Third Reader* by F. Baker and A. Thorndike (1920).

"Momotaro: Peach Boy" adapted from "The Adventures of Little Peachling," retold by A. B. Mitford, in *The Children's Hour: Folk Stories and Fables*, edited by Eva Tappan (1907).

"Pooh Goes Visiting and Gets into a Tight Place" by A. A. Milne, illustrated by E. H. Shepard, from *Winnie-the-Pooh* by A. A. Milne, illustrated by E. H. Shepard. Copyright 1926 by E. P. Dutton, renewed 1954 by A. A. Milne. Used by permission of Dutton Children's Books, a division of Penguin Books USA, Inc.

"Snow White" adapted from *Household Stories from the Brothers Grimm*, translated by Lucy Crane (1886).

"The Story of Jumping Mouse" is an original retelling of a Native American legend of the Northern Plains People by Rosie McCormick, copyright © 2013 Core Knowledge Foundation.

"The Three Billy Goats Gruff" adapted from versions in *Popular Tales from the Norse* by Peter Asbjornsen (translated by G. W. Dasent, 1908); *The Elson Readers: Book One* by W. Elson and L. Runkel (1920); and "The Three Piggy Wigs" in *The Progressive Road to Reading: Book Two* by G. Burchill et al. (1909).

"The Three Little Pigs" condensed and adapted from "The Story of the Three Little Pigs" in *English Folk Tales*, retold by Joseph Jacobs (1892).

"Tug-of-War" is an original retelling based on many versions of this tale, including "A Tug of War" in *Yes and No: The Intimate Folklore of Africa* by Alta Jablow (1961); "The Tug of War" in *African Village Folktales* by Edna Mason Kaula (1968); and "Tug of War" in *African Myths and Legends* by Kathleen Arnott (1962).

"The Ugly Duckling" adapted from the original story by Hans Christian Andersen (translated by C. Peachey, 1861) and from retellings in *Third Year Language Reader* by F. Baker et al. (1919) and *Everyday Classics: Third Reader* by F. Baker and A. Thorndike (1920).

"The Wolf and the Seven Little Kids" adapted from *Household Stories from the Brothers Grimm*, translated by Lucy Crane (1886).

While every care has been taken to trace and acknowledge copyright, the editors tender their apologies for any accidental infringement where copyright has proved untraceable. They would be pleased to insert the appropriate acknowledgment in any subsequent edition of this publication.

Index

Grimms' fairy tales
"The Bremen Town
Musicians," 77–80
"Little Red Riding
Hood," 68–71
"Snow White,"
106–14
"The Wolf and the
Seven Little Kids,"
97–100

H

half and half, 301–2
"Happy Thought," 31
"The Hare and the
Tortoise," 49
Hart, Betty, 17
Hawthorne, Nathaniel,
101
hearing, 362–63
heavy and light,
317–18
"Here We Go Round the
Mulberry Bush," 261
"Hey, Diddle,
Diddle," 32
"Hickory, Dicory,
Dock," 31
high and low, 257–58

higher-order thinking,
xxviii–xxix, xxxii, 11
history, 11, 147
China, 157
Christopher
Columbus, 182–88
Declaration of
Independence, 195
Europe, 159
first Americans,
173–82, 191–93
Fourth of July,
194–98
Pilgrims, 189–93
presidents, 200–208
slavery, 198–200
South America, 166
Thanksgiving,
192–93
"The Hokey Pokey," 267
"Hot Cross Buns!," 40
"How Many Spots Does
a Leopard Have?,"
115–18
Hughes, Shirley, 23
human body, 362–64
babies, 361
caring for your body,
364
five senses, 35, 362–63
"Humpty Dumpty," 39

Hunters in the Snow
(Brueghel), 218
"Hush, Little Baby," 259

I

"I Do Not Mind You,
Winter Wind," 351
"If You're Happy and
You Know It," 267
illustrators, 63
independent reading,
11–12
independent writing, 13
inferences, 16
instruments, 246–47, 249
Internet resources
(coreknowledge.org),
xxxiii, 20–21
"In Which Pooh Goes
Visiting and Gets into a
Tight Place," 120–24
"It's Raining, It's
Pouring," 34

J

"Jack and Jill," 37
"Jack Be Nimble," 38

About the Editors

E. D. HIRSCH, Jr., is the founder and chairman of the Core Knowledge Foundation and professor emeritus of education and humanities at the University of Virginia. He is the author of several acclaimed books on education issues including the bestseller *Cultural Literacy*. With his subsequent books *The Schools We Need and Why We Don't Have Them*, *The Knowledge Deficit*, and *The Making of Americans*, Dr. Hirsch solidified his reputation as one of the most influential education reformers of our time. He and his wife, Polly, live in Charlottesville, Virginia, where they raised their three children.

JOHN HOLDREN is senior vice president of content and curriculum at K^{12} Inc.—America's largest provider of online education for grades K–12. He lives with his wife and two daughters in Greenwood, Virginia.